T0267962

Additional Praise for *Enrich Your Future*

"If the conventional wisdom is, 'Don't just sit there. Do something,' Larry shows us that it should be 'Don't just do something. Sit there.' Indeed, consistently being long, the 'Larry factor' is how investors today can enrich their savings and their quality of life."
—Ross L. Stevens, *founder and CEO,*
Stone Ridge Holdings Group

"Larry Swedroe shows investors how to protect themselves against their own worst enemies—themselves. He buttresses his valuable advice with citations of the most rigorous quantitative research but explains it all in readily understandable—and highly entertaining—terms. This book is a tour de force!"
—Martin Fridson, *publisher,*
Income Securities Investor

"Classic Larry Swedroe: eminently readable and eminently important for anyone interested in their investments."
—Andrew L. Berkin, *head of research,*
Bridgeway Capital Management

"Many investors know that diversification, low cost, and tax awareness are the keys to being successful, but most can't resist the urge to chase returns, buy individual stocks, and use complicated and expensive investment products. In *Enrich Your Future*, esteemed author Larry Swedroe shows you how to construct a long-term investment portfolio, how to deal with difficult money emotions, and how to play the winner's game in life and investing. A must-read for all investors."
—Tom Cock, *cohost,* Talking Real Money

"Larry entertains as he busts toxic investing myths with illuminating personal stories and market histories: a wise and lively guide for investors to make the most of their resources."
—Ed Tower, *professor of economics,*
Duke University

"If you want to build wealth, read this book! Larry Swedroe's *Enrich Your Future* is a well-written, fabulously researched treasure-chest of wisdom that will give you the best investment education that you've likely ever had. Swedroe's lessons are worth a million times the price of this book."

—Andrew Hallam, *author of*
Millionaire Teacher, Millionaire Expat, *and* Balance

"Swedroe has nailed his revolutionary theses to the door of conventional finance wisdom. From the relationship of risk and return, randomness and behavioral finance, the book reveals state-of-the-art theory and grounds it in practical advice. Another rigorous work by the foremost investment researcher and writer working today."

—Tobias Carlisle, *managing director,*
Acquirers Funds®

Enrich Your Future

Enrich Your Future

The Keys to Successful Investing

Larry E. Swedroe

WILEY

Published by John Wiley & Sons, Inc., Hoboken, New Jersey.
Published simultaneously in Canada.

For general information on our other products and services or for technical support, please contact our Customer Care Department within the United States at (800) 762-2974, outside the United States at (317) 572-3993 or fax (317) 572-4002.

Wiley also publishes its books in a variety of electronic formats. Some content that appears in print may not be available in electronic formats. For more information about Wiley products, visit our web site at www.wiley.com.

Library of Congress Cataloging-in-Publication Data Is Available:

ISBN 9781394245444 (Cloth)
ISBN 9781394245468 (ePDF)
ISBN 9781394245451 (ePub)

Cover Design: Wiley
Cover Image: © DKosig/Getty Images
Author Photo: Courtesy of the Author

SKY10063997_010824

This book is dedicated to my grandchildren, Jonathan, Sophie, and Gracie Rosen; Ruby, Eloise, and Witt Morris; and William and Rosie Brennan, who bring joy into my life each and every day.

Contents

Also by Larry E. Swedroe   xiii

Foreword   xvii

Introduction   xxiii

Part One: How Markets Work: How Security Prices Are Determined and Why It's So Difficult to Outperform

Chapter 1:   The Determinants of the Risk and Return
              of Stocks and Bonds   3
Chapter 2:   How Markets Set Prices   9
Chapter 3:   Persistence of Performance   27
Chapter 4:   Why Is Persistent Outperformance So
              Hard to Find?   35
Chapter 5:   Great Companies Do Not Make
              High-Return Investments   39
Chapter 6:   Market Efficiency and the Case of Pete Rose   47
Chapter 7:   The Value of Security Analysis   51

Chapter 8:	Be Careful What You Ask For	55
Chapter 9:	The Fed Model and the Money Illusion	59

Part Two: Strategic Portfolio Decisions

Chapter 10:	When Even the Best Aren't Likely to Win the Game	67
Chapter 11:	The Demon of Chance	73
Chapter 12:	Outfoxing the Box	79
Chapter 13:	Between a Rock and a Hard Place	83
Chapter 14:	Stocks Are Risky No Matter How Long the Horizon	87
Chapter 15:	Individual Stocks Are Riskier Than Investors Believe	91
Chapter 16:	All Crystal Balls Are Cloudy	97
Chapter 17:	There Is Only One Way to See Things Rightly	105
Chapter 18:	Black Swans and Fat Tails	109
Chapter 19:	Is Gold a Safe Haven Asset?	115
Chapter 20:	A Higher Intelligence	121

Part Three: Behavioral Finance: We Have Met the Enemy and He Is Us

Chapter 21:	You Can't Handle the Truth	127
Chapter 22:	Some Risks Are Not Worth Taking	133
Chapter 23:	Framing the Problem	137
Chapter 24:	Why Do Smart People Do Dumb Things?	143
Chapter 25:	Battles Are Won Before They Are Fought	153
Chapter 26:	Dollar Cost Averaging	161
Chapter 27:	Pascal's Wager and the Making of Prudent Decisions	167
Chapter 28:	Buy, Hold, or Sell, and the Endowment Effect	173

Chapter 29: The Drivers of Investor Behavior   177
Chapter 30: The Economically Irrational Investor
                 Preference for Dividend-Paying Stocks   185
Chapter 31: The Uncertainty of Investing   193

Part Four: Playing the Winner's Game in Life and Investing

Chapter 32: The 20-Dollar Bill   199
Chapter 33: An Investor's Worst Enemy   205
Chapter 34: Bear Markets   211
Chapter 35: Mad Money   219
Chapter 36: Fashions and Investment Folly   227
Chapter 37: Sell in May and Go Away   233
Chapter 38: Chasing Spectacular Fund Performance   235
Chapter 39: Enough   239
Chapter 40: The Big Rocks   243
Chapter 41: A Tale of Two Strategies   249
Chapter 42: How to Identify an Advisor You Can Trust 253
Conclusion   257

Appendix A: Implementation: Recommended
                 Investment Vehicles   261
Notes   271
Acknowledgments   285
Index   287

Also by
Larry E. Swedroe

The Only Guide to a Winning Investment Strategy You'll Ever Need (first edition 1998, second edition 2005)

What Wall Street Doesn't Want You to Know

Rational Investing in Irrational Times

The Successful Investor Today: 14 Simple Truths You Must Know When You Invest

The Only Guide to a Winning Bond Strategy You'll Ever Need (coauthor Joe Hempen)

Wise Investing Made Simple: Larry Swedroe's Tales to Enrich Your Future

Wise Investing Made Simpler: Larry Swedroe's Tales to Enrich Your Future

The Only Guide to Alternative Investments You'll Ever Need: The Good, the Bad, the Flawed, and the Ugly (coauthor Jared Kizer)

The Only Guide You'll Ever Need for the Right Financial Plan: Managing Your Wealth, Risk, and Investments (coauthors Kevin Grogan and Tiya Lim)

Think, Act, and Invest Like Warren Buffett: The Winning Strategy to Help You Achieve Your Financial and Life Goals

Investment Mistakes Even Smart People Make and How to Avoid Them (coauthor R. C. Balaban)

The Quest for Alpha

Reducing the Risk of Black Swans: Using the Science of Investing to Capture Returns with Less Volatility (coauthor Kevin Grogan; first edition 2014, second edition 2018)

The Incredible Shrinking Alpha (coauthor Andrew Berkin; first edition 2015, second edition 2020)

Your Complete Guide to Factor-Based Investing (coauthor Andrew Berkin)

Your Complete Guide to a Successful and Secure Retirement (coauthor Kevin Grogan; first edition 2019, second edition 2021)

Your Essential Guide to Sustainable Investing (coauthor Sam Adams)

Quantitative Hedge Fund Investing (coauthor Marat Molyboga)

If you tell me a fact, I learn; tell me a truth and I'll believe; but tell me a good story and it will live in my heart forever.

—Anonymous

Foreword

Y ou will learn much about investing at the feet of Mr. Larry Swedroe while reading this fine book. Here are a few of the things he will teach you. First, intelligent, hard-working individual investors can reliably beat the stock market through stock picking and market timing. If you somehow disagree with that, then he will convince you that at least very-well-paid, overeducated professional money managers can consistently outperform. Okay, maybe you don't believe that's true, either. But Larry will convincingly argue that at least the subset who've reliably beaten the market in the past will again do so going forward. Okay, if you don't believe him about that, then at least believe him that sophisticated institutional investors, like pension funds and the investment committees of endowments and foundations, can make money manager hire-and-fire decisions that add a lot of value over the long term. Okay, enough about all the different ways Larry will show you how the pros can beat the market for you. Larry also teaches a lot of other important things about investing. For instance, he shows us that stocks become riskless but only if you hold them long enough. He clearly demonstrates that if you've built up a large nest egg by keeping your money in the stock of the company you work for, then continuing to do that going forward, provided that you really and truly love the company, is a prudent and low-risk strategy. He notes that dollar cost averaging is the real secret to investing success, and that owning gold hedges away your inflation risk, and how the stock market would be a paradise without bear markets. I could go on (and Larry does!). All vital pearls of wisdom.

Okay, in truth, this might actually be a somewhat painful (though important!) book to read for investors new to Mr. Larry Swedroe.[1] Many sacred oxen are gored (mixing my bovine aphorisms). Specifically, the book you are about to read will show you (quite persuasively) that everything I just listed in the previous paragraph is false. Larry teaches you the opposite of what I said, and that believing otherwise can be very damaging to your long-term financial health.

You can find this all out on your own.[2] All you have to do is read and understand a few hundred academic and practitioner research papers, some of them (unnecessarily?) mathematically difficult. Or you can come here and get it all in a few hours with some entertainment thrown in gratis. The math you'll find in Larry's book consists mainly of reporting average results, what tends to matter, what doesn't, what fraction of the time things happen in, and to what magnitude. Nothing too daunting and there is only as much math as you need to understand the concepts. Larry takes a few hundred serious research papers and turns them from mathematical exercises into understandable stories.

Like I said, the stories still have a little bit of math. The tales Larry tells are not quite the same as a 7th-century BC Greek

---

[1] Though if you have been an investor for a while and have not read some of Larry's other books, shame on you!

[2] You can also just read the dictionary straight through following the comedian Stephen Wright who says on his 1981 comedy album "I Have a Pony," "I was reading the dictionary. I thought it was a poem about everything." But I do not recommend it!

reciting Homer by the fire (sorry, Larry). But they are a lot closer to that than the papers he draws from! Larry uses stories, mostly as analogies, to make the difficult easy and the complex simple. Instead of regression analysis and matrix algebra, Larry teaches with examples ranging from Gaylord Perry to Sisyphus. You won't find that in the *Financial Analysts Journal*!

To play favorites, and get a little personal, out of the entirety of a great book, perhaps the chapter that resonated most with me was Chapter 24: Why Do Smart People Do Dumb Things?[3] No, it isn't because I think I'm a smart person who often does (very) dumb things, though that is certainly the case (and I'm definitely right about the second part). It's very personal and it's about the 2018–2020 horrendous period for most forms of quantitative stock selection (led by the famous "value factor"). Larry presents reams and reams of evidence that past performance doesn't predict future performance.[4] Wait. Actually, that's not quite right. He presents evidence that it does (mildly) predict future performance *but with the wrong sign!*[5] He discusses this for choosing mutual funds and for professionally managed pension funds choosing managers. He does so under a wide variety of rebalancing rules and a wide variety of ways to evaluate performance (e.g., benchmark relative performance, raw performance, risk-adjusted performance done a variety of ways). Quoting Larry:[6]

---

[3] If I had to pick a second favorite, it would be Chapter 35 on Jim Cramer of CNBC. Spoiler alert: watching his show can be very expensive.

[4] I have to be a bit careful here. Larry focuses on past active stock picking or market timing success not predicting the future—particularly when looking back over common time horizons. Larry shares my view that "evidence-based" investing, looking for what factors systematically outperform over very long periods with good economic explanations, is a very different (and potentially more attractive) beast.

[5] At the time horizons studied—mainly three- to five-year periods. Also, the word *mildly* is important. If you had to choose one, picking the three- to five-year losers would be better than the winners, but it would still not be a very reliable strategy and you should not bet the ranch on it.

[6] Though perhaps my favorite quote from the whole book is the staggeringly understated, "It is rare for a new fund to be brought to market when an asset class has performed poorly." Preach Larry! Hens' teeth should be so rare.

The bottom line is that so many investors are doing the same thing over and over again and expecting a different outcome. Most seem to never stop and ask the question: If the managers I hired based on their past outperformance have underperformed after being hired, why do I think the new managers I hire to replace them will outperform if I am using the very same criteria that have repeatedly failed? And, if I am not doing anything different, why should I expect a different outcome? I've asked these very questions, and never once received an answer—just blank stares.

Larry is not alone in making this point. To pick an utterly randomly chosen example of someone else making this point, in 2014 I wrote an article in the *Financial Analysts Journal* called "My Top 10 Peeves" and out of the 10 my number 3 was "had we but world enough, and time, using three- to five-year evaluation periods would still be a crime." It was a shorter, less evidence-based, more sarcastic take on what Larry is explaining here. Picking winning money managers[7] over three to five years isn't just wrong; it's *mildly backwards*. Picking the losers is (again, the predictive power is only mild, don't bet a lot on this either!) on average the right thing to do. Of course, I wrote this in 2014 when the prior three- to five-year period was quite good for us. You know why? Because you don't get to write about this when it's been a bad period for you. If you do, people roll their eyes and say you're just making excuses. You only get to scream this from the rooftops when the last three- to five-year period is great for you. I did that. Well, I didn't so much as scream as discuss it. But inside I was screaming.

Then, 2018–2020 rolled around and things got ridiculously tough for the academic factor-based strategies we favor. We could show precisely why it was so bad. We could put it into historical context. We could even measure how extreme was the pain and what we thought the concomitant opportunity. Yet exactly

---

[7] Or individual stocks, or asset classes, or "investment styles."

when, in a Vulcan world of rational investors, investors should've doubled up on value investing (and us!), we lost lots of clients and had (nearly) zero investors take up the opportunity (and our clients are, I dare say, of a high level of sophistication—remember Larry's admonition that this doesn't seem to help!).[8] Rather people, yet again, went the other way, adding what had worked recently and running from what had not despite its (sorry, I have to say) rather obvious attractiveness. It seems that despite overwhelming evidence of how crazy the world had gotten, despite my own prior statements in good times about not automatically selling after bad times, despite us surviving and thriving from a similar episode in 1999–2000 so we knew what the path looked like, and despite the gigantic and robust set of research Larry cites that people sell what they should be buying and buy what they should be selling, most still couldn't do it.[9] If I sound a bit bitter, well, it's not that much more than my average.[10]

From my description thus far, you might think this book is pure nihilism, glorying in shooting down harmful myths about

---

[8] Narrator:"It turned out it was an incredible opportunity and the next three years were excellent. Though, admittedly not as excellent as I would've thought in late 2020. The incredible record-setting bubble in what the market would imprecisely call 'growth vs. value stocks' that reached its heights in late 2020 has come down steadily in the nearly three years since it peaked, rewarding those who stuck with or even added to rational strategies, but it's come down slowly. The most comparable period to the last five-plus years is the 1999–2000 dot-com bubble and aftermath. That fully reversed in the next two to three years from the peak in March 2000. This one has only reversed by about 1/3 (meaning right now I would *not* fade three-year prior performance—remember doing so is only a mildly good strategy!). When you are historically unprecedented levels of cheapness even a 1/3 reversal can lead to multiple strong years. But it's still only 1/3. I want my other 2/3."

[9] I guess that's why the research exists but man it's different to live through!

[10] I pride myself on an exceptionally high bitterness-to-success ratio. As perhaps an odd coda to my ranting fervent wish that investors would listen to people like Larry and stop making mistakes like this, the very strategies I believe in, and that Larry advocates as structured systematic positions, would likely cease, in all or in part, to be long-term attractive if investors didn't do irrational things. What every investor wants is to profit from other investors' irrationality, but quickly and painlessly. Sadly, it just doesn't work that way. Perhaps there is some odd kind of fairness to the whole thing. The harder something good is to stick with, the better it is long term, if (if!) you can stay the course.

investing. There is a healthy dollop of that, and it's very valuable unto itself. But Larry doesn't end with nihilism, not at all. Yes, implicitly springing from nearly every chapter is indeed the depressing all-caps "YOU CANNOT WIN" by doing what so many self-interested experts tell you to do. But behind that there is also the ultimately uplifting "YOU DO NOT HAVE TO WIN TO WIN" as Larry convinces you that you mostly win by not playing. He even gives some good life advice along the way (not playing doesn't just leave you wealthier and more secure, it gives you some of your life back!).

So, what's Larry's prescription? Simple. Stay very diversified. Pay low costs. Do not chase performance or run from tough performance if you understand what drove it. Do not try to time the market. If you do try to beat the market, focus on the "factors" that have been discovered in academia and refined by applied researchers in industry.[11] Of this last piece of advice, I will say little save that I have no quarrel with him here.[12]

Do less. Pay less. Think about it all less. Don't put all your eggs in one basket. Think about the worst outcomes and make sure you aren't doomed if they occur.[13] If you're going to attempt to beat markets, do so using sound evidence-based academic findings consistent with behavioral finance or harvesting a risk premium. Stay the course.

I know. He could've just told you all that upfront, without the reams of academic evidence and the great stories/analogies, but would you have believed him? Nah. Well, you should now!

—Cliff Asness, managing and founding principal,
AQR Capital Management

---

[11] Though Larry rather rudely, though perhaps not inaccurately, says they're becoming "betas." Them's fightin' words!

[12] Astute readers will notice how staggeringly world-class-level self-serving I am being here.

[13] Chapter 27: Pascal's Wager.

Introduction

Most Americans, having taken a biology course in high school, know more about amoebas than they do about investing. Despite its obvious importance to every individual, our education system almost totally ignores the field of finance and investments. This is true unless you go to an undergraduate business school or pursue an MBA in finance. For example, my oldest daughter attended an excellent high school and graduated in the top 10 of her class. Having taken a biology course, she could tell you all you would ever need to know about amoebas. She could not, however, tell you the first thing about how financial markets work. She certainly could not tell you how markets set prices. Without that basic understanding, there is simply no way for her to know how to make informed investment decisions.

Most investors, many without realizing it, are in the same boat. They think they know how markets work. However, the reality is quite different. The following quote has been attributed to humorist Josh Billings: "It ain't what a man don't know as makes him a fool, but what he does know as ain't so." The result is that individuals are making investments without the basic knowledge required to understand the implications of their decisions. It is as if they took a trip to a place they have never been without a road map, directions, or a GPS. Lacking a formal education in finance, most investors make decisions based on the accepted conventional wisdom—ideas that have become so ingrained that few individuals question them.

Most of what you will read in this book directly contradicts the conventional wisdom that smart people, working diligently, can discover which stocks are mispriced by the market. Thus, they can buy stocks that are undervalued and avoid (or sell short) the stocks that are overvalued. This conventional wisdom also says these smart investors can also time the market—that is, they can get into the market before the bull enters the arena and sell before the bear emerges from its hibernation. This is what the practice of active management is all about—stock picking and market timing. Anything else is even considered by some to be un-American. To quote my ex-boss, "Diligence, hard work, research, and intelligence just have to pay off in superior results. How can no management be better than professional management?"

The problem with this thought process is that while these statements are correct generalizations (and as a result become conventional wisdom), success in beating the market is the exception to the rule. If hard work and diligence always produce superior results, how do you explain the failure of the majority of professional money managers (intelligent, capable, hard-working individuals) to beat the market year in and year out? Why is there no persistence of outperformance beyond the randomly expected? And why have not the leading consulting firms been able to identify the future outperformers?

If you keep an open mind, you will find that when exposed to the light of logic and evidence you will be convinced that not only is the conventional wisdom wrong—Moshe Levy, author of the article, "The Deadweight Loss of Active Management," evaluated the performance of US active equity funds and estimated that the aggregate annual loss to investors in US active equity funds was $235 billion—but it never made any sense in the first place.[1] In fact, it is illogical. I am confident that you will find the simple, yet compelling logic of the stories presented here, and the evidence supporting that logic, so overwhelming that you will be convinced of its accuracy. Remember "the Earth is flat" was once conventional wisdom, as was "the Earth is the center of the universe." As these examples make clear, however, just because something is conventional wisdom doesn't make it correct. In other words, even if millions of people believe a foolish thing, it is still a foolish thing.

Legends do die hard—especially when there is an establishment (Wall Street and the financial media) that is interested in perpetuating the legend. Thus, this book has three objectives. The first is to explain how markets really work, doing so in a way that makes it easy to understand even difficult concepts. I hope to accomplish this objective through the use of stories and analogies that present the logic in a paradigm with which you are already familiar, and relating that logic to the world of investing. If you understand the logic in the story, it should be just as clear when the logic is related to investing—especially when the evidence supports the logic.

If I am successful in meeting the first objective, I will have also achieved the second objective—to forever change the way you think about investing and how markets work.

The third objective is to provide you with sufficient knowledge to begin to make more informed and more prudent investment decisions.

The book was written with two audiences in mind. The first is individual investors. The second is financial advisors. Hopefully, my stories will provide advisors with the ammunition they need to convince their clients to stop throwing their hard-earned money away, to stop making brokers and fund families wealthy, and to start playing the winner's game.

The book is divided into four sections. The first is designed to help you understand how markets really work, how prices of securities are established, and why it's so difficult to outperform on a risk-adjusted basis. The second is designed to help you with the key decisions you have to make when designing your portfolio. The third is designed to help you understand how human nature leads us to make investment mistakes—being informed will help you avoid them. And the fourth is designed to help you play the winner's game by providing key insights.

You will learn that the winning strategy is actually simple and takes less energy. Thus, the strategy is not only likely to dramatically increase the odds of achieving your financial goals but also it will allow you to improve the quality of your life, as the tale of "The Big Rocks" illustrates. The way smart money invests today is by building a globally diversified portfolio of "passively managed" funds. Since there is some debate about exactly what is meant by passively managed, with some considering only index funds to be passively managed, my definition includes not only index funds but also other funds whose construction rules are evidence-based (as opposed to being based on opinions), transparent, and implemented in a systematic, replicable way. The key word is *systematic*. But owning only systematically managed funds is only the necessary condition for investing success. The sufficient condition is to be able to stay the course, ignoring the noise of the market and the investment propaganda put out by Wall Street and the financial media.

One of my favorite expressions is "If you think education is expensive, try ignorance." Hopefully this book will whet your appetite for a deeper understanding of the issues raised and create a desire to broaden your knowledge. If you find this book entertaining and educational, I have authored 18 other books on investing, each of which goes into greater depth than the scope of this book allowed, and they also cover many important topics not covered here.

Note that some of these tales appeared in *Wise Investing Made Simple*, published in 2007, or in *Wise Investing Made Simpler*, published in 2010. Those tales and all the data have been updated.

Part One

HOW MARKETS WORK: HOW SECURITY PRICES ARE DETERMINED AND WHY IT'S SO DIFFICULT TO OUTPERFORM

Chapter 1

The Determinants
of the Risk and Return
# of Stocks and Bonds

What the wise do in the beginning, fools do in the end.

—*Warren Buffett*

In 1977, Bill James self-published the book *1977 Baseball Abstract: Featuring 18 Categories of Statistical Information That You Just Can't Find Anywhere Else*. Seventy-five people found the book of sufficient interest to buy it.[1] Today James's annual edition (now called *The Bill James Handbook*) is considered a must-read for all serious fans of our national pastime.

James demonstrated, through rigorous research, that certain statistics are more meaningful than others in determining the effectiveness of a player. Among his many findings are that a player's batting average and the number of homers he hits are not as important as people had assumed. James found other statistics are more vital, namely, the total of a player's on-base percentage and his slugging average.

James revolutionized the way people think about baseball statistics and how to build a winning team. Today, every team in every major sport employs statistical experts (sabermetricians) on their staff. In his book *Moneyball*, Michael Lewis explained how Billy Beane, the general manager of the Oakland Athletics, used sabermetricians to build a winning team despite the constraint of a limited payroll.

By assessing which factors are the most significant in determining the impact a player has on the outcome of a game James changed the way we think about baseball. The 1992 publication of the paper "The Cross-Section of Expected Stock Returns," by Eugene Fama and Kenneth French in *The Journal of Finance*, had a similar impact on the field of financial economics.[2] The Fama-French research produced what has become known as the three-factor model. A factor is a common trait or characteristic of a stock or bond. The three factors are market beta (the return of the market minus the return on one-month Treasury bills), size (the return on small stocks minus the return on large stocks), and value (the return on value stocks minus the return on growth stocks). The model is able to explain more than 90% of the variation of returns of diversified US equity portfolios.

Lesser known is that professors Fama and French also provided us with a similar two-factor model that explains the variation of returns of fixed-income portfolios. The two risk factors are term and default (credit risk). The longer the term to maturity, the greater the risk; and the lower the credit rating, the greater the risk. Markets compensate investors for taking risk with higher *expected* returns. As is the case with equities, individual security selection and market timing do not play a significant role in explaining returns of fixed-income portfolios and thus should not be expected to add value.

Advances in our understanding of asset prices did not end there. Over the ensuing years, other common factors were found to add explanatory power. Among the leading ones are momentum (the tendency for securities that have outperformed in the recent past to continue to do so for a relatively short period), profitability (the tendency for more profitable companies to provide higher returns than less profitable ones despite higher valuations), and quality. Quality is a broader trait than profitability. Quality companies are those that are not only more profitable but also tend to have less financial and operating leverage (less debt and lower fixed costs), lower volatility of earnings, high asset turnover (they use their capital efficiently), and less idiosyncratic risk (risks not related to the broad economy).

An example of how the academic research has advanced our understanding of investment performance is the study "Buffett's Alpha."[3] The authors—Andrea Frazzini, David Kabiller, and Lasse Pedersen—examined the performance of the stocks owned by legendary investor Warren Buffett's Berkshire Hathaway and found that, in addition to benefiting from the use of cheap leverage provided by Berkshire's insurance operations, Buffett buys stocks that are safe, cheap, high-quality, and large. Their most interesting finding was that stocks with these characteristics tend to perform well in general, not just the stocks with these characteristics that Buffett buys. In other words, it is Buffett's strategy, or exposure to factors, that explains his success, not his stock-picking skills. That, and because he never engages in panicked selling.

The good news for investors is that the "discovery" of these common factors enables individuals to invest in the same type of stocks as legendary investors such as Warren Buffett—who had been successfully exploiting these factors for decades—without having to do all the research. Instead, they can simply invest in funds that provide exposure to these common factors. One example, the iShares MSCI USA Quality Factor ETF (QUAL), which buys quality stocks, has an expense ratio of just 0.15% and, as an ETF, is highly tax efficient.

Implications for Investors

The implication for investors is that the academic research has demonstrated that efforts to outperform the market by either security selection or timing are highly unlikely to prove productive after taking into account the costs, including taxes, of the efforts. For example, studies such as the "Luck Versus Skill in the Cross-Section of Mutual Fund Returns" have found fewer active managers (about 2%) are able to outperform their three-factor-model benchmark than would be expected by chance.[4] And that is even before considering the impact of taxes, which for taxable investors is typically the greatest expense of active management (greater than the fund's expense ratio and/or trading costs).

The prudent strategy, therefore, is to do the following:

- Develop a portfolio that reflects your unique ability, willingness, and need to take risk. The equity portion should be globally diversified across multiple asset classes. The fixed-income portion should be diversified in terms of credit and term risk, as appropriate.
- Avoid the use of actively managed funds. Instead, invest in funds (such as index funds) that provide systematic exposure to the factors you seek exposure to, and which are low cost and tax efficient. In the case of fixed-income assets (for those individuals who have sufficient assets to do so), build a portfolio of individual Treasury securities and/or FDIC-insured CDs, and for taxable accounts, AAA- and AA-rated municipal bonds that are also either general obligation or essential service revenue bonds. Doing so greatly reduces the credit risk and therefore the need for diversification (which is the benefit of a mutual fund). Those strategies will save you the expense of a mutual fund as well as allow you to tailor the portfolio to your unique state and tax situation.
- Have the discipline to stay the course, ignoring the noise of the markets as well as the emotions caused by the noise—emotions that cause investors to abandon even the most well-developed plans.

The Moral of the Tale

Intelligent people maintain open minds when it comes to new ideas. And they change strategies when there is compelling evidence demonstrating the "conventional wisdom" is wrong.

Why are some individuals unable to make a change in the face of what some would consider convincing evidence? One explanation is that when you are familiar with a certain way of thinking about a subject, whether it's investing or baseball, it is hard to make the leap to another model. Making the leap, however, is well worth the effort, as the Boston Red Sox demonstrated. In late 2002 they hired Bill James as a senior baseball operations advisor. In 2004, the Boston Red Sox won the World Series, breaking what some consider one of baseball's most famous curses, as well as my heart—I am a diehard Yankees fan and the Yankees are the only team in history to blow a 3–0 lead in the League Championship Series.

The next story is the most important one in the book. It explains how the market prices of securities are established. Understanding this is critical to determining a winning investment strategy.

Chapter 2

How Markets Set Prices

It is not easy to get rich in Las Vegas, at Churchill Downs, or at the local Merrill Lynch office.

—*Paul Samuelson*

On any given Saturday during the college basketball season, there may be 100 games being played. In some of those games, it is easy to identify the better team. For example, Duke is a perennial contender for the national college basketball championship. Mike Krzyzewski (Coach K), who coached Duke from 1980 through 2022, was a graduate of West Point. Each year he scheduled a game with Army as a favor to his alma mater. Though the likelihood of Army winning was about as likely as the sun rising in the west, the game did generate a large amount of revenue for West Point. These types of mismatches are known as "cupcake" games.

Every major school has a few cupcake games on their schedule, particularly early in the season. Even a fan with limited knowledge would be able to predict the winner of this type of game the majority of the time. A fan who was an "expert" would be able to predict the winner at least 90% of the time. The reason is simple: Duke has better shooters, better rebounders, better defenders, quicker athletes who can also jump higher, a better coach, better training facilities, and so on. This makes it easy to identify which team will likely win a game between Army and Duke.

However, there are many games in which it is more difficult to predict the winner. This is especially true later in the season when conference play begins. A good example of a game where it is typically difficult to predict the winner is the Duke Blue Devils versus their hated rival the Tar Heels of North Carolina. Since a monkey throwing darts would be expected to predict the winner of such games 50% of the time, a fan with limited knowledge should be expected to do no worse. A fan with "expert" knowledge should, however, be able to do better than monkeys. Perhaps such an expert might be able to forecast the winner of these types of games with an accuracy of 60%.

Most of us know at least a few individuals who think they are experts on sports. Some may even have an account with the website DraftKings. Again, such experts are likely able to predict the winners of the cupcake games with 90% accuracy, and the winners of the remainder of the games with an accuracy of 60%. Thus, they might be expected to predict the winner of all games with an accuracy of perhaps 75%. But the story gets even better— these experts don't have to bet on all the games. They can avoid betting on the games when it is difficult to predict the winner. They can limit the selection of games on which they place a bet to only those games where they are confident that they can predict the winner at least 90% of the time. Yet, despite that ability, it is unlikely you know even a single person who has become rich betting on sporting events. It is also unlikely you know anyone who knows anyone who has made their fortune that way. However, you might know someone who has made a small fortune betting on sporting events by starting out with a large one!

With the odds of success of predicting winners so high, why don't we know people who have achieved great wealth by betting on sports? The answer is quite simple: you cannot simply bet on Duke to beat Army. If you want to bet on Duke to beat Army, you might have to provide the counterparty to your bet with a handicap (known as the "point spread") of perhaps 40 points. In other words, Duke not only has to beat Army, they have to beat them by more than 40 points for you to win the bet. This point spread is the reason we don't hear about rich gamblers, only rich bookies. And the reason we hear about rich bookies is that gambling involves costs. Consider the following example.

Mark is a Duke fan and bets on the Blue Devils to beat Army by more than 40 points. In betting lingo, Mark "gives" points. Steve is a graduate of West Point, and even though he knows Duke is likely to beat Army, he doesn't think it likely they will do so by such a large margin. Thus, he "takes" the points and bets on Army. If Mark and Steve are friends and they bet against each other, we have what is known as a "zero-sum game." For example, if they bet $10, one would win $10 and the other would lose $10. The net of the two is zero. However, if they made a bet through a bookie, each would have to bet $11 to win just $10. This becomes a negative-sum game for Mark and Steve. The winner of the bet will win $10. The loser, however, is out $11. The difference of $1 is known as the "vigorish." It is a profit for the bookie. The game for Mark and Steve has become a negative sum. Note that the bookies win whether you win or lose; they just need you to play. I hope you are beginning to see the analogy to investing—we can compare broker-dealers and stockbrokers (including those who call themselves advisors) to bookies! They win whether you win or lose. Perhaps that is why Woody Allen has been quoted with the following observation: "A stockbroker is someone who invests your money until it is all gone." One translation: the objective of a stockbroker is to transfer assets from your account to their account. As my friend, and author of several wonderful books, Bill Bernstein, said, "The stockbroker services his clients in the same way that Bonnie and Clyde serviced banks."[1]

Continuing our story, it is important to understand who sets the point spreads. Most people believe it is the bookies that determine the spread. Although that is the conventional wisdom, it is incorrect. It is the market that determines the point spread. The bookies only set the initial spread. This is an important point to understand. Let's begin with an understanding of whether the bookies want to "make bets" or "take bets"—and there is a difference between the two.

If the bookies were to make bets, they might actually lose money by being on the wrong side of the bet. Again, think of a stockbroker. If you want to buy a stock (making a bet on the company), you have to buy it from someone. A stockbroker is not going to sell that stock to you because he might lose money. Instead, he finds someone who wants to sell the stock and matches the buyer with the seller. He is taking bets, not making bets. In the process, he earns the vigorish (a commission). Like stockbrokers, bookies want to take bets, not make them. Thus, they set the initial point spread at the "price" they believe will balance the forces of supply and demand (the point at which an equal amount of money will be bet on Duke and Army). To illustrate how the process works, consider the following example.

What would happen if a bookie made a terrible mistake and posted a point spread of zero in the Duke versus Army game? Obviously, gamblers would rush to bet on Duke. The result would be an imbalance of supply and demand. The bookies would end up making bets—something they are loath to do.

Like with any market, an excess of demand leads to an increase in price. The point spread would begin to rise, and it would continue to rise until supply equaled demand and the bookies had an equal amount of money bet on both sides (or at least as close to that as they could manage). At that point they are taking bets, not making them. And the bookies would win no matter the outcome of the game.

In one of my favorite films, *Trading Places*, Eddie Murphy makes a similar observation about the commodity brokerage firm of Duke and Duke. When the Duke brothers explain that they get a commission on every trade, whether the clients make money or not, Murphy exclaims, "Sounds to me like you guys are a couple of bookies."

As you can see, it is the market that determines the point spread (or the "price" of Duke). In other words, it is a bunch of amateurs like you and me (and I played college basketball) who think they know something about sports who are setting the spread. And even with a bunch of amateurs setting the spread (not the professional bookies), most of us don't know anyone who has become rich betting on sports. It seems that a bunch of amateurs are setting point spreads at prices that make it extremely difficult for even the most knowledgeable sports fan to exploit any mispricing, after accounting for the expenses of the effort. The important term here is "after expenses."

Because of the vigorish, it is not enough to be able to win more than 50% of the bets. With a vigorish of 10%, a bettor (investor) would have to be correct about 52.4% of the time to come out ahead. And that assumes there are no other costs involved (including the value of the time it takes to study the teams, analyze the spread, and make the bet).

In economic terms, a market in which it is difficult to persistently exploit mispricings after the expenses of the effort is called an "efficient" market. Because we don't know people who have become rich betting on sports, we know intuitively that sports-betting markets are efficient. However, intuition is often incorrect. It helps to have evidence supporting your intuition. Before we look at the evidence, however, we need a definition.

Point Spreads and Random Errors

An "unbiased estimator" is a statistic that is, on average, neither too high nor too low. The method of estimation does not always produce estimates that correspond to reality, but errors in either direction are equally likely. It turns out that the point spread is an unbiased estimate of the outcome of sporting events—while it is not expected to be correct in every instance, when it is incorrect, the errors are randomly distributed with a zero mean. To make this clear, we return to our Duke versus Army example in which

Duke was favored by 40 points. Duke does not have to win by exactly 40 points for the market in sports betting to be considered efficient. In fact, the likelihood of Duke winning by exactly that amount would be very low. However, that is not relevant to the issue of whether or not the market for sports betting is efficient. What is relevant is whether you can predict if Duke will win by more or less than 40. If half the time they win by more and half the time they win by less, and there is no way to know when they will be above or below the point spread, the point spread is an unbiased predictor—and the market is efficient. With this understanding, we are ready to examine the evidence.

Examining the Evidence

Research has found that point spreads are accurate in the sense that they are unbiased predictors. For example, in a study covering six NBA seasons, Raymond Sauer found that the average difference between point spreads and actual point differences was less than one-quarter of one point.[2] When you consider that, on average, the market guessed the actual resulting point spread with an error of less than one-quarter of one point, and the cost of playing is 10%, it is easy to understand why we don't know people who have become rich from betting on sports. And it is easy to see that the market in sports betting is efficient. The important lesson is that while it is often easy to identify the better team (in this case Duke), that is not a sufficient condition for exploiting the market; it is only a necessary condition. The sufficient condition is that you have to be able to exploit any mispricing by the market. For example, if you knew that Duke should be favored by 40 points but the point spread was only 30 points, and you could consistently identify such opportunities, the market would be inefficient. However, this is not the case.

Here's another example from the world of college basketball. Daniel C. Hickman studied the efficiency of betting on NCAA men's basketball tournament games from 1996 through 2019.

The NCAA men's basketball tournament is one of the most popular sporting events in the world and gives rise to a substantial betting market. Hickman examined the efficiency of this market to determine whether bettors display any significant biases and found that the market was highly efficient. For example, the higher-seeded team wins a high percentage of games but covers the spread just under 50% of the time. He also found that the market does a remarkably efficient job of forecasting the actual score for the higher-seeded teams in tournament games, with a mean forecast error of just 0.05 points. The score of the lower-seeded teams is underestimated by just 0.5 points.[3]

In case you think the betting market in basketball is just an anomaly, here's another example from English professional football. Guy Elaad, James Reade, and Carl Singleton, authors of the 2020 study "Information, Prices and Efficiency in an Online Betting Market," analyzed the odds (or prices) set by 51 online bookmakers for the result outcomes in more than 16,000 association football matches in England over the period 2010–2018. They found that "there is no statistically significant evidence at standard levels (5% or 1% level, two-tailed tests) that bookmaker odds excessively price in any particular match result outcomes."[4]

Horse racing presents an even more amazing outcome, especially when you consider the following. My mother loved to go to the track. Like many people, she chose the horses she would bet on by either the color of the jockey's outfit or the name of the horse. If the jockey wore purple, forget about it; she hated the color purple. And she always bet on the three horse in the first race. Now, there are fans who go to the track and make a "science" of studying each horse's racing history and under what racing conditions the horse did well or poorly. And perhaps these experts even attend workouts to time the horses. Thus, these "experts" are competing against people like my mother. Yet, the final odds, which reflect the judgment of all bettors, reliably predict the outcome—the favorite wins the most often, the second favorite is the next most likely to win, and so on. It gets even better in that a horse with 3-to-1 odds wins about one-fourth of the time![5] It seems that the collective wisdom of the crowd is a tough competitor indeed.

An Efficient Market

An efficient market is one in which trading systems fail to produce excess returns because everything currently knowable is already incorporated into prices (Duke is so much better than Army, they should be favored by 40 points, but not more). The next piece of available information will be random as to whether it will be better or worse than the market already expects. The only way to beat an efficient market is to either know something the market doesn't—such as the fact that a team's best player is injured and will not be able to play—or to be able to interpret information about the teams better than the market (other gamblers collectively) does. You have to search for a game where the strength of the favorite is underestimated or the weakness of the underdog is overestimated, and thus the spread, or the market, is wrong. The spread is really the competition. And the spread is determined by the collective wisdom of the entire market. This is an important point to understand. Let's see why.

Returning to our example of Mark and Steve betting on Duke versus Army. If there was no sports betting market to which Mark and Steve could refer, they would have to set the point spread themselves. Now, Mark might be a more knowledgeable fan than Steve, who also happens to be a graduate of West Point. Steve's heart might influence his thinking. Thus, when Mark offers to give Steve 30 points, Steve jumps at the chance and bets on Army. Mark has just exploited Steve's lack of knowledge. (Mark might still lose the bet, but the odds of winning have increased in his favor.)

The existence of an efficient public market in which the knowledge of all bettors (investors) is at work in setting prices serves to protect the less-informed bettors (investors) from being exploited. The flipside is that the existence of an efficient market prevents the sophisticated and more knowledgeable bettors (investors) from exploiting their less-knowledgeable counterparts. As we have seen, the spread is an unbiased predictor and the market is efficient. The result is that the market is a tough competitor.

There are other important points to understand about sports betting and how it relates to investing. The first is that in the world of sports betting, a bunch of amateurs are setting prices. Even though that is the case, we saw that it is difficult to find pricing errors that could be exploited. In the world of investing, however, professionals are setting prices.

Since about 90% of all trading is done by large institutional traders, it is these sophisticated investors who are setting prices, not amateur individual investors. With professionals (instead of amateurs) dominating the market, the competition is certainly tougher. Every time an individual buys a stock, they should consider that they are competing with these giant institutional investors. The individual investor should also acknowledge that institutions have more resources, and thus it is more likely they will succeed.

Another difference between sports betting and investing is best illustrated by returning to our example of Duke versus Army. Imagine that you were best friends with Coach K. As a birthday present, he invited you into the Duke locker room to meet the players and hear his pregame talk. As the players are exiting the locker room to start warming up, Duke's star point guard trips over a water bucket and breaks his ankle. Your mercenary instincts take over and you immediately pull out your cell phone and place a large bet on Army, taking 40 points. You possessed information that others did not have and took advantage of it. And the best part is that there is nothing illegal about that "trade." Now, remember it is likely that few, if any, of us know anyone who has become rich betting on sports despite the existence of rules that allow you to exploit what in the world of investing would be considered inside information. In that world, it is illegal to trade and profit from inside information, as Martha Stewart found out. But even individuals who have had inside information (such as Pete Rose, whose case we discuss in Chapter 6) and could influence the outcomes of sporting events don't seem to be able to persistently exploit such information.

The conclusion we can draw from the evidence is that the markets for betting on sports are highly efficient. This is true despite the lack of rules against insider trading and the fact that it is amateurs who think they know something about sports (and often bet on their home team or alma mater with their hearts and not their heads) who are setting prices. Conversely, there are specific rules against insider trading in investing, and it is professional investors who are setting prices, so the competition is tougher. In addition, as is the case with sports betting, it is not enough to be smarter than the market because there are costs involved. In sports betting, the cost is the vigorish.

The problem for those investors trying to exploit mispricings in the stock market is that there are also costs involved. Similar to sports betting, the "bookies" (broker-dealers) have to be paid when active investors place their bets. Trading involves not only commissions but also the spread between the bid (the price dealers are willing to pay) and the offer (the price at which dealers are willing to sell). If you place your assets with a mutual fund, you also have to pay its operating costs—which are generally higher for actively managed funds than for passively managed ones (such as index funds) that do not engage in individual stock selection or market timing. For institutional investors, costs may also include what are called "market-impact costs."

Market impact is what occurs when a mutual fund (or other investor) wants to buy or sell a large block of stock. The fund's purchases or sales will cause the stock to move beyond its current bid (lower) or offer (higher) price, increasing the cost of trading. For taxable accounts, there is also the burden of capital gains tax, which is created by actively trading the portfolio.

We continue with our analogy between sports betting and investing by examining how investors set the prices of individual stocks.

How Stock Prices Are Set

Stock prices are set in a similar manner to how point spreads are established. A good analogy to the point spread setting process is how underwriters set the price of a stock's initial public offering (IPO). Just as bookies survey the market to set the initial point spread so that supply will equal demand (so that they can take bets, not make them), underwriters survey potential investors and set the price based on their best estimate of the price needed to sell all the shares. Once the IPO is completed, the shares will trade in what is called the "secondary market." Just as with sports betting, in the secondary market the forces of supply and demand take over. The only difference is that instead of point spreads setting prices, they are determined by the price-to-earnings (P/E) ratio or the book-to-market (BtM) ratio. The P/E and BtM ratios act just like the point spread. The following example will make this clear.

Battle of the Discount Retailers

As an investor you are faced with the decision to purchase the shares of either Walmart or Kohl's. Walmart is generally considered to be one of the top retailers. It has great management, the best store locations, an outstanding inventory management system, a strong balance sheet, a strong online business, and so on. Because of its great prospects, Walmart is considered a growth stock. Kohl's, however, is a relatively weaker company. It has lower return on assets, lower return on equity, and a weaker balance sheet with a higher debt-to-equity ratio. Because of its relatively weaker prospects, Kohl's is considered a value stock. Just as it was easy to identify the better team in the Duke versus Army example, it is easy to identify the better company when faced with choosing between Walmart and Kohl's. Most individuals faced with having to buy one or the other would not even have to think about the decision— they would rush to buy Walmart. But is that the right choice?

As we saw in the sports betting story, being able to identify the better team did not help us make the decision as to which one was the better bet. Let's see if the ability to identify the better company helps us make an investment decision. Before reading on, think about which company is Duke and which one is Army.

Imagine that both Walmart and Kohl's have earnings of $1 per share. That is certainly possible even though Walmart generates far more profits. Walmart might have 1 billion shares outstanding, and Kohl's might only have 100 million shares outstanding. Now imagine a world where Walmart and Kohl's both traded at a price of $10. Which stock would you buy in that world? Clearly, you would rush to buy Walmart. The problem is that Walmart is Duke and Kohl's is Army. And Walmart and Kohl's trading at the same price is analogous to the zero-point spread set by the bookies in the Duke versus Army game. Hell will freeze over before either happens. Just as sports fans would rush in to bet on Duke, driving up the point spread until the odds of winning the bet were equal, investors would drive up the price of Walmart relative to the price of Kohl's until the *risk-adjusted* expected returns from investing in either stock were equal. Let's see how that might look in terms of prices for the shares of Walmart and Kohl's.

Being a weaker company with relatively poorer prospects, investors might be willing to pay just 10 times earnings for the stock of Kohl's. Thus, with earnings of $1 per share, the stock would trade at $10. The company might also have a book value of $10 per share. Thus, the BtM ratio would be 1 ($10 book value divided by its $10 market price). However, Walmart is not only a safer investment due to its stronger balance sheet but also it has stronger growth prospects. Thus, investors might be willing to pay 20 times earnings for Walmart stock. With $1 per share in earnings, the stock would trade at $20. The company might also have a book value of just $4 per share. Thus, the BtM would be 0.2 ($4 book value divided by its $20 market price). Walmart is trading at a P/E) ratio that is twice that of the P/E ratio of Kohl's. It is also trading at a BtM that is only one-fifth that of Kohl's. Walmart is Duke having to give Army 40 points to make Army an equally good bet.

The Financial Equivalent of the Point Spread

The P/E and the BtM ratios act just like point spreads. The only difference is that instead of having to give away a lot of points to bet on a great team to win, you have to pay a higher price relative to earnings and book value for a great glamour company than for a distressed value company. If you bet on the underdog (Army), you get the point spread in your favor. Similarly, if you invest in a value company (Kohl's), you pay a low price relative to earnings and book value. The great sports team (Duke) has to overcome large point spreads to win the bet. The great company (Walmart) has to overcome the high price you pay in order to produce above-market returns. In gambling, the middle people who always win as long as you play are the bookies. In investing, the middle people who always win as long as you play (try to pick mutual funds or stocks that will outperform) are the active fund managers and the broker-dealers.

Let's again consider the analogy between sports betting and investing in stocks. First, in sports betting sometimes it is easy to identify the better team (Duke versus Army) and sometimes it is more difficult (Duke versus North Carolina). The same is true of stocks. It is easy to identify which company, Walmart or Kohl's, is the superior one. However, it is harder when our choices are Walmart and Costco.

Second, in sports betting we don't have to bet on all the games. We can choose to bet only on the games in which we can easily identify the better team. Similarly, we don't have to invest in all stocks. We can choose to invest only in the stocks of the superior companies.

Third, in sports the problem with betting on the good teams is that the rest of the market also knows they are superior, and you have to give away lots of points. The point spread eliminates any advantage gained by betting on the superior team. The same is true with investing. The price you have to pay for investing in superior companies is a higher P/E ratio (offsetting the more rapid growth in earnings that are expected) and a lower BtM (offsetting the lesser risk of the greater company). In sports the pricing mechanism in place would make betting on either team an equally good bet. The same applies for investing: either stock would make an equally good investment. Thus, while being able to identify the better team (company) is a necessary condition of success, it is not a sufficient one.

Fourth, when a bet is placed between friends, it is a zero-sum game. However, when the bet is placed with a bookie, the game becomes a negative-sum one because of the costs involved (the bookies win). Since we cannot trade stocks between friends, trading stocks must be a negative-sum game because of the costs involved (the market makers earn the bid–offer spread, the broker-dealers charge commissions, the active managers charge large fees, and Uncle Sam collects taxes).

Fifth, in the world of sports betting, it should be relatively easy to exploit mispricing because amateurs are the competition setting prices. In the world of investing, the competition is tougher because it is mostly large institutional investors, not amateurs like you and me.

Sixth, in sports betting it is legal to trade on inside information. Yet, even with such an advantage, it is likely you don't know anyone who has become rich by exploiting this type of knowledge. However, it is illegal to trade on inside information regarding stocks. Thus, it must be even more difficult to win that game.

The evidence from the world of investing supports the logic of the previous arguments. Study after study demonstrate that the majority of individual and institutional investors who attempt to beat the market by either picking stocks or timing the market fail miserably, and do so with great persistence. The following is a brief summary of the evidence.

Individual Investors

University of California professors Brad Barber and Terrance Odean have produced a series of landmark studies on the performance of individual investors. One study found that the stocks individual investors buy underperform the market after they buy them, and the stocks they sell outperform after they sell them.[6] They also found that male investors underperform the market by about 3% per annum, and women (because they trade less and thus incur less costs) trail the market by about 2% per annum.[7] In addition, they found that those investors who traded the most trailed the market on a risk-adjusted basis by over 10% per annum.[8] And to prove that more heads are not better than one, they found that investment clubs trailed the market by almost 4% per annum.[9] Since all these figures are on a pretax basis, once taxes are taken into account, the story would become even more dismal. Perhaps it was this evidence that convinced Andrew Tobias to offer this sage advice: "If you find yourself tempted to ask the question what stock should I buy, resist the temptation. If you do ask, don't listen. And if you hear an answer, promise yourself that you will ignore it."[10]

Institutional Investors

Institutional investors don't fare much better than individual investors. Eugene Fama and Kenneth French found that only managers in the 98th and 99th percentiles showed evidence of statistically significant skill.[11] Similar results were found by Philipp Meyer-Brauns in his study, "Mutual Fund Performance Through a Five-Factor Lens."[12] Importantly, the research consistently finds that there is no persistence in performance beyond the randomly expected. And if there is no performance persistence, there is no way to identify the few future winners ahead of time. The figures here are all on a pretax basis as well. Thus, the effect of taxes on after-tax returns would make the story even worse.

For those interested in learning more about why outperforming the market on a risk-adjusted basis is so difficult, I recommend reading *The Incredible Shrinking Alpha*.[13]

The Moral of the Tale

The moral of this tale is that betting against an efficient market is a loser's game. It doesn't matter whether the "game" is betting on a sporting event or trying to identify which stocks are going to outperform the market. While it is possible to win by betting on sporting events, because the markets are highly efficient, the only likely winners are the bookies. In addition, the more you play the game, the more likely it is you will lose and the bookies will win. The same is true of investing. And the reason is that the securities markets are also highly efficient.

If you try to time the market or pick stocks, or hire managers to engage in that activity for you, you are playing a loser's game. Just as it is possible you can win by betting on sporting events, it is possible you can win (outperform) by picking stocks, timing the market, or using active managers to play the game on your behalf. However, the odds are poor. And just as with gambling, the more and the longer you play the game, the more likely it is you will lose (as the costs of playing compound). This makes accepting market returns (passive investing) the winner's game.

By investing in passively managed funds and adopting a simple buy, hold, and rebalance strategy, you are guaranteed to not only earn market rates of returns but also you will do so in a low-cost and relatively tax-efficient manner. You are also virtually guaranteed to outperform the majority of professional and individual investors. Thus, it is the strategy most likely to achieve the best results. The bottom line is that while gamblers make bets (speculate on individual stocks and actively managed funds), investors let the markets work for them, not against them.

This quote sums up this tale: "Information isn't in the hands of one person. It's dispersed across many people. So, relying on only your private information to make a decision guarantees that it will be less informed than it could be."[14]

Epilogue

Sometimes bookies lose their way and forget the winning strategy. Trouble begins when bookies are unable to "lay off" bets—make sure that an equal amount of money is bet on Duke and Army (in our running example). Thus, they end up making bets instead of taking them. And as we have seen, that is the loser's game. Consider the example of one bookie, the owner of the online casino Aces Gold.

The bookie had lost some money when he could not maintain a balanced book and ended up on the wrong side of the bet. Instead of trying to catch up gradually, he abandoned the winning strategy of only taking bets, not making them. He began to tilt his point spreads (relative to other bookmakers) to one team. This ensured that he would attract a lot of bets on one team and little to none on the other. Unfortunately, he kept losing. By the time of the 2002 NFL Super Bowl, the most heavily wagered sporting event, he owed his clients more than $1 million dollars. So, he went for the proverbial "Hail Mary." Prior to the game, the standard line favored the St. Louis Rams over the New England Patriots by 14 points. In order to attract a large volume of bets, Aces Gold offered those betting on the Patriots an extra one-half point, placing the spread at 14 1/2 points. Predictably, Aces Gold Casino took in a large volume of bets on the Patriots—and made no effort to "lay off" those bets. "Not only did the Rams not cover the spread, but they also lost the game in a stunning upset. Aces Gold owed gamblers more than $3 million, money they would never see. The bookie is now rumored to be living somewhere in Texas."[15] Or perhaps he is wearing "cement shoes."

The next story also relates to market efficiency and choosing the winning strategy.

Chapter 3

Persistence
of Performance

Athletes Versus Investment Managers

Despite volumes of research attesting to the meaninglessness of past returns, most investors (and personal-finance magazines) seek tomorrow's winners among yesterday's. Forget it. The truth is, much as you may wish you could know which funds will be hot, you can't—and neither can the legions of advisers and publications that claim they can.

—Fortune, *March 15, 1999*

Barry Bonds was arguably the best baseball player of his era. No one would consider him to have been lucky to generate the statistics he produced because they are persistently so much better than those of other players. What is important to understand is that his superior results were likely the result of relatively small differences in skills. He was perhaps a bit stronger than most players (though some were stronger). His bat speed was probably slightly faster (though there were others whose bat speed might have been just as fast or faster). His hand/eye coordination was also probably slightly superior (again, a few probably had similar skills). He was also one of the fastest runners in the game (though he was not that much faster than most, and others had superior speed). The small differences in each of these categories (and perhaps others) is what enabled him to be perhaps the best player of his era.

What is important to understand is that Bonds' competition was other individual players. In terms of individual skills, he was not stronger than every player. Nor was he faster than every player, and so on. The world of investing, however, presents a very different situation. The difference in the form of competition is why we do not see persistence of outperformance of investment managers. To understand this, we need to understand how securities markets set prices.

Dr. Mark Rubinstein, professor of applied investment analysis at the Haas School of Business at the University of California at Berkeley, provided the following insight:

> Each investor, using the market to serve his or her own self-interest, unwittingly makes prices reflect that investor's information and analysis. It is as if the market were a huge, relatively low-cost, continuous polling mechanism that records the updated votes of millions of investors in continuously changing current prices. In light of this mechanism, for a single investor (in the absence of inside information) to believe that prices are significantly in error is almost always folly. Public information should already be embedded in prices.[1]

Rubinstein was making the point that the competition for an investment manager is not other individual investment managers. Instead, it is the *collective wisdom* of the market—economist Adam Smith's famous "invisible hand." It's the same collective wisdom that prevents knowledgeable sports fans from exploiting the lack of knowledge of the casual fan when betting on sporting events.

The competition was the market, not the skills of each individual participant.

The implication for investors, as author Ron Ross points out in *The Unbeatable Market*, is that "the quest for market-beating strategy boils down to an information-processing contest. The entity you are competing against is the *entire* market and the accumulated information discovered by all the participants and reflected in prices."[2]

Here is another way to think about the quest for superior investment performance: "The potential for self-cancellation shows why the game of investing is so different from, for example, chess, in which even a seemingly small advantage can lead to consistent victories. Investors implicitly lump the market with other arenas of competition in their experience."[3] Rex Sinquefield, former co-chairman of Dimensional Fund Advisors (DFA) who retired in 2005, put it this way: "Just because there are some investors smarter than others, that advantage will not show up. The market is too vast and too informationally efficient."[4]

While the competition for Bonds is other individual players, the competition for investment managers is the entire market. It would be as if each time Bonds stepped up to the plate, he had to face a pitcher with the collective skills of Randy Johnson (fastball), Greg Maddux (control), Roger Clemens (split-finger pitch), Carl Hubbell (screwball), Bert Blyleven (curveball), and Gaylord Perry (spitball). If that had been the case, Bonds certainly would not have produced the same results.

In the world of investing, the competition is indeed tough. What so many people fail to comprehend is that in many forms of competition, such as chess, poker, or investing, it is the *relative* level of skill that plays the more important role in determining outcomes, not the *absolute* level. What is referred to as the "paradox of skill" means that even as skill level rises, luck can become more important in determining outcomes if the level of competition also rises.

Charles Ellis noted in a 2014 issue of the *Financial Analysts Journal* article "The Rise and Fall of Performance Management": "Over the past 50 years, increasing numbers of highly talented young investment professionals have entered the competition. . . . They have more-advanced training than their predecessors, better analytical tools, and faster access to more information."[5] Legendary hedge funds, such as Renaissance Technologies, SAC Capital Advisors, and D.E. Shaw, hire PhD scientists, mathematicians, and computer scientists. MBAs from top schools, such as Chicago, Wharton, and MIT, flock to investment management armed with powerful computers and massive databases.

For example, Gerard O'Reilly, the chief executive officer of DFA, has a PhD from Caltech in aeronautics and applied mathematics. Eduardo Repetto, the chief investment officer of Avantis Investors, has a PhD from Caltech and worked there as a research scientist. And Andrew Berkin, the head of research at Bridgeway Capital Management, has a Caltech BS and University of Texas PhD in physics, and is a winner of the NASA Software of the Year Award. According to Ellis, the "unsurprising result" of this increase in skill is that "the increasing efficiency of modern stock markets makes it harder to match them and much harder to beat them, particularly after covering costs and fees."[6]

Another problem for investors is that since today as much as 90% of the trading is done by institutional investors, even before expenses it is difficult to think of a large enough group of likely individuals to exploit. The reason is that for one group of investors to outperform another must underperform. The increasing share of trading done by institutional investors has resulted in the competition becoming increasingly more difficult, as demonstrated by Timothy Riley, author of "Can Mutual Fund Stars Still Pick Stocks? A Replication and Extension of Kosowski, Timmermann, Wermers, and White (2006)."[7] Riley began by reviewing the findings of the study "Can Mutual Fund 'Stars' Really Pick Stocks? New Evidence from a Bootstrap Analysis."[8] Using a bootstrap method, the authors, Kosowski, Timmermann, Wermers, and White (KTWW), found that over the period 1975 to 2002, "a sizable minority of managers pick stocks well enough to more than cover their costs; moreover, the superior alphas of these managers persist." Riley noted that "their work has subsequently been heavily cited as evidence in support of mutual fund manager skill and the value of active management in the mutual fund industry."[9]

Riley then tested whether KTWW's findings held outside of their 1975 to 2002 sample period—specifically the 15 years (2003 to 2017) after their sample ended. He next considered results generated using a combined sample formed from KTWW's original period and his extension (1975 to 2017). He concluded: "The results from this combined sample indicate what KTWW would have found if the full historical record available now was available at the time they completed their study."[10] His combined sample contained 3,151 unique funds. Following is a summary of his findings:

- When replicating KTWW inside their sample period (1975 to 2002), the results were similar to the original findings—funds in the top 10% of performance tended to produce alphas in excess of costs that could not be explained by luck alone.
- In the post-KTWW period, 2003–2017, there was no evidence of alphas greater than would be expected based solely on luck.
- Using the full sample from 1975 through 2017, there was little evidence to suggest high alphas are not due to luck.

His findings led Riley to conclude: "Consistent with the actions of investors and research since KTWW's publication, the 'sizable minority of managers [who] pick stocks well enough to more than cover their costs' appears to have substantially decreased in size—or perhaps disappeared entirely—during the last 15 years." He also noted that if he had limited his analysis to just the group of successful funds from the KTWW study, his conclusions would not change. Summarizing, Riley stated, "My results indicate that KTWW's study does not reflect the modern mutual fund industry or the full testable history of the industry."[11]

The Nature of the Competition

Understanding the true nature of the competition and the difficulty of achieving superior performance, Ralph Wanger, former chief investment officer of Liberty Wanger Asset Management and lead portfolio manager of the Liberty Acorn Fund, concluded:

> For professional investors like myself, a sense of humor is essential for another reason. We are very aware that we are competing not only against the market averages but also against one another. It's an intense rivalry. We are each claiming, "The stocks in my fund today will perform better than what you own in your fund." That implies we think we can predict the future, which is the occupation of charlatans. If you believe you or anyone else has a system that can predict the future of the stock market, the joke is on you.[12]

There is another important difference between sports and investing that explains the lack of persistence of superior investment performance. When Bonds was at the plate, he was engaged in a zero-sum game—either he won, or the pitcher did. However, investment managers trying to outperform are not engaged in a zero-sum game. In their efforts to outperform the market, they incur significantly higher expenses than passive investors accepting market returns. Those costs are research expenses, other fund operating expenses, bid-offer spreads, commissions, market impact costs, and taxes. It would be as if Bonds went up to the plate with a doughnut (a weight) on his bat while all other hitters had no such handicap.

The academic research on the subject of performance persistence is clear: there is little to no evidence of any persistent ability to outperform the market without taking on greater risk.

Summary

The conventional wisdom is that past performance is a good predictor of future performance. The reason it is conventional wisdom is that it holds true in most endeavors, be it a sporting event or any other form of competition. The problem for investors who believe in conventional wisdom is that the nature of the competition in the investment arena is so different that conventional wisdom does not apply—what works in one paradigm does not necessarily work in another. Peter Bernstein, consulting editor of the *Journal of Portfolio Management* and author of several highly regarded investment books, including *Against the Gods* and *Capital Ideas*, put it this way: "In the real world, investors seem to have great difficulty outperforming one another in any convincing or consistent fashion. Today's hero is often tomorrow's blockhead."[13]

The Moral of the Tale

To avoid choosing the wrong investment strategy, one must understand the nature of the game. In the investment arena, large institutional investors dominate trading. Thus, they are the ones setting prices. Therefore, the competition is tough. Making the game even more difficult is that the competition is not each individual institutional investor. Instead, it is the collective wisdom of all other participants. The competition is just too tough for any one investor to be able to persistently outperform.

The next story continues on the theme of market efficiency and why persistence of outperformance is so difficult to achieve.

Chapter 4

Why Is Persistent Outperformance So Hard to Find?

According to Christian mythology, the Holy Grail was the dish, plate, or cup with miraculous powers that was used by Jesus at the Last Supper. Legend has it that the Grail was sent to Great Britain, where a line of guardians keeps it safe. The search for the Holy Grail is an important part of the legends of King Arthur and his court.

For many investors the equivalent of the Holy Grail is finding the formula enabling them to successfully time the market. For others it is finding the mutual (or hedge) fund manager who can exploit market mispricings by buying undervalued stocks and perhaps shorting those that are overvalued. While it is easy to identify after the fact those with great performance (all one needs is a database), there is no evidence of the ability to do this before the fact. We don't see any evidence of that ability in the annual S&P Active versus Passive Scorecards. And research such as "The Selection and Termination of Investment Management Firms by Plan Sponsors" demonstrates that we don't see it in the performance of pension plans, either.[1] That is why the SEC requires the familiar disclaimer that a fund's past performance doesn't necessarily predict future results. Academic studies have found that beyond a year there is little evidence of performance persistence. The only place we find persistence of performance (beyond that which we would randomly expect) is at the very bottom—poorly performing funds tend to repeat. And the persistence of poor performance is not due to poor stock selection. Instead, it is due to high expenses.

The efficient market hypothesis (EMH) explains why the lack of persistence should be expected: it is only by random good luck that a fund is able to persistently outperform after the expenses of its efforts. But there is also a practical reason for the lack of persistence: successful active management sows the seeds of its own destruction.

Successful Active Management Sows the Seeds of Its Own Destruction

In his paper "Five Myths of Active Management," Jonathan Berk, professor at the University of California, Berkeley, suggested the following thought process:

> Who gets money to manage? Well, as investors know who the skilled managers are, money will flow to the best manager first. Eventually, this manager will receive so much money that it will impact the manager's ability to generate superior returns and expected return will be driven down to the second-best manager's expected return. At that point, investors will be indifferent between investing with either manager, so funds will flow to both managers until their expected returns are driven down to the third-best manager.
>
> This process will continue until the expected return of investing with any manager is driven down to the expected return investors can expect to receive by investing in a passive strategy of similar riskiness (the benchmark expected

return). At this point, investors are indifferent between investing with active managers or just indexing, and an equilibrium is achieved.[2]

Berk went on to point out that the manager with the most skill ends up with the most money. He added this important insight: "When capital is supplied competitively by investors, but ability is scarce, only participants with the skill in short supply can earn economic rents. Investors who choose to invest with active managers cannot expect to receive positive excess returns on a risk-adjusted basis. . . . [If they did,] there would be an excess supply of capital to that manager."[3]

Just as the EMH explains why investors cannot use publicly available information to beat the market (because all investors have access to that information, and it is therefore already embedded in prices), the same is true of active managers. Investors should not expect to outperform the market by using publicly available information to select active managers. Any excess return will go to the active manager (in the form of higher expenses).

The process is simple. Investors observe benchmark-beating performance and funds flow into the top performers. The investment inflow eliminates return persistence because fund managers face diminishing returns to scale.

The study "Scale Effects in Mutual Fund Performance: The Role of Trading Costs" provides evidence supporting the logic of Berk's theory. Authors Roger Edelen, Richard Evans, and Gregory Kadlec examined the role of trading costs as a source of diseconomies of scale for mutual funds.[4] They studied the annual trading costs for 1,706 US equity funds during the period 1995–2005 and found the following:

- Trading costs for mutual funds are on average even greater in magnitude than the expense ratio.
- The variation in returns is related to fund trade size.
- Annual trading costs bear a statistically significant negative relation to performance.

- Trading has an increasingly detrimental impact on performance as a fund's relative trade size increases.
- Trading fails to recover its costs—$1 in trading costs reduced fund assets by $0.41. However, while trading does not adversely affect performance at funds with a relatively small average trade size, trading costs *decreased* fund assets by roughly $0.80 for large relative trade size funds.
- Flow-driven trades were shown to be significantly more costly than discretionary trades. This nondiscretionary trade motive partially—but not fully—explained the negative impact of trading on performance.
- Relative trade size subsumed fund size in regressions of fund returns.

Edelen, Evans, and Kadlec concluded that "our evidence directly establishes scale effects in trading as a source of diminishing returns to scale from active management."[5]

There is another reason why successful active management sows the seeds of its own destruction. As a fund's assets increase, either trading costs will rise or the fund will have to diversify across more securities to limit trading costs. However, the more a fund diversifies, the more it looks and performs like its benchmark index. It becomes what is known as a "closet index fund." If it chooses this alternative, its higher total costs must be spread across a smaller number of differentiated holdings (reducing its active share), increasing the hurdle of outperformance.

The Moral of the Tale

The efficiency of the markets and the evidence of the effects of scale on trading costs explain why persistent outperformance beyond the randomly expected is so hard to find. Thus, the search by investors for persistent outperformance is likely to prove as successful as Sir Galahad's search for the Holy Grail.

The next story focuses on debunking one of the greatest investment fables.

Chapter 5

Great Companies Do Not Make High-Return Investments

Investors must keep in mind that there's a difference between a good company and a good stock. After all, you can buy a good car but pay too much for it.

—Loren Fox

It is July 1, 1963. John Doe is the greatest security analyst in the world. He is able to identify, with uncanny accuracy, the companies that will produce high rates of return on assets over the next 59 years. Unlike real-world analysts and investors, he never makes a mistake in forecasting which companies will produce great earnings. In the history of the world, there has never been such an analyst. Even Warren Buffett has made mistakes, such as investing in companies like US Airways and Salomon Brothers.

While John cannot see into the future as it pertains to the stock prices of those companies, following the conventional wisdom of Wall Street, he builds a portfolio of their stocks. He does so because he has confidence that, since these are going to be great-performing companies, they will make great investments. Relating this to our sports betting story, he has identified the Duke Blue Devils of the investment world. We can identify these great companies ourselves by the fact that growth companies have high price-to-earnings ratios and high prices-to-book value.

Jane Smith, however, believes that markets are efficient. She bases her strategy on the theory that if the market believes a group of companies will produce superior results, the market must also believe they are relatively safe investments. With this knowledge, investors (the market) will already have bid up the price of those stocks to reflect those great expectations and the low level of perceived risk. While the companies are likely to produce great financial results, their stocks are likely to produce relatively lower returns. Jane, expecting (though not certain) that the market will reward her for taking risk, instead buys a passively managed portfolio of the stocks of value, or distressed, companies. She even anticipates the likelihood that, on average, these companies will continue to be relatively poor performers in terms of financial metrics such as growth in revenue and earnings. Despite this, she does expect the stocks to provide higher returns, thereby rewarding her for taking risk.

As you will see, Jane believes that markets work—they are efficient. John does not. Relating this to our sports betting story, John believes that you can bet on Duke and not have to give any points when they play Army.

Faced with the choice of buying the stocks of "great" companies or buying the stocks of "lousy" companies, most investors would instinctively choose the former. Before looking at the historical evidence, ask yourself what you would do. Assuming your only objective is to achieve high returns, regardless of the risk entailed, would you buy the stocks of the great companies or the stocks of the lousy companies?

Let's now jump forward 59 years to the end of June 2022. How did John's and Jane's investment strategies work out? Who was right? In a sense, they both were. For the 59-year period ending

June 2022, the return on assets (ROA) for John's great growth stocks (Fama-French US growth research index) was 11% per year. This was almost three times the 4% ROA for Jane's lousy value stocks. The annualized return to investors in Jane's value stocks (Fama-French US value research index) was, however, 13.2% per annum—3.2 percentage points greater than the 10.0% annualized return to investors in John's growth stocks (Fama-French US growth research index). We see similar results when looking at return on equity (ROE). The ROE on growth stocks was 25.7%, almost three times that of the 9.7% ROE of value stocks.

If the major purpose of investment research is to determine which companies will be the great-performing companies, and you produce inferior results when you are correct in your analysis, why bother? Why not save the time and expense and just let the markets reward you for taking risk?

Small Companies Versus Large Companies

If the theory holds true that markets provide returns commensurate with the amount of risk taken, one should expect to see similar results if Jane invested in a passively managed portfolio consisting of small companies, which are intuitively riskier than large companies. Small companies don't have the economies of scale that large companies have, making them generally less efficient. They typically have weaker balance sheets and fewer sources of capital. When there is distress in the capital markets, smaller companies are generally the first to be cut off from access to capital, increasing the risk of bankruptcy. They don't have the depth of management that larger companies do. They generally don't have long track records from which investors can make judgments. The cost of trading small stocks is much greater, increasing the risk of investing in them. And so on.

When one compares the performance of the asset class of large companies with the performance of the asset class of small companies, one gets the same results produced by the great (growth) companies versus value companies comparison. For the same 59-year period ending June 30, 2022, while large companies produced ROA of 8% (1 percentage point more than the 7% ROA of small companies) and large companies produced ROE of 20.2% (4.1 percentage points more than 16.2% ROE of small companies), small companies (Fama-French US small research index) returned 11.5% per annum, outperforming the return of 10.0% of large stocks. What seems to be an anomaly actually makes the point that markets work. The riskier investment in small companies produced higher returns.

Why Great Earnings Don't Necessarily Translate into Great Investment Returns

The simple explanation for this anomaly is that investors discount the future expected earnings of value stocks at a higher rate than they discount the future expected earnings of growth stocks. This more than offsets the faster earnings growth rates of growth companies. The high discount rate results in low current valuations for value stocks and higher expected future returns relative to growth stocks. Why do investors use a higher discount rate for value stocks when calculating the current value? The following example should provide a clear explanation.

Let's consider the case of two identical (except for location) office buildings that are for sale in your town. Property A is in the heart of the most desirable commercial area, while Property B borders the worst slum in the region. Clearly, it is easy to identify the more desirable property. If you could buy either property at $10 million, the obvious choice would be Property A. This world, though, could not exist. If it did, investors would bid up the price of Property A relative to Property B.

Now let's imagine a slightly more realistic scenario, one in which Property A is selling at $20 million and Property B at $5 million. Based on projected rental cash flows, you project that (by coincidence) both properties will provide an expected rate of return of 10%—the higher rental income tenants pay for the better location is exactly offset by the higher price you have to pay to buy the property. Faced with the choice of which property to buy, the rational choice is still Property A. The reason is that it provides the same expected return as Property B while being a less risky investment. Being able to buy the safer investment at the same expected return as a riskier one would be like being able to buy a Treasury bond of the same maturity and yield as a junk bond. Thus, this world could not exist, either.

In the real world, Property A's price would continue to be bid up relative to Property B's. Perhaps Property A's price might rise to $30 million and Property B's might fall to $4 million. Now Property A's expected rate of return is lower than Property B's. Investors demand a higher expected return for taking more risk. It is important to understand that just because Property A provides a lower expected rate of return than Property B does not make it a worse investment choice—just a safer one. The market views it as less risky and thus discounts its future earnings at a lower rate. The result is that the price of Property A is driven up, which in turn lowers its expected return. The price differential between the two will reflect the perceived differences in risk. Risk and ex ante reward must be related. The way to think about this is that the market drives prices until the risk-adjusted returns are equal. It is true that Property B has higher expected returns. However, we must adjust those higher expected returns for the greater risk entailed.

Almost everyone understands the relationship between risk and expected return in the context of this example. However, it always amazes me that this most basic of principles is almost universally forgotten when thinking about stocks and how they are priced by the market.

With this understanding, we can now complete the picture by returning to our case of two similar companies, Walmart and Kohls. Think of Walmart as Property A and Kohl's as Property B. Most investors would say that Walmart is a better company and a safer investment. If an investor could buy either company at the same market capitalization, say $20 billion, the obvious choice would be Walmart. It would be like betting on Duke and not having to give away any points. Walmart not only has higher current earnings but also is expected to produce faster growth of earnings. If this world existed, investors owning shares in Kohl's would immediately sell those shares in order to buy shares in Walmart. Their actions would drive up the price of Walmart and drive down the price of Kohl's. This would result in lowering the risk premium demanded by investors in Walmart and raising it on Kohl's.

Now let's say that Walmart's price rises relative to Kohl's. Walmart is now selling at $100 billion and Kohl's at $10 billion. At this point the two have the same expected (not guaranteed) future rate of return—say, 10%. Given that Walmart is perceived to be the better company and therefore a less risky investment, investors should still choose Walmart. The reason is that, although we now have equal expected returns, there is less perceived risk in owning Walmart. The process of investors buying Walmart and selling Kohl's will continue until the expected return of owning Kohl's is sufficiently greater than the expected return of owning Walmart (to entice investors to accept the risk of owning Kohl's instead of owning Walmart)—say, a price of $200 billion for Walmart and $5 billion for Kohl's. The size of the differential (and thus the difference in future expected returns) between the price of the stocks of Walmart and Kohl's is directly related to the difference in perceived investment risk. Given that Walmart is perceived to be a much safer investment than Kohl's, the price differential (risk premium) may have to be very large to entice investors to accept the risk of owning Kohl's.

Would these price changes make Walmart "overvalued" or "highly valued" relative to Kohl's? The answer is "highly valued." If investors thought Walmart was overvalued relative to Kohl's, they would sell Walmart and buy Kohl's until equilibrium was reached. Instead, the high relative valuation of Walmart reflects low perceived risk. Walmart's future earnings are being discounted at a low rate, reflecting the low perceived risk. This low discount rate translates into low future expected returns. Risk and reward are directly related, at least in terms of expected future returns— "expected" because we cannot know the future with certainty. Kohl's future earnings are discounted at a high rate. Therefore, it has a relatively low valuation, reflecting the greater perceived risk. However, it also has high expected future returns.

Just as Property A is not a bad investment (it is a safe one) and Property B is not a good investment (it is a risky one), Walmart is not a bad investment (it is a safe one) and Kohl's is not a good investment (it is a risky one). Once we adjust for risk, the expected returns are the same, and they are equally good (or bad) investments.

The Moral of the Tale

There is a simple principle to remember that can help you avoid making poor investment decisions. Risk and expected return should be positively related. Value stocks have provided a premium over growth stocks for a logical reason: value stocks are the stocks of riskier companies. That is why their stock prices are distressed. Investors refuse to buy them unless the prices are driven low enough so that they can expect to earn a rate of return that is high enough to compensate them for investing in risky companies. For similar reasons small stocks have also provided a risk premium relative to large stocks.

Remember, if prices are high, they reflect low perceived risk, and thus you should expect low future returns; and vice versa. This does not make a highly priced stock a poor investment. It simply makes it an investment that is perceived to have low risk and thus low future returns. Thinking otherwise would be like assuming government bonds are poor investments when the alternative is junk bonds.

The next story continues with our focus on the efficiency of markets and how difficult it is to outperform.

Chapter 6

Market Efficiency and the Case of Pete Rose

The potential for self-cancellation shows why the game of investing is so different from, for example, chess, in which even a seemingly small advantage can lead to consistent victories. Investors implicitly lump the market with other arenas of competition in their experience.

—Mark Rubinstein, "Rational Markets:Yes or No? The Affirmative Case," Financial Analysts Journal (May–June 2001)

In 1998, when Charles Ellis wrote his famous book, *Winning the Loser's Game,*[1] about 20% of actively managed mutual funds were generating statistically significant alphas—they were able to outperform appropriate risk-adjusted benchmarks. The 2020 edition of *The Incredible Shrinking Alpha* presents the evidence demonstrating that despite the trend toward increasing market share for passive investment strategies, the percentage of active managers able to generate statistically significant alphas had collapsed—falling to about 2%, and that's even before considering the impact of taxes for taxable investors. My coauthor, Andrew Berkin, and I described several major themes behind this trend toward ever-increasing difficulty in generating alpha:

- Academic research is converting what once was alpha into beta (exposure to factors in which one can systematically invest, such as value, size, momentum, and profitability/quality). And investors can access those new betas through low-cost vehicles such as index mutual funds and exchange-traded funds.
- The pool of victims that can be exploited is persistently shrinking. Retail (naive) investors' share of the market has fallen from about 90% in 1945 to about 20%.
- The amount of money chasing alpha has dramatically increased. Twenty years ago, hedge funds managed about $300 billion; today, it's about $5 trillion.
- The costs of trading are falling, making it easier to arbitrage away anomalies.
- The absolute level of skill among fund managers has increased.

Despite the evidence, many investors have a difficult time understanding why smart investors working hard cannot gain an advantage over average investors who simply accept market returns. The world of sports betting provides an analogy that helps to explain why the "collective wisdom of the market" is a difficult competitor.

As we discussed in Chapter 2, we can define an efficient market as one in which trading systems fail to produce excess returns because everything *currently* knowable is already incorporated into prices. Because most of us don't know people who have become rich betting on sports, we know intuitively that sports betting markets are at least highly, if not perfectly, efficient. However, since intuition is often incorrect, it helps to have evidence supporting one's intuition. Thanks to the publication in 1989 of the Dowd Report to the commissioner of baseball, "In the Matter of Peter Edward Rose, Manager of Cincinnati Reds Baseball Club," we have evidence on the efficiency of the market for betting on sports.[2]

Pete Rose was one of the greatest players in the history of baseball, finishing his career with more hits than any other player. It seems logical that Rose would have a significant advantage over other bettors. Rose had 24 years of experience as a player and four years as a manager. In addition to having inside information on his own team, as a manager he also studied the teams he competed against. Yet, despite these advantages, Rose lost $4,200 betting on his own team, $36,000 betting on other teams in the National League, and $7,000 betting on American League games. Those losses, which included about $20,000 to $25,000 in transaction fees, are small relative to the total of $450,000 won and lost, and they are consistent with an informationally efficient market.[3] If an expert like Rose, often possessing nonpublic information, was unable to "beat the market," it seems unlikely that ordinary individuals without similar knowledge would be able to do so.

Chapter 2 presented other examples of the efficiency of sports betting markets. For example, in a study covering six NBA seasons, Professor Raymond Sauer, founder of *The Sports Economist*, found that the average difference between point spreads and actual point differences was astonishingly low—less than one-quarter of one point.[4]

The Moral of the Tale

James Surowiecki wrote a wonderful book, *The Wisdom of Crowds*.[5] Through many examples, Surowiecki demonstrated that as long as people are acting independently (not in herds), they exhibit what might be called "collective wisdom." With regard to sports betting, that means the market's collective wisdom in setting point spreads (or odds) is very difficult "competition" to overcome, especially after the expenses of the effort. Thus, while you may want to have a small entertainment account to bet on your favorite team (or the NCAA basketball tournament), you should not "invest" your retirement account on the outcome of sporting events. The same holds true of investing.

The market's collective wisdom in setting prices is difficult competition to overcome, especially after the expenses of the effort. Recognizing this, prudent investors don't attempt to beat the market by trying to exploit mispricings. Instead, they invest in a globally diversified portfolio of funds (such as index funds) that invest systematically and do so in a transparent and replicable manner. In that way, they earn market returns (less low costs), and do so in a highly tax-efficient manner. And the evidence demonstrates that they outperform the vast majority of investors, both institutional and individual.

The next story focuses on choosing the winning strategy in the face of uncertainty.

Chapter 7

The Value of Security Analysis

As children we are taught that joy should come from the effort, not necessarily from the result. Not everyone can win the game, climb to the top of the mountain, or finish a marathon. Hopefully, by the time we are adults we have learned that lesson. By contrast, one of the earliest lessons I learned in business was, as a manager of people, I should never confuse efforts with results. Some employees delivered outstanding results with seemingly little effort. They worked a normal day and their desks were never cluttered. They would take long lunch hours and would rarely seem harried. Sometimes they would come up with a single good idea that would provide great insights leading to improved profits. Other employees would put in tremendous amounts of hours, they were always busy, and their desks were always swamped with piles of paper. Yet, sometimes the results did not relate to the effort. In business, results are what matters—not effort. The same is true in the world of investing because we cannot spend efforts, only results.

The basic premise of active management is through their efforts, security analysts are able to identify and recommend stocks that are undervalued and avoid stocks that are overvalued. The result will be that investors following their recommendations will outperform the market. Is this premise myth or reality? The following example will help answer the question.

In May 1999, at a conference of financial economists at UCLA's Anderson School of Management, Bradford Cornell presented an example that provides insights into the value of the efforts of security analysts. As you will see, because much of the value of companies with high-growth rates comes from distant cash flows, the value of their stock is highly sensitive to the size of the equity risk premium (ERP)—the risk premium above the rate on riskless Treasury instruments investors demand for accepting the risks of equity ownership. In 1999, Intel was certainly considered a company with expectations for a high rate of growth.

At the time, Intel had accumulated over $10 billion of cash. The board of directors was trying to determine if it made sense to use a substantial portion of the cash to repurchase its stock. At the time, the stock was trading at about $120 per share (note that the stock split 2:1 on 4/12/1999 and again 2:1 on 7/31/2000). Based on publicly available forecasts of future cash flows, Cornell demonstrated that if the ERP were 3%, Intel's stock would be worth $204. If the ERP were 5%, the stock would be worth $130 (about the current price). And if the ERP were 7.2%, the stock would be worth just $82.

Buy, Sell, or Hold?

With such a wide range of estimated values, what should the board do? If the stock was worth $204, they should begin an aggressive repurchase program. However, if it was worth $82, they should take advantage of the current "overvaluation" and raise capital by issuing more shares. The board was faced with two problems. The first was that valuations assumed the cash flow projections were known. Not even the board (let alone some security analyst) can see the future with such clarity. Obviously, in the real world we can only make estimates of future cash flows. The second problem was why would the board believe it could predict the ERP any better than the market could? And you see how much the valuation changes with changes in the ERP.

In hindsight, the board should have issued a lot more shares. At the end of 2008 the stock was trading at about one-third of its split-adjusted price of $30 per share and it was not until 2014 that it exceeded that price.

We can also review the academic evidence on the value of security analysts.

Academic Evidence

In their paper "Analysts and Anomalies," Joseph Engelberg, David McLean, and Jeffrey Pontiff examined the recommendations of US security analysts over the period from 1994 through 2017 and found that analysts' predictions actually go in the opposite direction of the academic evidence—they conflict with well-documented anomalies.[1] And the results were statistically significant. They also found that buy recommendations did not predict returns, though sell recommendations did predict lower returns. Another interesting finding was that among the group of "market" anomalies (such as momentum and idiosyncratic risk), which are based only on stock returns, price, and volume data, analysts produce more favorable recommendations and forecast higher returns among the stocks that are stronger buys according to market anomalies. This is perhaps surprising, as analysts are supposed to be experts in firms' fundamentals. Yet, they performed best with anomalies that are not based on accounting data. Their evidence suggests that analysts even contribute to mispricing, as their recommendations are systematically biased by favoring stocks that are overvalued according to anomaly-based composite mispricing scores.

The only good news was that Engelberg, McLean, and Pontiff found that over time, as anomaly variables have become widely known, analysts have incorporated more of this information into their recommendations and price targets—the negative correlation weakened over their sample period. However, even during the later years of their sample, there was still a negative or, at best, neutral relationship. They concluded, "Analysts today are still overlooking a good deal of valuable, anomaly-related information."

The Moral of the Tale

If corporate insiders (e.g., boards of directors), with access to far more information than any security analyst is likely to have, have such great difficulty in determining a "correct" valuation, it is easy to understand why the results of conventional stock-picking methods (active management) are poor and inconsistent. While security analysts and active portfolio managers are putting forth great effort in attempts to beat the market, the historical evidence has shown that the majority of the time those efforts have proven counterproductive. We see that each time Standard & Poor's publishes their Active Versus Passive Scorecards. And smart investors, like smart businesspeople, care about results, not efforts. That is why "smart money" invests in "passively managed," structured portfolios that invest systematically in a transparent and replicable manner.

The next story discusses just how difficult it is to beat the market—even if you can forecast political and economic events with great accuracy.

Chapter 8

Be Careful What You Ask For

According to Greek mythology, Midas was a wealthy king of Phrygia. One day the satyr Silenus—a beast that was half man, half goat, and the tutor of Dionysos, the god of wine—lost his way and stumbled upon Midas and his palace. The king extended to Silenus his hospitality. Upon discovering this kindness, Dionysos granted Midas a wish. Midas asked that everything he touched would turn to gold. Midas reveled in his gift, thinking he would become the richest man in the world. His foolishness quickly became apparent. In hunger and despair, he embraced his young daughter for comfort, only to find that she too turned to gold. Midas begged Dionysos to take his golden touch away. Eventually the god relented and his daughter was restored to life.[1]

For today's investors, the equivalent of the "Midas touch" might be the ability to forecast economic growth rates. If you could forecast with 100% certainty which countries would have the highest growth rates, you could invest in them, avoiding the countries with low growth rates. And that would lead to abnormal profits. Or, perhaps not.

Historical Evidence

The historical evidence on the correlation of country economic growth rates and stock returns demonstrates this point. Researchers, including Jay Ritter (Economic Growth and Equity Returns), Jeremy Siegel (Stocks for the Long Run), and Antti Illmanen (Expected Returns) have found that there has actually been a slightly negative correlation between country growth rates and stock returns.

We have further evidence from a 2006 study on emerging markets done by Jim Davis of Dimensional Fund Advisors.[2] He chose the emerging markets because the widely held perception is that the markets of the emerging countries are inefficient.

Davis evenly divided the emerging market countries in the IFC Investable Universe database into two groups based on GDP growth for the upcoming year. The high-growth group consisted of the 50% of the countries with the highest real GDP growth for the year. He then measured returns using two sets of country weights—aggregate free-float-adjusted market-cap weights and equal weights. ("Free-float" refers to the amount of a company's shares outstanding available for purchase on the open market at any point in time.) Companies were market-cap-weighted within countries. The results are shown in the following table for the period from 1990 to 2005.

	Market-Cap-Weighted Countries Average Annual Return (%)	Equally Weighted Countries Average Annual Return (%)
High-growth countries	16.4	22.6
Low-growth countries	16.4	21.5

It seems that there is not much, if any, advantage to know in advance which countries will have the highest rates of GDP growth. The conclusion that we can draw is that the emerging markets are very much like the rest of the world's capital markets—they do an excellent job of reflecting economic growth prospects into stock prices. The only advantage would come from being able to forecast surprises in growth rates. For example, if a country was forecasted by the market to have 6% GDP growth, and you accurately forecasted a rate of growth of 7%, you might have been able to exploit such information (depending on how much it cost to make the forecasts and how much it cost to execute the strategy). Unfortunately, there is no evidence of the ability to forecast GDP rates any better than do the markets.

The Moral of the Tale

It seems intuitive that if you could accurately forecast which countries would have high GDP growth rates, you would be able to exploit that knowledge and earn abnormal returns. Unfortunately, relying on intuition leads to an incorrect conclusion. The reason is that markets are efficient in building information about future prospects into prices. And it is only surprises, which by definition are unpredictable, that provide an advantage. Obviously, forecasting is not free. There are costs (research expenses) involved in making the forecasts. And there are costs involved in trying to exploit those forecasts (operating expenses, trading costs, and taxes related to turnover). The evidence is that these efforts and expenditures serve only to reduce returns, not enhance them. Thus, the moral of our story is that the premise on which much of active management is based is a false one.

The next tale explains why another bit of conventional wisdom is based on a false premise.

Chapter 9

The Fed Model and the Money Illusion

There are well-dressed foolish ideas just as there are well-dressed fools.

—*Nicholas Chamfort*

Magic, or conjuring, is the art of entertaining an audience by performing illusions that baffle and amaze, often by giving the impression that something impossible has been achieved, as if the performer had supernatural powers. Practitioners of this art are called magicians, conjurors, or illusionists. Specifically, optical illusions are tricks that fool the eyes. Most magic tricks that fall into the category of optical illusions work by fooling the brain and the eyes at the same time.

Fortunately, most optical illusions don't cost the participants anything, except perhaps some embarrassment about having been fooled. However, basing investment strategies on illusions can lead investors to make all kinds of mistakes.

There are many illusions in the world of investing. The process known as data mining—torturing the data until it confesses—creates many of them. Unfortunately, identifying patterns that worked in the past doesn't necessarily provide you with any useful information about stock price movements in the future. As Andrew Lo, a finance professor at MIT, pointed out: "Given enough time, enough attempts, and enough imagination, almost any pattern can be teased out of any data set."[1]

The stock and bond markets are filled with wrongheaded data mining. David Leinweber, of First Quadrant, famously illustrated this point with what he called "stupid data miner tricks." Leinweber sifted through a United Nations CD-ROM and discovered the single best predictor of the S&P 500 Index had been butter production in Bangladesh.[2] His example is a perfect illustration that the mere existence of a correlation doesn't necessarily give it predictive value. Some logical reason for the correlation is required for it to have credibility. For example, there is a strong and logical correlation between the level of economic activity and the level of interest rates. As economic activity increases, the demand for money, and therefore its price (interest rates), also increases.

An illusion with great potential for creating investment mistakes is known as the "money illusion." The reason it has such potential for creating mistakes is that it relates to one of the most popular indicators used by investors to determine if the market is under- or overvalued—what is known as "the Fed Model."

The Fed Model

In 1997, in his monetary policy report to Congress, Federal Reserve Chairman Alan Greenspan indicated that changes in the ratio of prices in the S&P 500 to consensus estimates of earnings over the coming 12 months have often been inversely related to changes in long-term Treasury yields.[3] Following this report, Edward Yardeni, at the time a market strategist for Morgan, Grenfell & Co., speculated that the Federal Reserve was using a model to determine if the market was fairly valued—how attractive stocks were priced *relative* to bonds. The model, despite no acknowledgment of its use by the Fed, became known as the Fed Model.

Using the "logic" that bonds and stocks are competing instruments, the model uses the yield on the 10-year Treasury bond to calculate "fair value," comparing that rate to the earnings-price, or E/P, ratio (the inverse of the popular price-to-earnings, or P/E, ratio). For example, if the yield on the 10-year Treasury were 4%, fair value would be an E/P of 4%, or a P/E of 25. If the P/E is greater (lower) than 25, the market is considered overvalued (undervalued). If the same bond were yielding 5%, fair value would be a P/E of 20. The logic is that higher interest rates create more competition for stocks, and this should be reflected in valuations. Thus, lower interest rates justify higher valuations and vice versa.

For a long time after Yardeni coined the phrase, it seemed almost impossible to watch CNBC for more than a few days without hearing about the market relative to "fair value." The Fed Model as a valuation tool had become "conventional wisdom." However, conventional wisdom is often wrong. There are two major problems with the Fed Model. The first relates to how the model is used by many investors. Yardeni speculated that the Federal Reserve used the model to compare the valuation of stocks *relative* to bonds as competing instruments. The model says nothing about *absolute* expected returns. Thus, stocks, using the Fed Model, might be priced under fair value relative to bonds, and they can have either high or low expected returns. The expected return of stocks is not determined by their relative value to bonds. Instead, the expected *real* return is determined by the current dividend yield plus the expected real growth in dividends. To get the estimated nominal return, we would add estimated inflation. This is a critical point that seems to be lost on many investors. The result is that investors who believe low interest rates justify a high valuation for stocks without the high valuation affecting expected returns are likely to be disappointed (and perhaps not have enough funds on which to live comfortably in retirement). The reality is that when P/Es are high, expected returns are low and vice versa, regardless of the level of interest rates.

The second problem with the Fed Model, leading to a false conclusion, is that it fails to consider that inflation affects corporate earnings differently than it does the return on fixed-income instruments. Over the long term, the *nominal* growth rate of corporate earnings has been in line with the *nominal* growth rate of the economy. Similarly, the *real* growth rate of corporate earnings has been in line with the *real* growth of the economy.[4] Thus, in the long term the *real* growth rate of earnings is not affected by inflation. However, the yield to maturity on a 10-year bond is a *nominal* return—to get the real return, you must subtract inflation. The error of comparing a number that isn't affected by inflation to one that is leads to what is called the "money illusion." Let's see why it's an illusion.

Assume the real yield on a 10-year TIPS (Treasury inflation-protected security) is 2%. If the expected long-term rate of inflation were 3%, a 10-year Treasury bond would be expected to yield 5% (the 2% real yield on TIPS plus the 3% expected rate of inflation). According to the Fed Model, that would mean a fair value for stocks at a P/E of 20 (E/P of 5%). Let's now change our assumption to a long-term expected rate of inflation of 2%. This would cause the yield on the 10-year bond to fall from 5% to 4%, causing the fair value P/E to rise to 25. However, this makes no sense. Inflation doesn't affect the real rate of return demanded by equity investors; therefore, it shouldn't affect valuations. In addition, as stated, over the long term there is a very strong relationship between nominal earnings growth and inflation. In this case, a long-term expected inflation rate of 2% instead of 3% would be expected to lower the growth of *nominal* earnings by 1% but have no impact on real earnings growth (the only kind that matters). Because the real return on bonds is affected by inflation, while real earnings growth is not, the Fed Model compares a number that is affected by inflation with a number that isn't (resulting in the money illusion).

Let's also consider what would happen if the real interest rate component of bond prices fell. The real rate is reflective of the economic demand for funds. Thus, it's reflective of the rate of growth of the real economy. If the real rate falls due to a slower rate of economic growth, interest rates would fall, reflecting the reduced demand for funds. Using the same previous example, if the real rate on TIPS fell from 2% to 1%, that would have the same impact on nominal rates as a 1% fall in expected inflation and thus the same impact on the fair value P/E ratio—causing fair value to rise. However, this too does not make sense. A slower rate of real economic growth means a slower rate of real growth in corporate earnings. Thus, while the competition from lower interest rates is reduced, so are future earnings.

Since corporate earnings grow in line with the nominal GNP, a 1% lower long-term rate of growth in GNP would lead to a 1% lower expected growth in corporate earnings. The "benefit" of falling interest rates would be offset by the equivalent fall in future expected earnings. The reverse would be true if a stronger economy caused a rise in real interest rates. The negative effect of a higher interest rate would be offset by a faster expected growth in earnings. The bottom line is that there is no reason to believe stock valuations should change if the *real* return demanded by investors has not changed.

Clifford S. Asness studied the period 1881–2001. He concluded the Fed Model had no predictive power in terms of absolute stock returns—the conventional wisdom is wrong. (As we discussed, however, this is not the purpose for which Yardeni thought the Fed Model was used. Given the purpose for which the model was designed, it would have been more appropriate for Asness to study the relative performance of stocks versus bonds given the "signal"—under- or overvalued—the model was giving.) Asness also concluded that over 10-year horizons the E/P ratio does have strong forecasting powers. Thus, the higher the E/P ratio, the higher the expected returns to stocks *regardless* of the level of interest rates and vice versa.[5]

There is one other point to consider. A stronger economy, leading to higher real interest rates, should also be expected to lead to a rise in corporate earnings. A stronger economy reduces the risks of equity investing, which in turn could lead investors to accept a lower risk premium. Thus, it is possible that higher interest rates, if caused by a stronger economy and not higher inflation, could actually justify higher valuations for stocks. The Fed Model, however, would suggest that higher interest rates mean stocks are less attractive. The reverse is true if a weaker economy leads to lower real interest rates.

Before coming to the moral of this tale, it's worth noting that when the COVID-19 crisis drove the yield on 10-year Treasuries to under 1%, I did not hear a single reference to the Fed Model. That's because a yield below 1% would create a fair value P/E of more than 100! Which of course would not make any sense. In other words, the sharp fall in interest rates exposed the "wizard behind the curtain."

The Moral of the Tale

While gaining knowledge of how a magical illusion works has the negative effect of ruining the illusion, understanding the "magic" of financial illusions is beneficial because it should help you avoid mistakes. In the case of the money illusion, understanding how it is created will prevent you from believing an environment of low (high) interest rates allows for either high (low) valuations or high (low) future stock returns. Instead, if the current level of prices is high (a high P/E ratio), that should lead you to conclude that future returns to equities are likely to be lower than has historically been the case and vice versa. This doesn't mean investors should avoid equities because they are "highly valued" or increase their allocations because they have low valuations.

Hopefully, you are now convinced that the Fed Model should not be used to determine if the market is at fair value and that a much better predictor of future real returns is the E/P ratio.

We now move on to Part II, which focuses on strategic portfolio decisions. The first tale in this section is about choosing the winning strategy in the face of uncertainty.

Part Two

STRATEGIC PORTFOLIO DECISIONS

Chapter 10

When Even the Best Aren't Likely to Win the Game

*I believe the search for top-performing stock funds is an intellectu-
ally discredited exercise that will come to be viewed as one of the
great financial follies of the late-20th century.*

—*Jonathan Clements*

Awizard appears, waves his magic wand, and makes you the
11th best golfer in the world. Being the 11th best golfer
in the world earns you an invitation to the annual Super
Legends of Golf Tournament. That is the good news. The bad news
is that the competition is the 10 best players in the world. To even
the playing field you are given a major advantage. The rules of the
game are as follows. Each of the other players will play one hole at
a time and then return to the clubhouse and report their score. No
player gets to observe the others play—you cannot gain an advantage by watching the others play. After each of the other 10 players
completes the hole, you see their scores and are provided with
the following options. Option A is to choose to play the hole and

accept whatever score you obtain. Option B is to choose not to play that hole and accept par as your score.

The first hole is a par four. After each of the 10 best players in the world has completed the first hole you learn that eight of the 10 took five shots to put the ball in the cup—they shot a bogie. One player shot par, and the other scored a birdie, needing only three shots to put the ball in the cup. You now must decide to either accept par or play the hole. What is your decision?

The prudent choice would be to choose not to play, take par, and accept a score of four. The logic is that while it was not impossible to beat par (one player did) the odds of doing so are so low (10%) that it would not be prudent to try. And by accepting par you would have outperformed 80% of the best players in the world. In other words, when the best players in the world fail the majority of the time, you recognize that it is not prudent to try to succeed. The exception to this line of thinking would be if you could somehow identify an advantage you might have.

For example, if the 10 best players had played the day before you in a rainstorm, with 50-mile-an-hour winds, and you played the following day when the weather was perfect and the course was dry. Given that situation you might decide that the advantage was great enough that the odds of your shooting a birdie (a three) were greater than the odds of your shooting a bogie (a five, or perhaps even worse). Without such an advantage the prudent choice would be to not play if you do not have to.

What does this story have to do with investing? Consider the following. It seems logical to believe that if anyone could beat the market, it would be the pension plans of the largest US companies. Why is this a good assumption? First, these pension plans control large sums of money. They have access to the best and brightest portfolio managers, each clamoring to manage the billions of dollars in these plans (and earn large fees). Pension plans can also invest with managers that most individuals don't have access to because they don't have sufficient assets to meet the minimums of these superstar managers.

Second, it is not even remotely possible that these pension plans ever hired a manager who did not have a track record of outperforming their benchmarks, or at the very least matching them. Certainly, they would never hire a manager with a record of underperformance.

Third, it is also safe to say that they never hired a manager who did not make a great presentation, explaining why the manager had succeeded, and why they would continue to succeed. Surely the case presented was a convincing one.

Fourth, many, if not the majority, of these pension plans hire professional consultants such as Frank Russell, SEI, and Goldman Sachs to help them perform due diligence in interviewing, screening, and ultimately selecting the very best of the best. And you can be confident that these consultants have thought of every conceivable screen to find the best fund managers. Surely, they have considered not only performance records but also such factors as management tenure, depth of staff, consistency of performance (to make sure that a long-term record is not the result of one or two lucky years), performance in bear markets, consistency of implementation of strategy, turnover, costs, and so on. It is unlikely that there is something that you or your financial advisor would think of that they had not already considered.

Fifth, as individuals, it is rare that we would have the luxury of being able to personally interview money managers and perform as thorough a due diligence as do these consultants. And we generally do not have professionals helping us to avoid mistakes in the process.

Sixth, the fees they pay for active management are typically lower than the fees individual investors pay.

So, how have the pension plans done in their quest for finding the few managers that will persistently beat their benchmark? The evidence is compelling that they should have "taken par." For example, in his 2020 study "Institutional Investment Strategy and Manager Choice: A Critique" Richard Ennis found that public pension plans underperformed their benchmark return by 0.99% and the endowments underperformed by 1.59%. He also found that of the 46 public pension plans he studied, just one generated statistically significant alpha, compared to the 17 that generated statistically significant negative alphas. He calculated that "the likelihood of underperforming over a decade is 0.98—a virtual certainty."[1] It is evidence such as this that led legendary investor Charles Ellis, author of *Winning the Loser's Game: Timeless Strategies for Successful Investing*, to declare active investing a loser's game, one that is possible to win but the odds of doing so are so poor it isn't prudent to try.

Returning to our golf story, I hope you agree that just as it would be imprudent to try to beat par when 90% of the best golfers in the world failed, it would be imprudent for you to try to succeed if institutional investors, with far greater resources than you (or your broker or financial advisor), fail with great persistence. Remember, Ennis found that over the horizon of a decade, their likelihood of success was about 2%. The only reason for you to try for that birdie would be if you could identify a strategic advantage that you had over these institutional players. The questions you might ask yourself are Do I have more resources than they do? Do I have more time to spend finding future winners than they do? Am I smarter than all of these institutional investors and the advisors they hire? Unless when you look in the mirror you see Warren Buffett staring back at you, it doesn't seem likely that the answer to any of these questions is yes. At least it won't be yes if you are honest with yourself.

The Moral of the Tale

Wall Street needs and wants you to play the game of active investing. They need you to try to beat par. They know that your odds of success are so low that it is not in your interest to play. But they need you to play so that they (not you) make the most money. They make it by charging high fees for active management that persistently delivers poor performance.

The financial media also want and need you to play so that you "tune in." That is how they (not you) make money. However, just as you had the choice of not playing in the Super Legends of

Golf Tournament, you have the choice of not playing the game of active management. You can simply accept par and earn market (not average) rates of return with low expenses and high tax efficiency. You can do so by investing in low-cost, passive investment vehicles like index funds and other funds that are systematic and transparent in implementing their investment strategies. By doing so, you are virtually guaranteed to outperform the majority of both professionals and individual investors. In other words, you win by not playing. This is why active investing is called the loser's game. It is not that the people playing are losers. And it is not that you cannot win. Instead, it is that the odds of success are so low that it is imprudent to try.

The only logical reason to play the game of active investing is that you place a high entertainment value on the effort. For some people there might even be another reason—they enjoy the bragging rights if they win. Of course, you rarely, if ever, hear when they lose.

It's true that active investing can be exciting. Investing, however, was never meant to be exciting. Wall Street and the media created that myth. Instead, it is meant to be about providing you with the greatest odds of achieving your financial and life goals with the least amount of risk. That is what differentiates investing from speculating (gambling).

Many people get excitement from gambling on sporting events, horse races, or at the casino tables in Las Vegas. Prudent individuals, however, get entertainment value from gambling by betting only an infinitesimal fraction of their net worth on sporting events, etc. Similarly, even if you receive entertainment value from the pursuit of the "Holy Grail of Outperformance," you should not gamble more than a tiny fraction of the assets on which you wish to retire (or leave to your children or favorite charity) on active managers being able to overcome such great odds.

The next tale returns to the theme of persistence of performance and the need to understand the role of chance.

Chapter 11

The Demon of Chance

People often see order where it doesn't exist and interpret acciden-
tal success to be the result of skill.
—*Miriam Bensman,* Institutional Investor *(January 1997)*

t is January 2003, and the investment committee of a large
corporation meets to discuss the performance of the multi-
billion-dollar pension plan they are charged with overseeing.
Disappointed with the performance of its investments, the committee votes to fire the manager and initiates a search for a replacement.
The committee performs a thorough screening of potential candidates. Among the screens are a record of superior performance over
the 15-year period ending in 2002, a high persistency of superior
performance, tenure of the manager, and turnover. The due diligence

Fund	Annualized Returns 1988–2002 (%)
Larry Swedroe Investment Trust	14.3
Legg Mason Value	14.2
Washington Mutual	12.4
Fidelity Magellan	12.3
S&P 500 Index Fund	11.5
Janus Fund	11.3

process has narrowed the final candidates to the funds shown in the table on page 73 and a benchmark, the S&P 500 Index.

Based on its track record the winner of the performance derby is the Larry Swedroe Investment Trust. Not only has the fund outperformed its benchmark by a significant amount but also it has done so with a high degree of persistency, outperforming the S&P 500 Index in 9 of the 15 years (60%). In addition, the fund has had the same manager in charge for the entire period, and turnover has been extremely low.

After being presented with the data, the investment committee votes to award the management of the plan to the Larry Swedroe Investment Trust. At the last minute one member of the committee suggests that as one final bit of due diligence, Larry Swedroe should be brought in to explain his investment strategy.

Appearing before the committee, I am first congratulated on the superior results of the fund. I am then asked to explain my investment strategy. I respond by stating that since my wife's name is Mona, my lucky letter is M. Therefore, I construct a value-weighted portfolio of all US stocks that begin with the letter M and rebalance the portfolio annually. Skill, or the demon of luck?

This example was created by the technique known as data mining—a way to build predictive models of the real world by discerning patterns in masses of data. The computer was asked to find a "strategy" that delivered outperformance. It then *mined* (or tortured) *the data* and found one. Before ever concluding that because a strategy worked in the past it can be relied on to work in the future, we need to ask if there is a rational explanation for the correlation between the outcome and strategy. Obviously, in the case of the Larry Swedroe Investment Trust there is no rational explanation. Thus, no rational person should engage my fund to manage assets. Unfortunately, in the real world many investment products are based on ideas that have much in common (they are the result of data mining) with the strategy of the Larry Swedroe Investment Trust.

Mutual Funds to Drool Over

The financial media are forever seeking to anoint some mutual fund manager as the financial equivalent of the Michael Jordan of investment managers—the "next Peter Lynch." They, along with many investment advisors and individual investors, perform intensive searches of databases seeking to find a fund manager with a persistent long-term record of outperformance. The assumption is that while short-term outperformance might be a matter of luck, long-term outperformance *must* be evidence of skill. A basic knowledge of statistics, however, provides us with the knowledge that with thousands of money managers playing the game, the odds are that a few, not just one, will produce a long-term performance record similar to that of the Larry Swedroe Investment Trust.

Coin-Tossing Gurus?

Imagine the following scenario: 10,000 individuals are gathered together to participate in a contest. A coin will be tossed and the contestants must guess whether it will come up heads or tails. Contestants who correctly guess the outcome of 10 consecutive tosses are declared winners and receive the coveted title of "coin-tossing guru."

According to statistics, we can expect that after the first toss, 5,000 participants will have guessed the outcome correctly. The other 5,000 will have guessed incorrectly and thus are eliminated from the competition. After the second round, the remaining participants will be expected to be 2,500, and so on. After 10 repetitions we would expect to have 10 remaining participants who would have guessed correctly all 10 times and earned their guru status. What probability would you attach to the likelihood that those 10 gurus would win the next coin-toss competition? Would you bet on them winning again? The answers are obvious. What does this have to do with investing?

Today, there are more mutual funds than there are stocks. With so many active managers trying to win, statistical theory tells us that we should expect that some are likely to outperform the market. However, before expenses, beating the market is a zero-sum game— that is, since all stocks must be owned by someone, if some group of active managers outperforms the market there must be another group who underperforms. Therefore, the odds of any specific active manager being successful are at best 50/50 (before considering the burden of higher expenses active managers must overcome to outperform a benchmark index fund). Using our coin-toss analogy, we would expect that randomly half the active managers would outperform in any one year, about one in four to outperform two years in a row, and one in eight to do so three years in a row. Fund managers who outperform for even three years in a row are often declared to be gurus by the financial media. The question to consider is: Are they investment gurus or coin-tossing gurus? The answer is that it is hard to tell the difference between the two.

The reason for choosing 10,000 for the coin toss is that we are not far from having that number of actively managed funds. Using the formula from the previous example, after 10 years we should randomly expect that about 10 funds would outperform their benchmark every year. Without this knowledge of statistics investors are likely to confuse skill with "the demon of luck."

One fund manager who was acclaimed as the next Peter Lynch was Bill Miller, the manager of the Legg Mason Value Trust. He had managed to do what no other current manager has done— beat the S&P 500 Index 15 years in a row (1991–2005). Surely, that could be luck. Surely, you can rely on that performance as a predictor of future greatness. Before you come to that conclusion, consider the following evidence.

Those That Don't Know Financial History Are Doomed to Repeat It

For each of the 11 years from 1974 through 1984, the Lindner Large-Cap Fund outperformed the S&P 500 Index.[1] How were investors rewarded if they waited *11 years* to be sure that they had found a true genius and then invested in the fund? Over the next 18 years, the S&P 500 Index returned 12.6%. Believers in past performance as a prologue to future performance were rewarded for their faith in the Lindner Large-Cap Fund with returns of just 4.1%, an underperformance of over 8% per annum for 18 years. After outperforming for 11 years in a row, the Lindner Large-Cap Fund managed to beat the S&P 500 in just 4 of the next 18 years, and none of the last 9—quite a price to pay for believing that past performance is a predictor of future performance. The Lindner Fund was finally put out of its misery when it was purchased by the Hennessy Funds in October 2003 and eventually merged into the Hennessy Total Return Fund.

Not yet convinced? Consider the case of David Baker, and the 44 Wall Street Fund. Over the entire decade of the 1970s, 44 Wall Street was the top-performing diversified US stock fund—even outperforming the legendary Peter Lynch, who ran Fidelity's Magellan Fund. Faced with the decision of which fund to invest in, why would anyone settle for Peter Lynch when they could have David Baker? (We only know after the fact that Lynch continued to achieve superior results in the 1980s.)

How did investors fare after waiting 10 years to be sure that David Baker's results had to be the result of skill and not random good luck? Unfortunately, 44 Wall Street ranked as the single worst performing fund of the 1980s, losing 73%.[2] During the same period, the S&P 500 grew 17.6% per annum. Each dollar invested in Baker's fund fell in value to just $0.27. However, each dollar invested in the S&P 500 Index would have grown to just over $5. The fund did so poorly that in 1993 it was merged into the 44 Wall Street Equity Fund, which was then merged into the Matterhorn Growth Fund in 1996.

The Moral of the Tale

As evidenced by the examples of the Linder Large-Cap Fund and the 44 Wall Street Fund, belief in the "hot hand" and past performance as a predictor of the future performance of actively managed funds and their managers can be quite expensive. Unfortunately, both the financial media and the public are quick to assume that superior performance is a result of skill rather than the more likely assumption that it was a random outcome. The reason is that noise sells, and the financial media is in the business of selling. They are not in the business of providing prudent investment advice.

The bottom line is that while there will likely be future Peter Lynchs and future Bill Millers, we have no way to identify them ahead of time. Also, unfortunately, we can only buy future performance, not past performance. A perfect example of this obvious truism is that in 2006, Miller's streak was broken as the Legg Mason Value Trust underperformed the S&P 500 Index by almost 10%. In fact, the fund's performance was so poor that its cumulative three-year returns trailed the S&P 500 Index by 2.8% per annum. This provides further evidence of the fact that it is extremely difficult to tell whether past performance was the result of skill or the "demon of luck."

The conclusion that we can draw is that while relying on past performance as a guide to the future might lead you to investing with the next Peter Lynch, it is just as likely to lead you to investing with the next David Baker. That is a risk that a prudent, risk-averse investor (probably you) should not be willing to accept. If you do accept that risk, it is likely that you will be reciting the investor's lament: "I own last year's top performing funds. Unfortunately, I bought them this year." Investors interested in learning how easy it is to be fooled by what are often random outcomes would be well served to read *Fooled by Randomness*, an excellent book by Nassim Nicholas Taleb.[3]

The next tale demonstrates that when confronted with a loser's game the prudent decision is to choose not to play.

Chapter 12

Outfoxing the Box

The greatest advantage from gambling comes from not playing it at all.

—*Girolamo Cardano, 16th-century physician,
mathematician, and quintessential Renaissance man*

My good friend Bill Schultheis, author of *The Coffeehouse Investor*, devised "outfoxing the box" to help investors understand that the winning investment strategy is to accept market returns. It depicts a game that you can choose to either play or not play.

In this game you are an investor with the following choice to make. The following table contains nine percentages, each representing a rate of return your financial assets are guaranteed to earn for the rest of your life.

%	%	%
0	5	23
6	10	14
−3	15	20

You are told that you have the following choice: you can either accept the 10% rate of return in the center box or you will be asked to leave the room, the boxes will be shuffled around, and you will have to choose a box, not knowing what return each box holds. You quickly calculate that the average return of the other eight boxes is 10%. Thus, if thousands of people played the game and each one chose a box, the expected average return would be the same as if they all chose not to play. Of course, some would earn a return of negative 3% per annum while others would earn 23% per annum. This is like the world of investing, where if you chose an actively managed fund and the market returns 10%, you might be lucky and earn as much as 23% per annum, or you might be unlucky and lose 3% per annum. A rational risk-averse investor should logically decide to "outfox the box" and accept the average (market) return of 10%.

In my years as an investment advisor, whenever I present this game to an investor, I have never once had an investor choose to play. Everyone chooses to accept par, or 10%. While they might be willing to spend a dollar on a lottery ticket, they become more prudent in their choice when it comes to investing their life's savings.

Now consider the following. In the outfoxing the box game, the average return of all choices was the same 10% as the 10% that would have been earned by choosing not to play. And 50% of those choosing to play would be expected to earn an above-average return and 50% a below-average return. The academic research on the performance of actively managed mutual funds, as presented in my book, *The Incredible Shrinking Alpha*, coauthored with Andrew Berkin, shows that the odds are far worse than 50%. In fact, today only about 2% of actively managed funds generate statistically significant alphas on a pretax basis. If you would choose to not play a game when you have a 50% chance of success, what logic is there in choosing to play a game where the most sophisticated investors have a much higher failure rate? Yet, that is exactly the choice those playing the game of active management are making.

The research has shown that even the big institutional investors, with all of their resources, fail to outperform appropriate risk-adjusted benchmarks.[1] In addition to their other advantages, institutional investors have one other major advantage over individual investors—their returns are not subject to taxes. However, if your equity investments are in a taxable account, the returns you earn are subject to taxes. The incremental tax cost of active funds further reduces your odds of success.

The Moral of the Tale

You don't have to play the game of active investing. You don't have to try to overcome abysmal odds—odds that make the crap tables at Las Vegas seem appealing. Instead, you can outfox the box and accept market returns by investing passively. Charles Ellis, author of *Investment Policy: How to Win the Loser's Game*, put it this way: "In investment management, the real opportunity to achieve superior results is not in scrambling to outperform the market, but in establishing and adhering to appropriate investment policies over the long term—policies that position the portfolio to benefit from riding with the main long-term forces in the market."[2]

The next story demonstrates just how strong the conventional wisdom is on past performance being a predictor of the future.

Chapter 13

Between a Rock and a Hard Place

The definition of insanity is doing the same thing over and over and expecting different results.

—Benjamin Franklin

According to Greek mythology, Sisyphus was the son of Aeolus (the king of Thessaly). Sisyphus was a clever and evil man, who would waylay travelers and murder them. He also betrayed the secrets of the gods and bound Thanatos, the god of death, so the deceased could not reach the underworld. Hades eventually intervened, severely punishing Sisyphus. He was forced to remain in the realm of the dead and complete the same task for eternity. The task—push a boulder up a steep hill only to watch the boulder roll back down just before it reaches the top. Then he must begin the whole process again. Are investors who search for outperformance via active management condemned to a similar fate?

The majority of financial advisors, investment policy committees, and trustees of pension and retirements plans select investment managers based on historical performance. The selection process includes thorough due diligence, often with the assistance of a "gatekeeper"—a consulting firm such as Frank Russell or SEI. These firms have tremendous resources. Unfortunately, on average, the active managers chosen based on outstanding track records have failed to live up to expectations. The underperformance relative to passive benchmarks invariably leads decision-makers to fire the active manager. And the process begins anew. A new round of due diligence is performed and a new manager is selected to replace the poorly performing one. And, almost invariably, the process is repeated a few years later.

The Evidence

Among the studies finding that the fired managers go on to outperform the new hires that replace them are *The Trust Mandate* by Herman Brodie and Klaus Harnack[1]; "Institutional Investor Expectations, Manager Performance, and Fund Flows" by Howard Jones and Jose Vicente Martinez[2]; and "The Selection and Termination of Investment Management Firms by Plan Sponsors" by Amit Goyal and Sunil Wahal.[3] And Tim Jenkinson, Howard Jones, and Jose Vicente Martinez, authors of the "Picking Winners? Investment Consultants' Recommendations of Fund Managers,"[4] found no evidence that consultant recommendations add value to plan sponsors. Sadly, so many individual investors go through the same motions. And they end up with the same results—a high likelihood of poor performance.

The conventional wisdom that past performance is a strong predictor of future performance is so strongly ingrained in our culture that it seems almost no one stops to ask if the conventional wisdom is correct, even in the face of persistent failure. Why aren't investors asking themselves, "If the process I used to choose a manager that would deliver outperformance failed, and I use the exact same process the next time, why should I expect anything but failure the next time?" The answer is painfully obvious. If you don't do anything different, you should expect the same result. Yet, so many have not thought to ask this simple question.

It is important to understand that neither the purveyors of active management nor the gatekeepers want you to ask that question. If you did, they would go out of business. You, however, should ask that question. Your obligation is to provide the best returns, either to yourself or to members of the plan for which you are a trustee, not to provide the fund managers, or the consultants, with a living.

As head of economic and financial research at Buckingham Strategic Wealth I have asked hundreds of people this simple question. Not once have I ever received an answer that explains either why they should expect a different outcome, or what they will be doing differently the next time to avoid the prior outcome. It is as if those who select active managers believe that they will be able to "push Sisyphus's rock over the top of the mountain."

The Moral of the Tale

Like Sisyphus, both individual and institutional investors seem condemned to a life of repeating an action that has proven to be highly likely to fail—though the odds are not quite as bad as they are for Sisyphus. As the story goes, Sisyphus is doomed to a failure rate of 100%. The odds against selecting active managers that will outperform on a risk-adjusted basis over the long term are not quite that bad. However, they are so poor that while it was possible to win the game, the odds of doing so are so poor that it is not prudent to try. Of course, it doesn't have to be that way. Investors would benefit from taking George Santayana's advice: "Those who cannot remember the past are condemned to repeat it."[5]

The next story tackles another bit of conventional wisdom— that stocks are only risky if your investment horizon is short.

Chapter 14

Stocks Are Risky No Matter How Long the Horizon

Buying stocks today is not the easy choice that it would be if we had a time machine and could go back into U.S. history.
—*Terry Burnham*, Mean Markets and Lizard Brains

Thirteen Days in October is the story of the Cuban Missile Crisis. Fortunately, the crisis was resolved in a favorable way. However, that outcome was not preordained. In fact, we now know that during a confrontation between the US and Soviet ships, two Soviet commanders gave orders to launch nuclear weapons. Noam Chomsky, professor at the Massachusetts Institute of Technology, described the event as follows:

> We learned that the world was saved from nuclear devastation by one Russian submarine captain, Vasily Arkhipov, who blocked an order to fire nuclear missiles when Russian submarines were attacked by US destroyers near Kennedy's "quarantine" line. Had Arkhipov agreed, the nuclear launch would have almost

certainly set off an interchange that could have "destroyed the Northern hemisphere," as Eisenhower had warned.[1]

History would have played out differently had Arkhipov not blocked the launch order. And while the history of equity returns for US stocks has been extremely favorable, it is likely they would not have been as attractive if the events that played out from October 16 through October 28, 1962, had played out differently.

For the period 1926–2022, the S&P 500 Index returned 10.1% per year, 6.9 percentage points above the 3.2% rate of inflation. During the same period, long-term government bonds returned 5.2% per year before inflation and 2.0% after. It was favorable returns such as these that led Jeremy Siegel, in his best-selling book *Stocks for the Long Run*, to declare that stocks are only risky if one's investment horizon is short. Siegel presents the evidence on returns in the US all the way back to the early 1800s to back up his claim.[2]

The claim that stocks are not risky if one's horizon is long is based on just one set of data (the US) for one period (albeit a long one). It could be that the results were due to a "lucky draw." In other words, if stocks are only risky when one's horizon is short, we should see evidence of this in other markets. Unfortunately, investors in many other markets did not receive the kind of returns US investors did. US returns might just have been the result of what has been called "the triumph of the optimists." Let's go to the videotape.

It is January 1, 1949, and US investors are looking back on the last 20 years of equity returns. They find the S&P 500 Index had returned 3.1% per year, underperforming long-term government bonds by 0.8% per year—so much for the argument that stocks always beat bonds if the horizon is 20 years or more. And how did the world look to US investors at that time? Did it appear to be an encouraging environment for investing in stocks? In fact, the world looked like a very risky place. There had been two World Wars and the Great Depression, the Iron Curtain had fallen across Europe and the Cold War was heating up, trouble was brewing in Korea (which would again throw much of the world into war on

June 25, 1950), and there was even the threat of nuclear war. The world looked so risky that the S&P 500 Index was trading at a P/E of just 6.6 in January 1949!

It is only today that we know capitalism triumphed, the Korean War did not escalate into a global war, the Iron Curtain and the USSR collapsed, and capitalism and democracy spread over most of the world. It turned out to be a far less risky place than it appeared to investors in 1949. The result was that US investors enjoyed spectacular returns, partly as a result of the dramatic fall in the equity risk premium demanded by investors. For the period 1949–2022, the S&P 500 Index returned 11.3% per year, well above the 5.5% return on long-term government bonds. Was this preordained?

While we do not know what US equity returns would have been had Arkhipov not blocked the launch, it is probably safe to assume there would not have been a book called *Stocks for the Long Run*. The lesson we should learn is that while it is true that the longer your investment horizon, the greater your ability to take the risk of investing in stocks (because you have greater ability to wait out a bear market without having to sell to raise capital), stocks are risky no matter the length of your investment horizon. In fact, that is exactly why US stocks have *generally* (but not always) provided such great returns over the long term—investors know that stocks are always risky and, thus, they price stocks in a manner that provides them with an expected (but not guaranteed) risk premium. In other words, stocks have to be priced low enough that they will attract investors with a risk premium large enough to compensate them for taking the risk of equity ownership. In 1949, because the world looked like a very risky place in which to invest, the risk premium was very large (P/E ratios were very low).

If you are not yet convinced that stocks are risky no matter the investment horizon and that the US may just have gotten the "lucky draw," consider the case of investors in Egyptian equities. In 1900, the Egyptian stock market was the fifth largest in the world. Those investors are still waiting for the return *of* their capital, let alone the return *on* their capital. Or consider that in the

1880s there were two promising countries in the Western Hemisphere receiving capital inflows from Europe for development purposes. One was the US; the other was Argentina. One group of long-term investors was well rewarded, while the other was not. If an alternate universe (to use a *Star Trek* term) had shown up, the results might have been reversed, and Professor Siegel's book might have been published in Spanish.

Finally, consider the case of Japanese investors. In December 1989, the Nikkei Index reached an intraday all-time high of 38,957. From 1990 through 2022, Japanese large-cap stocks (MSCI/Nomura) returned just 0.2% a year—a total return of just 6%. Consider that cumulative inflation over the period was about 15%, Japanese large-cap stocks lost about 9% in real terms over the 33-year period. Do you think that long-term Japanese investors believe that stocks are not risky if one's horizon is long?

The Moral of the Tale

Stocks are risky no matter the length of your investment horizon. Rational investors know that stocks are *always* risky. Therefore, markets price stocks in a manner that provides investors with an expected risk premium. Because the majority of investors are risk averse, the equity risk premium has historically been large.

Investors should never take more risk than is appropriate to their personal situation. It is also important to remember these words of caution from Nassim Nicholas Taleb: "History teaches us that things that never happened before do happen."[3] If the events of September 11, 2001, taught you nothing else, they should have taught you that. With that in mind, you will be well served if you remember to never treat the highly unlikely (a very long or even permanent bear market) as impossible.

The next tale explains why investing in individual stocks is much riskier than investors believe.

Chapter 15

Individual Stocks Are Riskier Than Investors Believe

Individual stock ownership offers both the hope of great returns (finding the next Google, for instance) and the potential for disastrous results (ending up with the next Enron). Because investors are not compensated for taking the risk that their result will be the disastrous one—the market doesn't compensate investors with higher expected returns for taking risks that are easily diversified away—the rational strategy is not to buy individual stocks. Unfortunately, the evidence is that the average investor, while being risk averse, doesn't act that way. In a triumph of hope over wisdom and experience, they fail to diversify.

Given the obvious benefits of diversification, the question is, Why don't investors hold highly diversified portfolios? One reason is that it's likely most investors don't understand just how risky individual stocks are. To correct that lack of knowledge, we'll review the literature, beginning with a study by Longboard Asset Management called "The Capitalism Distribution" covering the period from 1983 through 2006 and the top 3,000 stocks.[1] The authors found that while the Russell 3000 Index provided an annualized return of 12.8% and a cumulative return of 1,694% the following also was true for individual stocks:

- The median annualized return was just 5.1%, 7.7% below the return of the market.
- The *average* (mean) annualized return was −1.1%.
- 39% of stocks lost money (even before inflation) during the period.
- 19% of stocks lost at least 75% of their value (again, before considering inflation).
- 64% of stocks underperformed the Russell 3000 Index.
- Just 2% of stocks were responsible for all the market's gains.

Investors picking stocks had almost a two-in-five chance of losing money (they underperformed by at least 1,694% even before considering inflation, which was a cumulative 107%) and almost a one-in-five chance of losing at least 75% of their investment, again even before considering inflation. And there was just greater than a one-in-three chance of picking a stock that outperformed the index.

You may be wondering how the Russell 3000 Index can have an overall positive rate of return when the average annualized return for all stocks is negative. The answer lies mostly in the index's construction methodology. The Russell 3000 is market-capitalization weighted. This means that successful companies with rising stock prices receive larger weightings in the index. Likewise, unsuccessful companies with declining stock prices receive smaller and smaller weightings. In addition, stocks with a negative annualized return had shorter life spans than their successful counterparts—losing stocks have shorter periods of time to negatively affect index returns.

Here's another great example of the riskiness of individual stocks. While the 1990s witnessed one of the greatest bull markets of all time, with the Russell 3000 providing an annualized return of 17.7% and a cumulative return of almost 410%, 22% of the

2,397 US stocks in existence throughout the decade had negative returns. Not negative real returns, but negative absolute returns (meaning they underperformed by at least 410%). And, over the decade, inflation was a cumulative 33.5%, meaning they lost at least 33.5% in real terms. Even this shocking figure is inaccurately low because the data includes only stocks that were in existence throughout the decade—there is a large survivorship bias.

Hendrik Bessembinder contributed to our understanding of the risky nature of individual stocks with his study, "Do Stocks Outperform Treasury Bills?"[2] His study covered the period from 1926 through 2015 and included all common stocks listed on the NYSE, Amex, and NASDAQ exchanges. He found the following:

- Only 47.7% of returns were larger than the one-month Treasury rate.
- Even at the decade horizon, a minority of stocks outperformed Treasury bills.
- From the beginning of sample or first appearance in the data through the end of sample or delisting, and including delisting returns when appropriate, just 42.1% of common stocks had a holding period return greater than one-month Treasury bills.
- While more than 71% of individual stocks had a positive arithmetic average return over their full life, only a minority (49.2%) of common stocks had a positive lifetime holding period return, and the median lifetime return was −3.7%. This is because of volatility and the difference in arithmetic (annual average) returns versus geometric (compound or annualized) returns. For example, if a stock loses 50% in the first year and then gains 60% in the second, it has a positive arithmetic return but has actually lost money (20%) and has a negative geometric return.
- Despite the existence of a small-cap premium (an annual average of 2.8%), smaller capitalization stocks are more likely to have returns that fall below the benchmarks of zero or the Treasury bill rate. Just 37.4% of small stocks had holding period returns that exceed those of the one-month Treasury bill. By contrast, 80% of stocks in the largest decile had positive decade

holding period returns and 69.6% outperformed the one-month Treasury bill.

- Reflective of the positive skewness in returns, only 599 stocks, just 2.3% of the total, had lifetime holding period returns that exceed the cross-sectional mean lifetime return.
- The median time that a stock was listed on The Center for Research in Security Prices database was just more than seven years.
- Only 36 stocks were present in the database for the full 90 years.
- A single-stock strategy underperformed the value-weighted market in 96% of bootstrap simulations (a test that relies on random sampling with replacement) and underperformed the equal-weighted market in 99% of the simulations.
- The single-stock strategy outperformed the one-month Treasury bill in only 28% of the simulations.
- Only 3.8% of single-stock strategies produced a holding period return greater than the value-weighted market, and only 1.2% beat the equal-weighted market over the full 90-year horizon.

The bottom line is that most common stocks (more than four out of every seven) did not outperform Treasury bills over their lifetimes. Bessembinder's findings highlight the high degree of positive skewness (lottery-like distributions), and the riskiness, found in individual stock returns. He noted that the 86 top-performing stocks, less than one-third of 1% of the total, collectively accounted for more than half of the wealth creation. And the 1,000 top-performing stocks, less than 4% of the total, accounted for all of the wealth creation. The other 96% of stocks just matched the return of riskless one-month Treasury bills! The implication is striking: while there has been a large equity risk premium available to investors, a large majority of stocks have negative risk premiums. This finding demonstrates just how great the uncompensated risk is that investors who buy individual stocks, or a small number of them, accept—risks that can be diversified away without reducing expected returns.

Bessembinder concluded that his results help to understand why active strategies, which tend to be poorly diversified, most often lead to underperformance. At the same time, he wrote that the results potentially justify a focus on less-diversified portfolios by investors who particularly value the possibility of "lottery-like" outcomes, despite the knowledge that the poorly diversified portfolio will most likely underperform. Bessembinder showed the impact of the preference for lottery tickets with this finding: only 31.5% of monthly returns to stocks in the lowest share price decile exceeded one-month Treasury bill rates, as compared to 59.1% of monthly returns to stocks in the highest share price decile.

The results from the studies we have examined serve to highlight the important role of portfolio diversification. Diversification has been said to be the only free lunch in investing. Unfortunately, most investors fail to use the full buffet available to them. Bessembinder added this observation: "The results here focus attention on the fact that poorly diversified portfolios may underperform because they omit the relatively few stocks that generate large positive returns. The results also help to explain why active portfolio strategies, which tend to be poorly diversified, most often underperform their benchmarks. Underperformance is typically attributed to transaction costs, fees, and/or behavioral biases that amount to a sort of negative skill. The results here show that underperformance can be anticipated more often than not for active managers with poorly diversified portfolios, even in the absence of costs, fees, or perverse skill."[3]

Investors have the false perception that by limiting the number of stocks they hold they can manage their risks better.

The Moral of the Tale

Investors make mistakes when they take idiosyncratic (unique), diversifiable, uncompensated risks. The field of behavioral finance provides us with explanations for this economically irrational behavior. They do so because they are overconfident of their skills, they overestimate the worth of their information, they confuse the familiar with the safe, they have the illusion of being in control, they don't understand how many individual stocks are needed to effectively reduce diversifiable risks, and they don't understand the difference between compensated and uncompensated risks (some risks are uncompensated because they are diversifiable).

Another likely explanation from the field of behavioral finance is that investors have a preference for skewness. They are willing to accept the high likelihood of underperformance in return for the small likelihood of owning the next Google. In other words, they like to buy lottery tickets. If you have made any of these mistakes, you should do what all smart people do: once they have learned that a behavior is a mistake, they correct their behavior.

The next tale demonstrates how important it is to understand that investors live in a world filled with uncertainty—a world where the odds of negative outcomes cannot be calculated, only estimated. It also demonstrates why the potential for unfavorable outcomes must be considered and built into an investment plan. Finally, it shows how valuable a tool a Monte Carlo simulation can be.

Chapter 16

All Crystal Balls Are Cloudy

The consequences of our decisions must always dominate the probabilities [of outcomes].

—*Peter Bernstein*

In 1977, heavy spring rains caused the people of Grand Forks, North Dakota, to become concerned about the potential for the Red River of the North to flood. Unfortunately, the predictions of scientists that the river would crest at 49 feet lulled the population into a false sense of security. The river eventually crested at 54 feet, forcing 50,000 people to rapidly abandon their homes.

The mistake was not in the scientists' forecast. The mistake was that the population regarded the forecast as a precise one. Instead, the forecast should have been looked on as one potential outcome within a range of potential outcomes. Perhaps a more accurate forecast would have been that there was a 50% chance of the river cresting at 49 feet, a 20% chance of cresting at 54 feet, and a 10% chance of cresting at 60 feet. Had the full range of potential outcomes been considered, it is likely actions would have been taken that would have allowed more people to preserve their possessions.[1]

Predictions can be useful if we understand they contain a large degree of uncertainty. This is true whether we are dealing with a forecast of the height at which a river will crest or a forecast of investment returns in developing a financial plan. A common error is to treat a forecast of returns as a single point—deterministic rather than probabilistic. As the flooding of Grand Forks illustrates, the failure to consider alternative outcomes creates the potential for disastrous outcomes that could have been avoided. Consider the following example.

From 1926 through 1972, the S&P 500 Index returned 9.9% per year in nominal returns and 8% in real terms. Based on this experience, a 65-year-old investor planning his retirement in 1973 might forecast that future real returns will also be 8% per year. To be conservative, he plans to withdraw only 7% of his $1 million portfolio each year, adjusting it for cumulative inflation. In 1973 the remaining average life expectancy for a 65-year old male was 13 years (by 2020 it had increased to about 18). Being conservative, and knowing that half the people live beyond life expectancy, he plans on having sufficient assets to live for 27 years, through the end of the century.

Now let's provide our hypothetical investor with a crystal ball that allows him to foresee the total real return of the S&P 500 through 1999. Thus, he knows with certainty that over the next 27 years (1973–1999) the S&P 500 Index will return 13.9% per year and inflation will rise 5.2% a year, providing him with a real return of 8.% per annum. Now he is even more confident in his plan to withdraw just 7% in real terms, well below the certain real return of 8.7%. How did that turn out?

The Threat of Sequence Risk

As you can see in the following table, despite providing an 8.7% per annum real return over the 27-year period, because the S&P 500 Index declined by more than 37% from January 1973 through December 1974, withdrawing an inflation-adjusted 7% per annum in the portfolio caused it to be depleted by the end of 1982—in just 10 years! (Note that from January 1973 through October 1974, when the bear market ended, the S&P 500 lost 48%.)

	Beginning Portfolio	Return of S&P 500(%)	Ending Portfolio	Inflation (CPI) (%)	Funding Requirement for Following Year
1973	930,000	−14.7	793,000	8.8	76,160
1974	716,840	−26.5	526,877	12.2	85,451
1975	441,426	37.2	605,637	7.0	91,432
1976	514,205	23.8	636,585	4.8	95,821
1977	540,764	−7.2	501,830	6.8	102,337
1978	399,493	6.6	425,859	9.0	111,547
1979	314,312	18.4	372,146	13.3	126,383
1980	245,763	32.4	325,390	12.4	142,054
1981	183,336	−4.9	174,352	8.9	154,697
1982	19,655	21.4	23,861	3.9	160,730

One lesson is that the order of returns matters a great deal in the decumulation phase because systematic withdrawals work like a dollar cost averaging program in reverse—market declines are accentuated. This can cause principal loss from which the portfolio may never recover. In this case the combination of the bear market and relatively high inflation caused the portfolio to shrink by almost 56% in the first two years. In order for the portfolio to be restored to its original $1 million level, the S&P 500 Index would have had to return 127% in 1975. And because of the inflation experienced, the amount to be withdrawn would have needed to increase from $70,000 to over $90,000. In cases such as this, if adjustments are not made to the plan (such as increasing savings, delaying retirement, or reducing the spending goal), the odds of outliving one's assets greatly increase.

Since 1975 we have had five "crashes" in market values: September 1987–November 1987 (−29.5%), April 2000–September
2002 (−43.8%), November 2007–February 2009 (−51.0%), January–
March 2020 (−19.6%), and January 2022–September 2022 (−23.9%).
Clearly such risks should be incorporated into a withdrawal strategy.

The mistake our investor made was the same one the residents
of Grand Forks made. They both treated the single-point estimate
as if it were a certain outcome and not a single potential outcome
within a wide spectrum of potential outcomes.

Another mistake our investor made was to fail to consider that
his investment experience might be different than the return over
the entire period because of the impact on his portfolio of his
withdrawals. In other words, the order of returns matters, not just
the returns over the full period.

Since we know we live in a world with cloudy crystal balls, and
all we can do is estimate returns, it is best not to treat a portfolio's
estimated return as a certain return. It is better to consider the
possible dispersion of likely returns, and estimate the odds of successfully achieving the financial goal. The goal is generally, though
not always, defined as achieving and maintaining an acceptable
lifestyle—not running out of money while still alive. Said another
way, the goal is not to retire with as much wealth as possible, but
to be as sure as possible one does not retire poor and risk running
out of assets while still alive.

The task of considering the potential dispersion of returns is
best accomplished through the use of a Monte Carlo simulator—a
computer simulation with a built-in random process, allowing one
to see the probabilities of different possible outcomes of an investment strategy. The computer program will produce numerous random iterations (usually at least 1,000 and often many thousands),
letting one see the odds of meeting a goal. Since thousands of
iterations are run, one is forced to think in terms of probabilities
instead of just one outcome.

In simple terms, your investment life is divided into an accumulation phase, when you're working and making contributions,

and a distribution phase that begins when you retire and lasts as long as you live. The inputs into the Monte Carlo simulation are the investment assumptions (expected returns, standard deviations, and correlations), future deposits into the investment account, the desired annual withdrawal amount, and the number of years the account must last. The output is summarized by assigning probabilities to the various investment outcomes. For example, in looking at final wealth at a target age (which should be at least as long as life expectancy), the following probabilities might be shown:

- You have a 50% probability of having more than $1 million at age 90.
- You have a 20% probability of having $0 at age 90.

Because the cost of losing is so great, most investors should concentrate on the downside risk (the cost if the "flood" occurs) of outliving their portfolio. There are two uncertainties one faces in forecasting returns. First, as we have seen, while future returns may approximate the expected returns, the year-to-year returns can vary dramatically. Low or negative returns in the early years of retirement, combined with the impact of withdrawals from the portfolio, can have a devastating impact on the ability of an investor to achieve their goals. Second, the realized returns over the period may be less than the expected returns. A Monte Carlo simulation incorporates these uncertainties by selecting a return each year that is drawn from a distribution that encompasses the expected average annual return and expected volatility of the portfolio.

The ultimate goal is to make sure you are comfortable with the projected likelihood of success—the odds you will be able to withdraw sufficient funds from the portfolio each year and still achieve your financial goal. The goal might be to maintain a desired lifestyle and not run out of money while still alive. Or it might be to leave a certain size estate to your heirs. Each investor is different in how they perceive the probabilities and final wealth figures. For some individuals, odds of success of 80% might be sufficient. For others, 95% would be required to allow them to sleep at night. Investors with flexibility (such as the ability to delay retirement and work longer, the willingness and ability to live a lesser lifestyle, or the ability to sell assets such as a second home) can accept lower odds of success than those without such options.

Because there are often trade-offs that must be made between the lifestyle desired and the odds of success, the output of a Monte Carlo simulation provides an important benefit. The process allows for the examination of the pros and cons of alternative strategies in an unemotional manner. For example, after examining the output, you might decide that you are taking more risk than needed to achieve your goals. This is an easy situation to deal with. It involves lowering the allocation to risky investments. The more difficult case is when you find that you are not taking enough risk to provide acceptable odds of success. If this is the case, the decisions are more difficult. For example, you have to decide whether to take more risk than you would otherwise like to take, lower your goal, save more by lowering your current lifestyle, or live with the estimated risk of failure.

An important benefit of a Monte Carlo simulation is that it allows for an analysis of how marginal changes in input affect the odds of achieving the financial goal. For example, let's assume the input results in an 80% chance of success. The program allows you to see the impact on those odds of increasing savings by $X a month. If a change increases the odds of success to 85%, you might decide it's worthwhile to reduce current consumption by that amount. However, if it only raises the odds of success to 81%, a different conclusion might be drawn.

The output also allows for the analysis of how changes in the asset allocation affect the odds of success. If increasing the equity allocation from 70% to 80% increases the odds of success from 80% to 90%, you might decide it's worth the extra risk of more equity ownership (and the extra stomach acid it will likely produce along the way). Alternatively, if it only increases the odds of success to 81%, a different decision might be made.

An analysis can also be done for changes in withdrawal rates (impact on future lifestyle). For example, if a 4% withdrawal rate produces a 95% chance of success, and a 5% withdrawal rate lowers the odds of success to 90%, you might choose to raise the withdrawal rate, accepting a somewhat lower likelihood of success in return for greater consumption. However, if that decision is made and the risks do show up, you must be prepared to accept an even lower lifestyle in the future.

Another use of the simulation program is to look at how delaying retirement by X years affects various issues, such as the need to save, the withdrawal rate, or the equity allocation required. The same analysis can be done for taking retirement at an earlier age. This allows you to determine if a greater lifestyle is worth working an extra year. It also allows you to see how an extra year of work affects the need to take risk. For example, each extra year of work might allow for a reduced need to save of $X per year, or allow for a Y% increase in the withdrawal rate, or allow for a reduction in the equity allocation of Z%.

There are many software programs available that provide the ability to perform Monte Carlo simulations. As you can see, the process is complex. It is, however, an extremely valuable tool. A good financial advisor with experience using these models can add significant value to the process.

The Moral of the Tale

Casey Stengel, the great manager of the New York Yankees and the provider of many pearls of wisdom, said, "Forecasting is very difficult, especially if it involves the future." When it comes to forecasting the future, be it the weather or stock market returns, our crystal balls are always cloudy. As Alan Greenspan noted, this is the best you can do: "Learn everything you can, collect all the data, crunch all the numbers before making a prediction or a financial forecast. Even then, accept and understand that nobody can predict the future when people are involved."[2]

The inability to accurately forecast the future does not render forecasting a useless effort. However, it does mean we must accept this shortcoming and take it into account. Another important moral to learn from this tale is to never make the mistake of treating even the highly likely as if it were certain—whether a river will crest at no more than 49 feet or the stock market will provide 10% returns over the long term.

The next tale explains why it is important to understand that one should not view the risk of an asset in isolation. Instead, the only right way to view an asset is to consider how its addition affects the risk and return of the entire portfolio.

Chapter 17

There Is Only One Way to See Things Rightly

You've got to look at the portfolio as a whole, not just position by position. And if you're trying to reduce the volatility or uncertainty of your portfolio as a whole, then you need more than one security obviously, but you also need securities which don't go up and down together.

—*Harry Markowitz*

Steve Nash played 18 seasons in the National Basketball Association (NBA). He was an eight-time All-Star and a seven-time All-NBA selection. He was also a two-time NBA Most Valuable Player while playing for the Phoenix Suns. And in 2006 ESPN named him the ninth-greatest point guard of all time. If you looked at his career statistics (other than his assists) in many ways they are pedestrian. Over his career he averaged 14.3 points and just 3 rebounds per game—though he did average 8.5 assists per game. Certainly, there are those with far gaudier statistics and whom many would consider better players.

The reason Nash won such accolades is that his contributions go well beyond his individual statistics, especially points and rebounds. Nash's main contribution was that he made everyone around him a better player. This attribute is why Nash is generally considered the greatest point guard of his era. Nash's example demonstrates why it is so important to not make the mistake of viewing a player's value to the team by viewing his statistics in isolation. One needs to consider how the player affects the team's overall performance.

The same thing applies to investing. A common mistake made by investors and even professional advisors is to view an asset class's returns and risk in isolation. Just as the only right way to consider the value of Steve Nash is to consider how his play affects the entire team, the only right way to view an asset is to consider how its addition affects the risk and return of the entire portfolio.

Modern Portfolio Theory

In 1990, Harry Markowitz was awarded the Nobel Prize in economics for his contributions to modern portfolio theory. Markowitz demonstrated that one could add risky, but low correlating, assets to a portfolio and actually increase returns without increasing risk (or, alternatively, reduce risk without reducing returns). The following example, using Vanguard's popular index funds, the largest index funds in their respective categories, will demonstrate just how important it is to consider investments in the whole.

From 1998 through 2022, the Vanguard 500 Index Fund (VFINX) returned 7.53% per annum, outperforming Vanguard's Emerging Markets Index Fund (VEIEX), which returned 6.14% per annum. VFINX also experienced lower volatility of 15.7% versus 22.6% for VEIEX. The result was that VFINX produced a much higher Sharpe ratio (risk-adjusted return measure) of 0.43 versus 0.30 for VEIEX. Looking at the data, would you have preferred to have at least some allocation to emerging markets?

Despite including an allocation to the lower returning and more volatile VEIEX, a portfolio of 90% VFINX/10% VEIEX, rebalanced annually, would have outperformed, returning 7.59%.

And it did so while also producing the same Sharpe ratio of 0.43. Perhaps surprisingly, a 20% allocation to VEIEX would have done even better, returning 7.61% with a 0.43 Sharpe ratio. Even a 30% allocation to VEIEX would have returned 7.59%, higher than the 7.53% return of VFINX (though the Sharpe ratio would have fallen slightly to 0.42 from 0.43). The portfolios that included an allocation to the lower returning and more volatile emerging markets benefited from the imperfect correlation of returns (0.77) between the S&P 500 Index and the MSCI Emerging Markets Index.

The Moral of the Tale

John Ruskin was an author, poet, and artist best known for his work as an art and social critic. His essays on art and architecture were influential in the Victorian and Edwardian eras. He stated, "Not only is there but one way of *doing* things rightly, but there is only one way of seeing them, and that is seeing the whole of them."[1] Ruskin's advice applies to investing. There is only one right way to build a portfolio—by recognizing that the risk and return of any asset class by itself should be irrelevant. The only thing that should matter is considering how the addition of an asset class affects the risk and return of the *entire portfolio*.

It's also important to remember that if markets are efficient (and the persistent failure of active managers to exploit inefficiencies as evidenced in the annual Standard & Poor's Active Versus Passive (SPIVA) reports demonstrates that they are highly, if not perfectly, efficient), all risky assets should have very similar risk-adjusted returns. And that argues for broad global diversification, avoiding the home country bias that leads so many investors to underweight non-domestic equities. The logical starting place for you to consider is the global market capitalization.

The next tale explains the importance of never treating the unlikely as impossible and making sure your plan includes the near certainty that black swan events will appear. Thus, your plan should consider their risks and how to address them.

Chapter 18

Black Swans and Fat Tails

Measures of uncertainty that are based on the bell curve simply disregard the possibility, and the impact, of sharp jumps . . . Using them is like focusing on the grass and missing out on the (gigantic) trees. Although unpredictable large deviations are rare, they cannot be dismissed as outliers because, cumulatively, their impact is so dramatic.

—*Nassim Taleb,* The Black Swan: The Impact of the Highly Improbable *(Random House, 2007)*

Over the course of the first two decades of the 21st century, equity markets faced three "black swan" events: the attacks of September 11, 2001; the Great Financial Crisis that began in late 2007; and the COVID-19 pandemic. Each resulted in steep falls in equity prices. The term *black swan* was a common expression in 16th-century London as a statement that described impossibility. It derived from the "Old World" presumption that all swans must be white—because all historical records of swans reported that they had white feathers. Thus, a *black swan* was something that was impossible, or near impossible, and could

109

not exist. After the discovery of black swans in Western Australia in 1697 by a Dutch expedition led by explorer Willem de Vlamingh on the Swan River, the term metamorphosed to connote that a perceived impossibility may later be found to exist.

With the publication of Nassim Nicholas Taleb's 2001 book *Fooled by Randomness,* the term *black swan* became part of the investment vernacular—virtually synonymous with the term *fat tail.* In terms of investing, fat tails are distributions in which very low and high values are more frequent than a normal distribution predicts.[1] In a normal distribution, the tails to the extreme left and extreme right of the mean become smaller, ultimately reaching zero occurrences. However, the historical evidence on stock returns is that they demonstrate occurrences of low and high values that are far greater than theoretically expected by a normal distribution. Thus, an understanding of the risk of fat tails is an important part of developing an appropriate asset allocation and investment plan. Unfortunately, many investors fail to account for the risks of fat tails. Let's look at some evidence on the existence of fat tails.

Javier Estrada, author of the 2007 study, "Black Swans and Market Timing: How Not to Generate Alpha," examined the returns of 15 stock markets and over 160,000 daily returns.[2] He sought to determine the likelihood that investors can successfully predict the best days to be in and out of the market. Following is a summary of its findings:

1. Stock Returns Are Not Normally Distributed

Black swans appear with far greater frequency than predicted by normal distributions. For example, for the Dow Jones Industrial Index, 29,190 trading days (107 years) produced a daily mean return of 0.02% and a standard deviation of 1.07%. Under the assumption of normality, 39 days would produce returns above 3.22% and 39 would produce returns below −3.17%. However, there were six times the number of returns outside that range—253 daily returns below −3.17% and 208 above 3.22%. Note that the maximum and minimum daily returns were +15.34% and −22.61%. The returns exhibited a high degree of negative skewness (the left tail of the distribution curve is larger) and excess kurtosis (fat tails)—clear departures from normality.

2. The Tails Are Fat

While the daily mean return was 0.02%, the mean returns of the best 10, 20, and 100 days were 11.10%, 9.37%, and 5.92%, respectively—10.4, 8.8, and 5.5 standard deviations above the mean. The mean return of the worst 10, 20, and 100 days were −10.46%, −8.73%, and −5.87%, respectively—9.8, 8.2, and 5.5 standard deviations below the mean. Even the lowest of the best 100 daily returns (4.20%) was 3.9 standard deviations above the mean. While less than two of these should have been expected, the market produced 100. Similarly, the highest of the worst 100 daily returns (−4.28%) was 4 standard deviations below the mean. While less than one should have been expected, the market produced 100.

3. Impact of Missing the Best and Worst Days

While 10 days account for 0.03% of the days, missing the best 10, 20, and 100 best days results in a reduction of terminal wealth of 65%, 83%, and 99.7%—the terminal value is less than the original investment. However, avoiding the worst 10, 20, and 100 days increased the terminal wealth 206%, 532%, and 43,397%, respectively. The author concluded: "These figures speak for themselves and should help investors notice the odds they are against when trying to successfully time the market. A negligible proportion of days determine a massive creation or destruction of wealth. The odds against successful market timing are just staggering."[3]

4. International Markets Produce Same Results

The departure from normal distributions was clear in all 15 countries studied. The countries and the numbers of years through 2006 follows: Australia, 49; Canada, 31; France, 38; Germany, 47; Hong Kong, 37; Italy, 34; Japan, 52; New Zealand, 37; Singapore, 41; Spain, 35; Switzerland, 38; Taiwan, 40;

Thailand, 31; UK, 38; US, 79. Across all 15 markets the number
of outliers was over five times more than expected—investors
assuming normal distributions of returns substantially underestimated risk. Interestingly, with Australia as the lone exception,
missing the best 100 days (less than 1%) resulted in a terminal
wealth lower than the initial capital invested.

Estrada's results were not new information. Professor Eugene
Fama, in his 1964 thesis at the University of Chicago, demonstrated that market returns were not normally distributed.[4] And
Nassim Nicholas Taleb discussed the problem of what he called
black swans in his 2001 book *Fooled by Randomness*. His second
book, *The Black Swan*, was published in 2007. Taleb called a black
swan an event with the following three attributes:

> First, it is an outlier, as it lies outside the realm of regular
> expectations, because nothing in the past can convincingly
> point to its possibility. Second, it carries an extreme impact.
> Third, in spite of its outlier status, human nature makes us
> concoct explanations for its occurrence after the fact, mak-
> ing it explainable and predictable. I stop and summarize the
> triplet: rarity, extreme impact, and retrospective (though not
> prospective) predictability. A small number of Black Swans
> explain almost everything in our world, from the success of
> ideas and religions, to the dynamics of historical events, to
> elements of our own personal lives.[5]

Given that the existence of fat tails was well known, when one
arrives it certainly shouldn't be a surprise to investors. Yet, it is safe
to say that the depth and breadth of the bear market we experienced from November 2007 through March 9 of 2009 came as a
shock to many, if not most, investors—as did the crash caused by
COVID-19, which resulted in the sharpest decline in history with
the MSCI World Index falling 34% from February 19 to March 23.

The Moral of the Tale

Just as shipbuilders know that, in most cases, the seas are relatively safe, they also know that typhoons and hurricanes happen. Therefore, they design their ships not just for the 95% of the sailing days, when the weather is clement, but also for the other 5%, when storms blow and their skill is tested.

The existence of fat tails doesn't change the prudent strategy of being a passive buy, hold, and rebalance investor. Active managers have demonstrated no ability to protect investors from fat tails. However, the existence of fat tails is extremely important because of the effect they can have on portfolios. The risks of black swans, and the damage they can do to portfolios, especially for those in the withdrawal phase, must be considered when designing your asset allocation. With that in mind the following advice is offered:

- Make sure your investment plan accounts for the existence of fat tails.
- Don't take more risk than you have the ability, willingness, or need to take.
- Never treat the unlikely as impossible or the likely as certain.

Chapter 19

Is Gold a Safe Haven Asset?

Gold has long been used as a store of value, a unit of exchange, and as jewelry. More recently, many investors have come to believe that gold should be thought as an investment asset, playing a potential role in the asset allocation decision by providing a hedge against currency risk and against inflation, and being a haven of safety during serious economic recessions. We'll review the research findings to determine if the evidence supports those beliefs.

In their June 2012 study, "The Golden Dilemma," Claude Erb and Campbell Harvey found that in terms of being a currency hedge, changes in the real price of gold were largely independent of the change in currency values—gold is not a good hedge against currency risk.[1] As for gold serving as a safe haven (it is stable during bear markets in stocks), they found gold isn't quite the safe haven some might think as 17% of monthly stock returns fell into the category where gold dropped while stocks posted negative returns. If gold acted as a true safe haven, we would expect very few, if any, such observations. Still, 83% of the time on the right side isn't a bad record. With that said, even the safe-haven hypothesis was tarnished, as gold prices declined over 30% during the worst of the financial crisis of 2007–2009—when the hedge was needed most, it failed. In 2022 when both stocks and bonds produced double-digit losses, even though gold outperformed stocks and bonds, it once again failed to provide a true hedge, as it fell slightly, closing at $1,824 in 2022 after closing at $1,829 in 2021.

In terms of gold's value as an inflation hedge, the following example provides the answer. On January 21, 1980, the price of gold reached a then-record high of $850. On March 19, 2002, gold was trading at $293, well below its price 20 years earlier. The inflation rate for the period from 1980 through 2001 was 3.9%. Thus, gold's loss in real purchasing power was about 85%. Gold cannot be considered an inflation hedge over most investors' horizons when it lost 85% in real terms over 22 years. Here's an example with a longer horizon. With gold trading at less than $2,000 in July 2023 it had lost more than 20% of its real value (inflation-adjusted) from its peak of about $2,533 in February 1980. That's more than 42 years with a significant loss in real value.

Their analysis led Erb and Harvey to conclude that although there is little relation between the nominal price of gold and inflation when measured over even 10-year periods, the evidence suggests that gold does hold its value over the very long run. For example, in their 2019 update to "The Golden Constant," they presented historical evidence that the wage of a Roman centurion (in gold) was approximately the same as the pay a US Army captain earned today. They also showed that the price of bread (again in gold) thousands of years ago was about the same as we would pay today at an upscale bakery.[2]

As additional evidence that gold is not a good hedge against inflation, Goldman Sachs' *2013 Investment Outlook* included the following finding: during the post–World War II era, in 60% of episodes when inflation surprised to the upside, gold underperformed inflation.[3] That said, gold has been a good inflation hedge over the very long run (such as a century). Unfortunately, that's a much longer horizon than that of most investors.

Safe Haven

Pim van Vliet and Harald Lohre, authors of the 2023 study, "The Golden Rule of Investing," examined the strategic role of gold in investment portfolios, focusing on its marginal downside risk-reduction benefits relative to bonds and equities.[4] They also considered longer horizons and accounted for inflation. Their analysis covered the period from 1975 (when gold became truly tradable) through 2022. Following is a summary of their key findings:

- Equities and gold jointly declined in 17% of the months. Conversely, equities were down and gold was up in 19% of the months, roughly resonating with a 50/50 chance for gold to show negative returns in a given negative equity month—gold is not a perfect safe haven when evaluated at a one-month horizon.
- At the three-year horizon, gold would have served as a safe haven in about three-quarters of down markets for equities—again, not a perfect safe haven. In addition, the somewhat limited protection came at a clear cost because gold was down half of the times when equities were up.

Van Vliet and Lohre next examined the effectiveness of gold in lowering downside risk and found:

- The real returns for equities (US total market), bonds (10-year Treasuries), and gold were 8.0%, 3.3%, and 1.5%, respectively.
- The risk of gold was high on a stand-alone basis—its downside volatility was 11.3% compared to 7.9% for equities and 5.3% for bonds.
- The Sortino ratio, which measures the return per unit of downside volatility, was 1.01 for equities, 0.62 for bonds, and only 0.13 for gold.
- Judging by the loss probability over a one-year horizon, gold was riskier (49.% chance of loss) than both equities (24.9% chance of loss) and bonds (34.6% chance of loss). Notably,

bonds had a greater probability of loss than equities, though lower than that of gold.

- Judging by the expected loss over a one-year horizon, gold was riskier (−6.1%) than both equities (−3.1%) and bonds (−2.5%).
- Judging by the minimum return over a one-year horizon, gold was riskier (−46.1%) than both equities (−42.2%) and bonds (−25.3%).

When van Vliet and Lohre examined adding an increasing allocation of gold to a traditional stock and bond portfolio (with annual rebalancing), they found very little evidence of any real net benefits. For example, while adding a small allocation to gold (5%–10%) slightly reduced downside volatility (from 3.9% to 3.7%), slightly improved the Sortino ratio (from 1.56 to 1.61), and reduced the probability of loss (from 26.6% to 22.4%) and the expected loss (from 1.6% to 1.3%), it also reduced the real return from 6.1% to 5.9%. They also found that increasing the gold allocation to above 10% generally led to even lower real returns and increased downside risk as well.

Their findings led van Vliet and Lohre to conclude: "Our empirical study corroborates that a portfolio's loss probability, its expected loss, and downside volatility can be brought down with modest allocations (5%–10%) to gold. However, hedging downside risk via gold investing comes at the cost of lower return."

The Moral of the Tale

Investors are often attracted to gold because they believe it provides hedging benefits—hedging inflation, hedging currency risk, and acting as a haven of safety in bad times. The evidence demonstrates that investors should be wary. First, while gold might protect against inflation in the very long run, 10 or 20 years is not the long run. And there is no evidence that gold acts as a hedge against currency risk. As to being a safe haven, gold is a volatile investment that is capable and likely to overshoot or undershoot any notion of fair value. Evidence of gold's short-term volatility is that over the 17-year period of 2006–2022, the annual standard deviation of the iShares Gold Trust ETF (IAU), at 17.2%, was higher than the 15.6% annual standard deviation of Vanguard's 500 Index Investor Fund (VFINX). In addition, it experienced a maximum drawdown of almost 43%—safe havens don't experience losses of that magnitude.

The next tale addresses the issue of what defines prudent investing.

Chapter 20

A Higher Intelligence

There is one thing stronger than all the armies of the world, and that is an idea whose time has come.

—*Victor Hugo*

For many years, a group of higher beings had monitored the advancement of society on Earth through radio waves that reached their distant planet. Although the beings agreed that Earth's civilization had generally progressed over the last millennium, they had become interested in certain communications emitting from the United States. Specifically, communications regarding investment propaganda—seemingly popular theories espousing that the way to prudently invest was to pick stocks and time the market. They wondered why investors would believe such foolish theories when the evidence from their own experiences clearly demonstrated that those benefiting from such strategies were the purveyors of these theories (brokers, investment bankers, mutual fund sponsors, and especially hedge fund managers). Still, the beings assumed that US investors would eventually realize the errors of their ways and abandon the prevailing investment theories.

Watching investors continue to subscribe to such investment strategies (often with disastrous results) eventually compelled the

beings to visit the United States to investigate this strange investment culture. They were intent on discovering whether all residents
of Earth had lost the ability to recognize investment fiction from fact.

Upon arriving in the United States, they visited Wall Street
and the New York Stock Exchange. After watching CNBC, the
beings were convinced that their worst fears had been confirmed.
There was, however, one hopeful being. She pleaded with the rest
of the reconnaissance group that before they abandoned all hope
they should find out what the legal statutes had to say about investment strategy. This would be a good test of what Earthlings truly
believed about investing—at least those who took the time to
study the evidence instead of listening to the hype. She convinced
the group to visit the New York Public Library before heading
back to their galaxy.

The beings visited the library after closing and scoured the legal
reference section. They found that embedded within the American legal code is a doctrine known as the Prudent Investor Rule.
They also found something called the Third Restatement of Trusts.
The Restatement (Third), written in 1992 by the American Law
Institute (ALI), made clear that it recognized that active management delivers inconsistent and poor results. They were especially
happy to find that the ALI had the following to say about market
efficiency:

- Economic evidence shows that the major capital markets of
  this country are highly efficient, in the sense that available
  information is rapidly digested and reflected in market prices.
- Fiduciaries and other investors are confronted with potent evidence that the application of expertise, investigation, and diligence in efforts to "beat the market" ordinarily promises little
  or no payoff, or even a negative payoff after taking account of
  research and transaction costs.
- Empirical research supporting the theory of efficient markets
  reveals that in such markets skilled professionals have rarely
  been able to identify underpriced securities with any regularity.

- Evidence shows that there is little correlation between fund managers' earlier successes and their ability to produce above-market returns in subsequent periods.

They also found that there was something called the Uniform Prudent Investor Act. The act governs the investment activities of trustees and is the law in virtually all states. They learned that the act effectively makes passive investing the standard by which fiduciaries should be judged. They were pleased to see that the act incorporated two important tenets of prudent investment management. The first is that because broad diversification is fundamental to the concept of risk management, it is incorporated into the definition of prudent investing. The second is that cost control is an essential part of prudent investing.

They also noted that the act gives trustees the authority to delegate their responsibilities as a prudent investor would. Thus, trustees/investors who do not have the knowledge, skill, time, or interest to prudently manage a portfolio should delegate that responsibility to an advisor who does.

They were also interested to find the following analysis from Michael G. Sher of the University of Minnesota's Carlson School of Management:

> Ethical malfeasance occurs when an investment manager does something deliberately or conceals it (e.g., the manager knows that it's too drunk to drive, but drives anyway). For example, consider the manager who invests intentionally at a higher level of risk than the client chose without informing the client and then subsequently generates a higher return than expected. . . . The manager attributes the excess return to its superior investment skill [instead of the acceptance of incremental risk].
>
> "Ethical misfeasance" occurs when an investment manager does something by accident (e.g., the manager really believes that it's sober enough to drive). . . . Thus, the

manager doesn't know what it's doing and shouldn't be managing money.

Sher concluded, "Managing money in an efficient market without investing passively is investment malfeasance." He then noted, "Not knowing that such a market is efficient is investment misfeasance." In either case, he believed that "such conduct may be imprudent per se (i.e., there's no excuse for the manager to be driving)."[1] The bottom line is that Sher felt that passive investing is the more ethical way to invest.

After reading these various documents the beings realized that most investors did have ready access to the prudent investment approach. They felt assured that not all was lost. The beings left New York with the knowledge that investors need not accept the popular but flawed investment strategy of active management. They were pleased that investors were at least able to access the prudent investment alternative of passive asset class investing. However, they were sorry to see how long it was taking for the majority of Earth's investors to learn what they had known for thousands of years. They were also sad to see that so many of the yachts that were anchored in the marinas of lower Manhattan belonged to the brokers. They should have belonged to the investors.

The Moral of the Tale

The prudent investment strategy is available to all investors. All anyone needs to do is take a trip to the public library.

We now move to Part III, which discusses some of the most important behavioral errors investors make, beginning with a tale demonstrating that investors have the ability to delude themselves about their own skills and performance, leading to persistent and costly investment mistakes.

Part Three

BEHAVIORAL FINANCE: WE HAVE MET THE ENEMY AND HE IS US

Chapter 21

You Can't Handle the Truth

That is the famous line Jack Nicholson shouted at Tom Cruise in the film *A Few Good Men*. Evidence from the field of behavioral finance suggests investors can't handle the truth—many delude themselves about their own skills and performance. The ability to delude oneself leads to persistent and costly investment mistakes. Consider the following.

In 1965, 50 drivers were asked to rate their skill and ability the last time they were behind the wheel. About two-thirds said they were at least as competent as usual. Many even described their most recent drive as "extra good." What is particularly interesting about this study performed by two psychologists was that all the participants had ended their last driving trip in an ambulance. Police reports showed almost 70% of the drivers were directly responsible for their crashes, almost 60% had at least two past traffic violations, a similar number had totaled their cars, and almost 50% faced criminal charges.

This data may seem strange in light of the unique group of participants. However, overconfidence is an all-too-human trait. The same psychologists interviewed people with clean driving records and found that over 90% believed themselves to be above average.[1]

Overconfidence

In a *New York Times* article, Jonathan Fuerbringer cited professors Richard Thaler and Robert Shiller, who noted that individual investors and money managers persist in their belief that they are endowed with more and better information than others, and they can profit by picking stocks.[2] This insight helps explain why individual investors believe they can do the following:

- Pick stocks that will outperform the market.
- Time the market so they're in it when it's rising and out of it when it's falling.
- Identify the few active managers who will beat their respective benchmarks.

Even when individuals think it is hard to beat the market, they are confident they themselves can be successful. Here is what noted economist Peter Bernstein had to say: "Active management is extraordinarily difficult, because there are so many knowledgeable investors and information does move so fast. The market is hard to beat. There are a lot of smart people trying to do the same thing. Nobody's saying that it's easy. But possible? Yes."[3] That slim possibility keeps hope alive. Overconfidence leads investors to believe they will be among the few who succeed. Consider the data from a study on individual investors.

Money magazine conducted a study on more than 500 individual investors. Almost 30% stated their portfolios had outperformed the Dow Jones Industrial Average over the previous 12 months. About one-third stated their portfolios had risen between 13% and 20%, another third stated they earned between 21% and 28%, and about one-fourth stated they earned at least 29%. Four percent admitted they had no idea what they had earned. Over that period, the Dow actually returned more than 46% and outperformed more than three-quarters of all the investors.[4] Now consider the evidence from a similar study.

The study "Positive Illusions and Forecasting Errors in Mutual Fund Investment Decisions" sought the answer to the question, "Why do investors spend so much time and money on actively managed mutual funds despite the fact the vast majority of these funds are outperformed by passively managed index funds?" The authors concluded the reason is that investors delude themselves. They found most participants had consistently overestimated both the future performance and past performance of their investments. In fact, more than a third who believed they had beaten the market had actually underperformed by at least 5%, and at least a fourth lagged by at least 15%. Biases such as this contribute to suboptimal investment decisions.[5]

We turn now to the results of the study "Why Inexperienced Investors Do Not Learn: They Do Not Know Their Past Portfolio Performance."[6] The authors, Markus Glaser and Martin Weber, analyzed the actual performance of the online brokerage accounts of individual investors. Following is a summary of their findings:

- Investors are unable to give a correct estimate of their own past portfolio performance. The correlation coefficient between return estimates and realized returns was not distinguishable from zero.
- People overrate themselves. Only 30% considered themselves average. Investors overestimated their own performance by an astounding 11.5% a year. And portfolio performance was negatively related with the absolute difference between return estimates and realized returns—the lower the returns, the worse investors were when judging their realized returns. It seems likely investors are unable to admit how badly they have done. While just 5% believed they had experienced negative returns, the reality was that 25% had done so.

- On average, investors underperform relevant benchmarks. While the arithmetic average monthly return of the benchmark was 2.0%, the mean gross monthly return of investors was just 0.5%. And more than 75% of investors underperformed.

Psychologists have also found that investors who have the "I'm in charge feeling" have an even greater ability to delude themselves. A study of US retirement plan investors who could either choose their own mutual funds or permit someone else to decide for them found that both groups deluded themselves about their performance. The investors who allowed others to make the selections on their behalf only overstated their returns by more than 2%. The group that was "in charge" overstated returns by almost 9%.[7]

Possible, Not Likely

It is certainly possible for investors to outperform the market. However, the evidence demonstrates that the vast majority would be better off simply accepting market returns. At the very least, investors should know the odds of outperforming. For example, S&P Dow Jones Indices SPIVA U.S. 2022 Report found that over the 20-year period ending December 2022, 95% of large-cap funds and 94% of midcap and small-cap funds underperformed their benchmark S&P indices. In just three (large value, midcap value, and real estate) of 18 categories did less than 90% underperform. In no case was the percentage of underperformers below 86.5%.

Unfortunately, it seems most investors delude themselves about those odds. One reason might be that they are unaware of the evidence. Another is that they don't know their own track records. This type of self-delusion helps to explain why investors exhibit the common human trait of overconfidence. Most people want to believe they are above average; thus, the disconnect investors have between reality and illusion persists.

The Moral of the Tale

It is important to measure your investment returns and also compare them to appropriate benchmarks. Doing so will force you to confront reality rather than allow an illusion to undermine your ability to achieve your financial objectives.

The next tale demonstrates the importance of being able to distinguish between risks that are worth taking and ones that are not.

Chapter 22

Some Risks Are Not Worth Taking

Content makes poor men rich; discontent makes rich men poor.
—*Benjamin Franklin*

In his wonderful book *Deep Survival*, author Laurence Gonzalez described the following situation. Eight snowmobilers had just completed a search and rescue mission. They stopped at the base of a hill well known for climbing and hammer-heading—a competitive game to see who can reach the highest point. The idea is to race up the hill until either gravity stops you or you turn back. This particular hill had a reputation for being especially dangerous and prone to avalanches. Hammer-heading was out of the question. Still, one of the snowmobilers could not resist temptation. Then a second couldn't. An avalanche occurred, and tragically, the two members of the team died.[1] This story reminds us that some risks are just not worth taking. It is certainly true in the world of investing, as the following example illustrates.

I was visiting Atlanta to give a seminar based on my first book, *The Only Guide to a Winning Investment Strategy You'll Ever Need.* While there, I met with an Intel executive. His net worth at the time exceeded $10 million. With the exception of his home, almost all of the $10 million was in Intel stock. At the time, Intel was trading at a split-adjusted price of about 40 (in July 2000, the stock split 2:1). Despite his acknowledging the risks of this concentrated strategy, he was so confident in the outlook for his company that he would not consider selling even a small percentage of his stock in order to diversify his portfolio. Despite my best efforts, which included many examples of individuals in similar situations who had seen their net worth suffer greatly (employees of once-great companies like Digital Equipment, Polaroid, and Xerox), there was no convincing him to sell.

I met the Intel executive again about two and a half years later. Intel's stock was trading at about 10, having fallen about 75%. However, there was still no convincing him to diversify his holdings. Nine years after the original meeting, in March 2009, the stock was still trading at about 10—and there was still no convincing him. He said, "Surely Intel will come back." I pointed out that executives from now-bankrupt companies had said the same thing. I reminded him that investing is about risk; there are no sure things. Fortunately, Intel eventually recovered. However, it was not until late in 2017 that it once again reached 40. And over the period from March 2000 through September 2020, while an investment in Vanguard's 500 Index Fund (VFINX) returned 6.4% per annum, Intel returned just 1.8% per annum. There are some risks not worth taking. You should never have more than a small percentage, perhaps 10%, of your assets in the stock of any one company, especially that of your employer, because your labor capital could then be highly correlated with the performance of the stock.

The Moral of the Tale

Investing is about taking risk. However, prudent investors know there are some risks that are worth taking, and some that are not.

And they know the difference. Thus, when the cost of a negative outcome is greater than you can bear, the risk should not be taken, no matter how great the odds appear to be of a favorable outcome. In other words, the consequences of your investment decisions should dominate the probabilities, no matter how favorable you think the odds.

The next tale explains why many of the mistakes investors make are the result of the failure to view problems through the correct lenses.

Chapter 23

Framing the Problem

You are the commanding officer of 600 troops surrounded by the enemy. After careful analysis, you determine you have two alternatives. Alternative A is to fight it out until reinforcements arrive. If you adopt that strategy, you estimate 200 of your troops will survive. Alternative B is to attempt to surprise the enemy by sneaking out under cover of darkness. You estimate there is a one-third chance that everyone will be saved and a two-thirds chance that everyone will die. Which do you choose?

Now consider the same exact scenario, though the wording is different. In this case, your estimate for alternative A is that 400 of your troops will die. The estimate for alternative B is that there is a one-third chance that everyone will be saved and a two-thirds chance that everyone will die. Which do you choose?

While the two situations are identical, in the first case, the majority of people will choose alternative A. In the second case, the majority will choose alternative B. Psychologists explain this result by the way the alternative was posed: in the first case, the focus was on how many lives would be saved (200), while in the second case, the focus was on how many would die (400).

Each of us likes to believe we are rational when we make decisions. As rational people, when faced with equivalent situations, we should come to equivalent decisions. However, psychologists have found that is not the case for most people. Depending on how a problem is framed, we often come to very different conclusions, and mistakes are often made. That includes investment mistakes.

Consider the following examples from Jason Zweig's excellent book, *Your Money & Your Brain*:

- One group of people was told that ground beef was "75% lean." Another was told the same meat was "25% fat." The "fat" group estimated the meat would be 31% lower in quality and taste 22% worse than the "lean" group estimated.
- Pregnant women are more willing to agree to amniocentesis if told they face a 20% chance of having a Down syndrome child than if told there is an 80% chance they will have a "normal" baby.
- A study asked more than 400 doctors whether they would prefer radiation or surgery if they became cancer patients themselves. Among the physicians who were informed that 10% would die from surgery, 50% said they would prefer radiation. Among those who were told that 90% would survive surgery, only 16% chose radiation.[1]

The evidence from the three examples shows that if a situation is framed from a negative viewpoint, people focus on that. However, if a situation is framed in a positive way, the results are quite different. Let's now look at two investment-related situations that illustrate how our decisions can be influenced by the way they are presented.

Indexed Annuities

Indexed annuities (IAs) are products described by those selling them as providing "the best of both worlds"—the potential rewards of equity investing without the downside risks. The typical IA offering has the following characteristics:

- A link to a *portion* of the positive changes in an index (typically the S&P 500)
- Principal protection
- A minimum guaranteed return, regardless of the performance of the index
- Tax-deferred growth potential
- Income options to meet your specific needs
- A death benefit guaranteeing beneficiaries 100% of the annuity's indexed value

Investors seem to find these characteristics irresistible. In 2019, Limra, an insurance industry group, projected that sales of indexed annuities would rise to $96 billion by the end of 2023, $26 billion more than in 2018. In 2022, sales actually reached $80 billion. Unfortunately for investors, IAs contain many negative features, any one of which could lead investors to conclude they should not buy an IA. The negatives can include the following:

- Large commissions reduce the returns that can be earned.
- The return is limited by either capping it or providing as little as 50% of the return of the benchmark index (though 70% to 90% is more typical). Thus, investors can miss out on much of the potential rewards of equity investing.
- The return is based on the price-only return of the index and does not include dividends. (Historically, dividends have provided a significant portion of the total return of stocks.)
- The return is reduced by some margin that is subtracted from the return of the index.
- The return is based on simple interest instead of compound interest.
- Most IAs have significant early surrender charges that can exceed 20%.
- The issuer can change some of the terms, such as the rate cap.

The typical IA is so complex, and filled with negative features that are difficult for most investors to fully understand, that in July

2020 the SEC issued a bulletin warning about them. The following warnings were contained in that bulletin.

Please Note

Indexed annuities are complex products. Before you decide to buy an indexed annuity, read the contract and, if the annuity is a security, read the prospectus. You should understand how each feature works, and what impact it and the other features may have on the annuity's potential return. You can lose money buying an indexed annuity. Ask your insurance agent, broker, or other financial professional questions to understand how the annuity works.

Please Note

Indexed annuity contracts commonly allow the insurance company to change some of these features periodically, such as the rate cap. Changes can affect your return. Read your contract carefully to determine what changes the insurance company may make to your annuity.

With all the negatives, why do investors seem to love this product, buying tens of billions year after year? The reason is simple. The insurance industry frames the investment decision in a manner that gets investors to focus on the potential for large gains, the principal protection, and the guaranteed minimum return provided by annuities. Investors lose sight of the costs and the lost upside potential. In other words, "you've been framed." Consider the following regarding the guaranteed minimum return and the protection of principal.

Most IAs do come with a guaranteed minimum return, historically 1% to 3%. However, that guarantee is not always on the entire investment. Frequently, the company guarantees investors will receive at least x% of just 90% of their investment. Why 90%? The reason is the insurer has paid 10% in commissions. The result is investors can still lose principal investing in an IA, especially if they need to cancel their annuity early—the guarantee only applies if held to maturity. And then there are those nasty early withdrawal penalties.

There is another important point to consider regarding the benefit of the guaranteed minimum return. Because the guarantee is based on nominal (not real, or inflation-adjusted) returns, the insurance has historically had almost no value. From 1931 through 2007, there was not any 10-year period when the S&P 500 Index did not produce positive nominal returns—no principal protection was needed. And from 1932 through 2007, there was only one single 10-year period when the S&P 500 Index did not produce a return in excess of 3%. The single exception was 1965–1974, when the S&P 500 Index returned 1.2% per year. The bear market of 2008 added to that list—and that is how investors get framed by recent events.

One can only wonder how many investors would have actually bought these IAs if they were presented with the focus on the upside potential they had given up instead of being pitched on the downside protection (historically of little value). How the problem was framed (and lack of investor knowledge) led to costly investment mistakes.

Let's now look at another situation where framing can lead to mistakes.

Monte Carlo Simulations

Since we live in a world with cloudy crystal balls and all we can do is estimate returns, it is best not to treat a portfolio's estimated return as a certain return. It is better to consider the possible dispersion of likely returns, and then estimate the odds of successfully achieving the financial goal. The task is best accomplished through the use of a Monte Carlo (MC) simulator.

The output of an MC simulation is summarized by assigning probabilities to the various investment outcomes. How the output is framed can make all the difference in how people look at risk. For example, the output might be presented as the individual having a 90% chance of never running out of money (their financial goal). Given what we have learned, it is highly likely that far more people will find that an acceptable risk than if the situation were framed from the negative perspective—a 10% chance of running out of assets. Since MC output is almost always shown from the positive perspective (the odds of success are shown), it is likely people are taking more risks than appropriate. The research, and my own anecdotal experience, demonstrates that people who say that 90% odds of success are acceptable will answer differently if they're told 1 out of 10 of them will run out of assets. Are you willing to accept that risk? That's why I have learned that when dealing with issues related to risks, I always pose the questions from the negative perspective.

The Moral of the Tale

Individuals and financial advisors alike must be careful to frame problems in a way that enables analyzing them from various perspectives. That is the best way to ensure that all the pros and cons have been thought through. Understanding the ways in which human beings can make mistakes, and helping them avoid such mistakes, is also a way a financial advisor can add value.

The next tale demonstrates that otherwise intelligent people persistently make investment mistakes, even when presented with warnings from regulatory agencies.

Chapter 24

Why Do Smart People Do Dumb Things?

If you want to see the greatest threat to your financial future, go home and take a look in the mirror.

—Jonathan Clements

f you are like most people, you probably have wondered why you have done some really foolish things. Perhaps you have used a folding chair as a stepladder, tried cleaning an oven with the burners still on, or left your car with the engine still running (something I have done twice). The facts of life are that even smart people occasionally do dumb things—it is one of the things that makes us human. When it comes to investing most of us make mistakes, often caused by behavioral errors like overconfidence. Being overconfident can cause us to take too much risk, trade too much, and confuse the familiar with the safe. Those are explainable errors. But here is one I find hard to explain.

While most smart people don't ignore the surgeon general's warning about the hazards of smoking cigarettes, they do ignore the SEC's required warning that accompanies all mutual fund advertising: "Past performance does not guarantee future results." Despite both an overwhelming body of evidence, including the annual SPIVA Scorecards, that demonstrates that the past mutual fund returns of active managers are not prologue, and the SEC's warning, investors still flock to funds that have performed well in the recent past. Fund companies exploit and encourage this by advertising their top-performing funds. And studies such as the 2021 research paper, "Ratings-Driven Demand and Systematic Price Fluctuations," show that fund flows follow advertising.[1]

We'll review some of the most powerful evidence on performance persistence—evidence that I hope will lead you to ask why investors ignore the evidence. We'll begin with the 2017 study "Does Past Performance Matter in Investment Manager Selection?"[2] The authors examined "whether selecting managers based on recent simple outperformance against the stated benchmark (the dominant manager selection heuristic) can lead to subsequent simple outperformance against the benchmark (the desired outcome for most institutional investors)." To simulate the impact of the popular manager selection heuristic, they compared the performance of hypothetical pension portfolios that follow policies that mandate investing in products based on recent benchmark-adjusted returns.

The authors started with the commonly employed "winner strategy," defined as follows: at the beginning of each three-year period, investors purchase equal positions in products that rank in the top decile of benchmark-adjusted returns. At the end of three years, monies are reallocated to a new portfolio that is once again equal-weighted among the top-decile performers.

They then compared the investment results of their winner strategy with those of a "median strategy," whose three-year asset allocation policy is to invest in products that rank between the 45th and 55th percentile of benchmark-adjusted returns. They also examined the counterintuitive "loser strategy," which follows the same procedure but invests in products that rank in the bottom decile of benchmark-adjusted returns.

The winner-strategy bucket would generally consist of fund managers that investment consultants would recommend to their pension clients. Managers in the loser-strategy bucket would generally be put on a "watch list" and actively replaced in client portfolios by managers on the recommended list.

Finally, they also compared the investment performance produced by an unorthodox strategy of investing in products that underperformed their benchmarks by more than 1% per year, as well as the even more extreme case of investing in products that underperformed their benchmarks by more than 3% per year. These portfolios provide insight into the impact of the common manager firing heuristic. Their sample excluded funds that did not have at least $1 billion in assets under management (AUM) and also those that ranked in the top decile of expense ratio (research shows that expensive mutual funds tend to be persistent underperformers because of costs). Their study covers the period from 1994 through 2015. The following is a summary of their findings:

- The average benchmark-adjusted return for the median strategy beat that of the winner strategy by 1.32 percentage points per year (−1.07% versus −2.39%), and the loser strategy outperformed the median strategy by 0.96 percentage points per year (the loser strategy had a benchmark-adjusted return of −0.11%). Thus, the loser strategy outperformed the winner strategy by 2.28 percentage points per year.
- In addition to benchmark-adjusted returns, the median strategy outperformed the winner strategy across all other performance metrics commonly employed in academic studies while the loser strategy outperformed the median strategy.
- The Sharpe ratio of the median strategy was 0.42 versus 0.25 for the winner strategy, while the loser strategy produced a Sharpe ratio of 0.48. Thus, investors would have nearly doubled their mean–variance efficiency by switching from chasing winners to investing in loser funds.
- The CAPM alpha generated by the median strategy beats that of the winner strategy by a statistically significant 2.76 percentage points per year (−0.85% versus −3.61%) and its Carhart

four-factor (market beta, size, value, and momentum) alpha beat that of the winner strategy by a statistically significant 1.03 percentage points a year (−2.16% versus −3.19%). The loser strategy managed to do even better, producing an annual CAPM alpha of just −0.11% and a Carhart four-factor alpha of −0.17%, though neither was statistically significant.

Similar results were found when examining the performance of the extreme loser portfolios. "At the 3% threshold, the fired funds outperform the kept funds by over one percentage point per year based on benchmark-adjusted return, raw return, CAPM alpha, and Carhart four-factor model alpha. The Sharpe ratios indicate that the fired funds also exhibit greater mean-variance efficiency than their counterparts. The results are largely similar when we use a 1% threshold in place of the 3% threshold. Once again, the fired funds outperform the kept funds across all performance metrics."[3]

For example, they found the funds that underperformed by more than 1% (fired managers) produced four-factor alphas of −0.69%, which compares favorably to the −1.88% alpha of funds that did not underperform by more than 1% (managers who were kept). For funds that underperformed by more than 3%, the four-factor alpha was −0.48% versus −1.64% for those that did not underperform by more than 3%.

As a test of robustness, they found similar results using a two-year evaluation period instead of three years. They also found similar results when they eliminated the $1 billion AUM requirement, and when they looked at only institutional share classes (which have lower costs). They even found the same results when looking at funds by benchmark performance decile (in general, moving from the funds in the best-performing deciles to the worst, performance became worse on both a raw and risk-adjusted basis). Such outcomes help to explain the often-reported "performance gap"—the finding that, on average, performance-chasing behavior can cause investors to underperform the very funds in which they invest.

Their findings led the authors to conclude: "We find that the common selection methodology turns out to be a detriment to performance." They added: "The greater benchmark-adjusted return to investing in 'loser funds' over 'winner funds' is statistically and economically large and is robust to reasonable variations in the evaluation and holding periods, as well as to standard risk adjustments. We also found that the standard practice of firing managers who have recently underperformed actually eliminates those managers that are more likely to outperform in the future."[4]

These findings are entirely consistent with prior research. Take note of the publication dates of the studies cited in the next section. You'll see that the evidence on using past performance to select actively managed funds has been there for a long time for all to see, yet the evidence continues to be ignored by a large majority of investors, both institutional and individual.

Supporting Evidence

Rob Bauer, Rik Frehen, Hurber Lum, and Roger Otten, authors of the 2008 study "The Performance of U.S. Pension Plans," examined the performance of 716 defined benefit plans (over the period from 1992 through 2004) and 238 defined contribution plans (over the period from 1997 through 2004).[5] They found that returns relative to benchmarks were close to zero. They also found no persistence in performance.

Importantly, the authors also found fund size, degree of outsourcing, or company stock holdings were factors driving performance. This refutes the claim that large pension plans are handicapped by their size. Smaller plans did no better. They concluded, "We show striking similarities in net performance patterns over time, which makes skill differences highly unlikely."

Bauer, Frehen, Lum, and Otten also studied the performance of mutual funds, adding to our body of evidence on them. As you should expect, the news for individual investors is even worse. While pension plans failed to outperform market benchmarks, on a risk-adjusted basis mutual funds underperformed pension plans by about 2% per year. Pension plans are able to use their size (negotiating power) to minimize costs and reduce the risks of any conflicts of interest between fund managers and investors. The authors attributed the underperformance to the incremental costs incurred by mutual fund investors.

Counterproductive Activity

The 2008 study "The Selection and Termination of Investment Management Firms by Plan Sponsors" by Amit Goyal and Sunil Wahal provided further evidence on the inability of plan sponsors to identify investment management firms that will outperform the market after they are hired.[6] In their study, Goyal and Wahal examined the hiring and firing of investment management firms by plan sponsors (public and corporate pension plans, union pension plans, foundations, and endowments). They built a dataset of the selection and termination decisions of about 3,400 plan sponsors from 1994 to 2003. The data represented the allocation of over $627 billion in mandates. The following is a summary of their findings:

- Plan sponsors hired investment managers after large, positive excess returns coming up to three years prior to hiring.
- Such return-chasing behavior did not deliver positive excess returns thereafter.
- Post-hiring, excess returns were indistinguishable from zero.
- Plan sponsors terminated investment managers after underperformance, but the excess returns of these managers after being fired were frequently positive.
- If plan sponsors had stayed with the fired investment managers, their returns would have been larger than those actually delivered by the newly hired managers.

It is important to note that these results did not include any of the trading costs that would have accompanied transitioning a portfolio from one manager's holdings to the holdings preferred by the new manager. The bottom line: all of the activity was counterproductive.

Having reviewed the evidence, it's time to return to our question: Why do investors ignore both the warning and the evidence?

Why Are Warnings Worthless?

The study "Worthless Warnings? Testing the Effectiveness of Disclaimers in Mutual Fund Advertisements" provided some interesting results.[7] The authors created an experiment in which participants were shown a version of a performance advertisement for a mutual fund that had outperformed its peers in the past. They were then asked about their propensity to invest in the fund and about their expectations regarding the fund's future returns. Versions of the advertisement differed in the strength and prominence of the disclaimer contained in the advertisement.

The authors found that "people viewing the advertisement with the current SEC disclaimer were just as likely to invest in a fund, and had the same expectations regarding a fund's future returns, as did people viewing the advertisement with no disclaimer whatsoever." The authors concluded, "The SEC-mandating disclaimer is completely ineffective. The disclaimer neither reduces investors' propensity to invest in advertised funds nor diminishes their expectations regarding the funds' future returns. . . . The current disclaimer fails because it is too weak. [It fails because] "it only conveys that high past returns don't *guarantee* high future returns and that investors in the fund *could* lose money, things that almost all investors already know. It fails to convey what investors really need to understand: high past returns are a poor predictor of high future returns."

The authors did find "that a stronger disclaimer—one that informs investors that high fund returns generally don't persist (they are often a matter of chance)—would be much more effective."

Investors are also ignoring the American Law Institute's Prudent Investor Rule, which states that "there is little correlation between fund managers' earlier successes and their ability to produce above-market returns in subsequent periods."

There are hundreds of studies on the subject of past performance of money managers as a predictor of future performance. The following from the March 15, 1999, issue of *Fortune* effectively summarizes the conclusions of a publication that regularly touts top-performing funds: "Despite the solemn import that fund companies attribute to past performance, there's no evidence that the 4 percent who beat the index owe their record to anything other than random statistical variation. The whole industry is built up around a certain degree of black magic." *Fortune* continued: "Despite volumes of research attesting to the meaninglessness of past returns, most investors (and personal finance magazines) seek tomorrow's winners among yesterday's. Forget it. The truth is, much as you wish you could know which funds will be hot, you can't—and neither can the legions of advisers and publications that claim they can."

If Not Past Performance?

There's an axiom in finance that when the evidence (past performance of active funds is not prologue) conflicts with the theory, no matter how logical and intuitive it may be, throw out the theory, not the evidence. Unfortunately, most investors continue to ignore the evidence that makes it clear a policy of hiring recently outperforming managers and firing recently underperforming managers is a losing strategy. The results you have seen in the research pose a significant challenge for investors who continue to base decisions on beliefs that run counter to the evidence.

The bottom line is that so many investors are doing the same thing over and over again and expecting a different outcome. Most seem to never stop and ask the question, If the managers I hired based on their past outperformance have underperformed after being hired, why do I think the new managers I hire to replace them will outperform if I am using the very same criteria that have repeatedly failed? And, if I am not doing anything different, why should I expect a different outcome? I've asked these very questions, and never once received an answer—just blank stares.

The practical implication is that investors should change the criteria they use to select managers. Instead of relying mainly, if not solely, on past performance, they should use criteria such as fund expenses and the fund's degree of exposure to well-documented factors (such as size, value, momentum, profitability, and quality) that have been shown to have provided premiums. These premiums should have evidence that they have been persistent, pervasive, robust to various definitions, implementable (they survive transaction costs), and that they have intuitive explanations for why you should expect the premium to persist.

A set of criteria like that will almost certainly lead investors to avoid actively managed funds and increase their likelihood of superior results.

The Moral of the Tale

Whether the advice comes from the Surgeon General, the SEC, or the American Law Institute, smart people know that it should not be ignored. They also know that if they choose to ignore the advice, they do so at their own peril.

The next tale demonstrates the importance of planning—wars are won in the planning stage, not on battlefield.

Chapter 25

Battles Are Won Before They Are Fought

S un Tzu was an honorific title bestowed on Sūn Wǔ. Tzu, lived from 544 to 496 BCE and authored *The Art of War*, an immensely influential ancient Chinese book on military strategy. The book is composed of 13 chapters, each devoted to one aspect of military warfare. It has long been considered one of the definitive works on military strategies. And it has also had an influence on business tactics. Investors can also benefit from its wisdom. In particular, they may benefit from the insight provided by one of the book's most often cited phrases: "Every battle is won before it is ever fought."

The bear market that was caused by the COVID crisis began on February 20, 2020. Over the next 23 trading days the S&P 500 Index fell 34%, the largest drop ever over such a short period. However, those with knowledge of historical events knew that such losses should not have been entirely unexpected. We'll review a few key episodes, as well as the historical evidence, to demonstrate why that is true.

On July 19, 2007, the S&P 500 Index closed at 1553. By August 15, it had fallen to 1407, a drop of almost 10% in less than a month. The drop was fueled by a dual flight-to-quality and a flight-to-liquidity. Headlines from the financial media reported huge losses in hedge funds as investors fled all risky assets, the kind of assets hedge funds often buy.

The media (and not just the financial media) also commented about how this was an unprecedented event. The following statement is a good example. It was made by Matthew Rothman, global head of quantitative equity strategies for Lehman Holdings Inc. and a University of Chicago PhD. After three days of huge losses for equities all around the globe Rothman stated, "Wednesday is the type of day people will remember in quant-land for a very long time. Events that models only predicted would happen once in 10,000 years happened every day for three days."[1]

Lehman's models (as well as the models of many other hedge funds) may have made such a forecast, but all that proved was that the models were wrong. Such events had occurred in the past, and they had done so with a fair amount of frequency. In fact, we had a very similar crisis in summer 1998, just 10 years earlier.

The hedge fund Long-Term Capital Management (LTCM) was founded in 1994 by John Meriwether (former vice chairman and head of bond trading at Salomon Brothers). Myron Scholes and Robert Merton, who shared the 1997 Nobel Memorial Prize in Economics, sat on its board. LTCM had early successes producing annualized returns of over 40% in its first years. Then, in 1998, it lost $4.6 billion in less than four months and became the most popular example of the risk that exists in the hedge fund industry. In early 2000, the fund folded. LTCM failed because its models told them the same thing that Rothman's model had told him.

The Historical Evidence

Professor Eugene Fama (the thesis advisor to LTCM's Myron Scholes at the University of Chicago) studied the historical distribution of stock returns. Here is what Fama found: "If the population of price changes is strictly normal, on the average for any stock . . . an observation that is more than five standard deviations from the mean should be observed about once every 7,000 years. In fact, such observations seem to occur about once every three or four years."[2] That is a long way from once every 10,000 years. Consider also the following:

- From 1926–2022, in 26 out of the 97 years the S&P 500 Index produced negative returns. In 11 of those years the losses were greater than 10%. In six of the years the losses exceeded 20%. In three of the years the losses exceeded 30%. And in one year the loss exceeded 40%.
- During the same period, out of 388 quarters, there were 34 (9% of the quarters) in which losses exceeded 10%. There were also eight quarters (2%) when losses exceeded 20%. And there were two quarters when losses exceeded 30% (1%).

What the data is telling us is that stocks are risky assets, risks that appear more than would be randomly expected given historical volatility. The data also tells us that investors must expect that they will experience severe losses at some point. In fact, the risk of severe losses is the reason why stocks have provided higher returns historically than have safe bonds—on average, investors are highly risk averse. To entice them to take the risks of equity investing, stocks must be priced to provide high expected returns. And it is not a question of *if* the risks will show up. The only questions (to which no one has the answers) are when the risks will show up, how sharp the declines will be, and when they will end.

The Anatomy of a "Crisis"

Some bear markets are caused by specific events, such as what occurred on September 11, 2001, the oil crisis of 1973, or the COVID crisis. These are random events that cannot be forecasted. However, others follow a fairly consistent pattern that goes as follows. When economic times are good investors become more willing to take risks. Prices begin to rise. The longer the times remain good, the more confident investors become, and the more risk they become willing to take. Eventually stocks may even become "priced for perfection." Eventually, risks do show up. Losses appear, credit tightens, margin calls have to be met, and a flight-to-quality ensues. We might say that "a tipping point" was reached. Prices don't just fall, they often collapse as a vicious cycle develops as selling begets more selling. Some investors are forced to sell to meet margin calls. Others simply panic as the pain of losses exceeds their tolerance for that pain.

When Risks Show Up

It is important to note that during bear markets most equity and risky bond assets have a strong tendency to become highly correlated. Thus, while global diversification across equity asset classes is the prudent strategy because it reduces risk over the long term, during crises this benefit "takes a holiday." The only safe haven during such periods is fixed income investments of the highest quality (for example, Treasuries, government agency securities, and FDIC-insured CDs). Riskier fixed income assets such as junk bonds and emerging market bonds also suffer from flights-to-quality and liquidity. This is why the prudent strategy is to make sure that your portfolio contains a sufficient amount of safe bonds to dampen the risk of the overall portfolio to an acceptable level—winning the battle before the fight begins.

It is also important to note that the risks of hedge funds, which supposedly offer the benefit of low correlation, tend to rise during crises. The reason is that many hedge funds attempt to achieve high returns by investing in risky and illiquid assets. Thus, just when you need them to provide their so-called hedge, the risk appears. This is exactly what happened in summer 1998, with encore performances in 2008 and in 2022. This is just one of the many reasons why investors should avoid hedge funds. (There are many others including their failure to deliver on their "promise" of greater risk-adjusted returns.)

These crises also show the why investors should avoid strategies that employ significant leverage to high-volatility assets like equities. Leverage works well until risk shows up. Then the use of leverage often leads to the inability to wait out a bear market because margin calls must be met. Leverage has been the factor leading to the demise of many investment strategies. The perfect example is LTCM. It went belly-up despite the fact that many of its trades proved to be correct if only it could have held on to its positions. Unfortunately, margin calls had to be met, and LTCM was forced to liquidate. Those who shorted GameStop were provided with a remedial course on that lesson.

Let's now turn to the issue of whether investors can successfully avoid the inevitable periods of sharp losses by timing the market.

Timing the Market

The evidence on efforts to successfully time the market is compelling. For example, in his book *The Portable MBA in Investment*,[3] Peter Bernstein cited a study of 100 large pension funds and their experience with market timing that found that while they all had engaged in at least some market timing, not a single one had improved its rate of return as a result.

Let's look at some evidence on why market timers get such poor results. Keep in mind that when you try to time the market you have to be right not just once, but twice. You have to sell at the right time and you also have to get back in at the right time. We saw earlier that of the 388 quarters from 1926 through 2022, there were 34 in which losses exceeded 10%. Out of those 34 quarters, 21 were followed by quarters when the S&P 500 Index rose at least 5%. There was also 12 quarters when it rose at least 10%, five when it rose at least 20%, three when it rose at least 30%, and two when it rose at least 80%. Yes, 80%. Thus, following quarters when the market fell at least 10%, the next quarter it rose at least 5% almost two-thirds of the time. There were also three other quarters when the market rose, though less than 5%. Thus, over 70% of the time after experiencing a quarter of a sharp decline, the market actually rose. Evidence such as this is why legendary investor Peter Lynch stated, "Far more money has been lost by investors preparing for corrections, or trying to anticipate corrections, than has been lost in corrections themselves."[4] And Warren Buffett's favorite time frame for holding a stock is forever.

If bear markets cannot be anticipated, what is the prudent strategy?

The Winner's Game

The quote, "Most battles are won or lost [in the preparation stage] long before the first shot is fired," is attributed to Napolean, perhaps history's greatest general. For investors the battle is also won in the planning stage. Successful investors know both that bear markets will happen and that they cannot be predicted with a high degree of accuracy. Thus, they build bear markets into their plans. They begin by determining their ability, willingness, and need to take risk. They make sure that their asset allocation does not cause them to take so much risk that when a bear market inevitably shows up they might sell in a panic. They also make sure that they don't take so much risk that they lose sleep when emotions caused by bear markets run high.

The Moral of the Tale

Life is just too short for individuals to spend time worrying about their portfolio. If investors make sure that they don't take too much risk, they will be able to rebalance (buy more of the investments that have performed the worst) in the face of large losses. Unfortunately, many investors, especially those who take excessive risk, let emotions drive their decisions and they end up buying high and selling low—the opposite of what you are doing when rebalancing. Prudent investors who stay disciplined and rebalance, buying low and selling high, clearly adhere to a superior strategy.

Stocks are risky investments, no matter the time horizon. Smart investors recognize that. They also know that they cannot predict when the bear [market] will emerge from its hibernation or how large the losses will be. They know that just as battles are won in the planning stage, the winning investment strategy is to have a well-developed investment plan in the form of an investment policy statement. However, they also know that having such a plan is only a *necessary* condition for investment success. The *sufficient* condition is that they must have the discipline to stick to the plan, acting like a postage stamp. The postage stamp does only one thing, but it does it exceedingly well. It adheres to its package until it reaches its destination. To be successful, investors must have the discipline to avoid having their well-developed plan end up in the trash heap of emotions.

In closing, the next time the emotions caused by a bear market tempt you to sell you should consider the following from Stephen Gould. Gould, who died in May 2002, was professor of zoology and geology at Harvard University. In his book, *Full House*, he wrote: "Probably more intellectual energy has been invested in discovering (and exploiting) trends in the stock market than in any other subject—for the obvious reason that stakes are so high, as measured in the currency of our culture. The fact that no one has ever come close to finding a consistent way to beat the system—despite intense efforts by some of the smartest people in the world—probably indicates that such causal trends do not exist, and that sequences are effectively random."[5]

The next tale addresses one of the more popular investment myths—the best way to address the volatility of the stock market is to invest equal amounts on a regularly scheduled basis (dollar cost averaging) over a predetermined period of time (such as on the first of each month for one year).

Chapter 26

Dollar Cost Averaging

It is undesirable to believe a proposition when there is no ground whatsoever for supposing it true.
—*Bertrand Russell, British philosopher, mathematician, and historian*

We can define a myth as a traditional story, typically based on the activities of gods and heroes, which purports to explain a natural phenomenon or cultural practice. Based on the number of questions I get on the subject, one of the most popular myths is that the best way to address the volatility of the stock market is to invest equal amounts on a regularly scheduled basis—dollar cost averaging (DCA)—over a predetermined period of time (such as on the first of each month for one year). Like much conventional wisdom, it seems to be based on a commonsense idea: in an unpredictable and high-volatility world, you will be buying at both high and low prices.

The issue of DCA typically arises when an investor has received a large lump sum of money. They wonder if they should invest it all at once or spread the investment out over time. The same problem arises when an investor has panicked and sold when confronted with a bear market, but then there are two questions: How does the investor decide when it is safe to reenter the market? And do they reinvest all at once or by DCA?

From an academic perspective, the answer to the question of which is the winning strategy, lump-sum investing or DCA, has been known for a long time. The June 1979 issue of *The Journal of Financial and Quantitative Analysis* published an article by University of Chicago professor George Constantinides, "A Note on the Suboptimality of Dollar Cost Averaging as an Investment Policy."[1] Constantinides demonstrated that DCA is an inferior strategy to lump-sum investing. This was followed in 1992 by a paper by John Knight and Lewis Mandell, "Nobody Gains from Dollar Cost Averaging: Analytical, Numerical and Empirical Results."[2]

Knight and Mandell compared DCA to a buy-and-hold strategy and then analyzed the strategies across a series of investor profiles from risk averse to aggressive. The authors stated,

> Brokerage firms endorse DCA for two reasons. First, they state that returns are increased because more shares are purchased when prices are low and fewer when prices are high. Secondly, they assert that DCA enhances investor utility by preventing an ill-timed lump sum investment. Our results do not support either of these contentions. . . . Using three separate methods of comparison, we have shown the lack of any advantage of DCA relative to two alternative investment strategies. Our numerical trial and empirical evidence, in consonance with our graphical analysis, both favor optimal rebalancing and buy and hold strategies over dollar cost averaging.

The 2011 paper by the firm Gerstein Fisher, "Does Dollar Cost Averaging Make Sense for Investors?," took another look at the subject.[3] The authors begin by asking, "When will the DCA strategy not work? It won't work when, in general, prices rise. Since markets are moving up, every time more cash is invested, it is being invested at a higher cost. On the flip side, this strategy will work over the long run if markets are moving downward—every new purchase is made at a lower cost than the previous one." So, which is more likely? The S&P produced positive returns in over 60% of the months between January 1926 through December 2010 and in over 70% of the years between 1926 and 2010. Updating the data through 2022 shows that 63% (73%) of the months (years) produced positive returns. Thus, if you want to put the odds in your favor, the answer should be obvious.

The authors then set up the following test. To compare the performance of DCA versus LSI (lump-sum investing), the two strategies were back-tested between 1926 and 2010. Transactions costs were ignored (favoring DCA, which involves more trading). The initial portfolio was assumed to be $1 million in cash, and the only investment available was the S&P 500 Index:

- DCA strategy: One-twelfth of the initial portfolio was invested each month at the beginning of the month—the entire $1 million was invested by the beginning of the 12th month.
- LSI strategy: The entire $1 million portfolio was invested on day one.

The study covered 781 rolling 20-year periods. The LSI strategy outperformed in 552 of them—over 70% of the time. In addition, in the roughly 30% of instances in which DCA outperformed, the magnitude of that outperformance was less than when LSI outperformed. Specifically, during the 552 20-year periods in which LSI did better than DCA, the average cumulative outperformance was $940,301 on the initial $1 million investment. During the 229 periods in which DCA did better than LSI, the average cumulative outperformance was $769,311.

The authors even looked at how the two strategies performed during the 10-year period 2001–2010. For the 109 rolling 12-month periods, LSI outperformed in 70 (64%). The average outperformance was 1.3%.

Unfortunately, despite all the evidence, I still hear investors and advisors recommending DCA. They are either unaware of the evidence or the simple logic—since there is always an equity risk premium (stocks have higher expected returns than bonds), common sense tells us to invest all at once. Unfortunately, many investors, and even many financial advisors, do not always base decisions on logic or evidence. In fact, the stomach (emotions) often plays a far greater role in decision-making than the head (logic).

The Lesser of Two Evils

Despite the evidence and logic presented, there is one exception to the rule of avoiding DCA. There is an argument to be made in its favor when it is the lesser of two evils—when an investor simply cannot "take the plunge" because they are sure that if they were to invest all at one time, that day would turn out to be the high not exceeded until the next millennium. That fear causes paralysis. If the market rises after they delay, how can they buy now at even higher prices? And if the market falls, how can they buy now because the bear market they feared has arrived? Once a decision has been made to not buy, exactly how do you make the decision to buy?

There is a solution to this dilemma, one that addresses both the logic and the emotional issues. An investor should write down a business plan for their lump sum. The plan should lay out a schedule with regularly planned investments. The plan might look like one of these alternatives:

- Invest one-third of the investment immediately and invest the remainder one-third at a time during the next two months or next two quarters.
- Invest one-quarter today and invest the remainder spread equally over the next three quarters.
- Invest one-sixth each month for six months or every other month.

Once an investor has written up the schedule, they should sign the document. If the investor has an advisor, they should instruct the advisor to implement the plan regardless of how the market performs. Otherwise, they might be tempted by the latest headlines or guru forecasts.

Having accomplished these objectives, the investor should adopt a "glass is half full" perspective. If the market rises after the initial investment, they can feel good about how their portfolio has performed. They can also feel good about how smart they were not to delay investing. If, however, the market has fallen, they can feel good about the opportunity they now have to buy at lower prices and about being smart enough not to have put all of their money in at one time. Either way, they win from a psychological perspective. Because we know that emotions play an important role in how individuals view outcomes, this is an important consideration.

The Moral of the Tale

Once an investor is convinced that a gradual approach is the correct one, it is important to ask the following question: "Having made your initial partial investment, do you now want to see the market rise or fall?" The logical answer is that one should root for the market to fall so that one gets to make future investments at lower prices.

The next tale demonstrates the importance of understanding that the consequences of your decisions should always dominate the probabilities of outcomes, no matter how confident you are in those probabilities.

Chapter 27

Pascal's Wager and the Making of Prudent Decisions

Pascal's wager is a suggestion posed by the French philosopher Blaise Pascal that even though the existence of God cannot be determined through reason, a person should wager as though God exists—because the consequences of being wrong with each belief are very different. As author William Bernstein explained in his forward to Jonathan Clements's book, *The Little Book of Main Street Money*, "If a supreme being doesn't exist, then all the devout has lost is the opportunity to fornicate, imbibe, and skip a lot of dull church services. But if God does exist, then the atheist roasts eternally in hell."[1]

What does Pascal's wager have to do with investing and financial decision-making? Pascal demonstrated that the consequences of decisions should be carefully considered before you accept the risks involved in case you are wrong in your choice. Pascal's wager can be used to help you make all kinds of financial decisions. Let's take a look at some of them.

Asset Allocation

If you have already achieved sufficient wealth to support a quality lifestyle, you face a similar wager to the one Pascal proposed. You can choose to either focus on the preservation of capital by having a low allocation to risky assets like equities, or you can choose to try to accumulate even more wealth by having a large allocation to risky assets. While it is likely that a high allocation to risky assets such as equities will result in greater wealth, that outcome is not a certainty. And, not only do we know that for most people the pain of a loss is at least twice the magnitude of the good feelings generated by an equivalent gain, we also know that consequences of going from rich to poor are intolerable for most people. Therefore, if you have reached the point where your marginal utility of wealth is low, your portfolio should be dominated by high-quality fixed-income assets. As Pascal demonstrated, there are some risks that are just not worth taking. This was a lesson the market taught many investors in the Great Financial Crisis of 2008 and provided remedial courses during the COVID-19 crisis and in 2022 when both stocks and bonds experienced double-digit losses.

If you are deciding on which side of Pascal's wager you want to be with your portfolio, you should consider this insight from author Nassim Nicholas Taleb: "One cannot judge a performance in any given field by the results, but by the costs of the alternative (i.e., if history played out in a different way). Such substitute courses of events are called *alternative histories*. Clearly the quality of a decision cannot be solely judged based on its outcome, but such a point seems to be voiced only by people who fail (those who succeed attribute their success to the quality of their decision)."[2]

Let's look at how Pascal's wager applies to the decision to buy life insurance.

Whether or Not to Buy Life Insurance

Consider a young, healthy couple with a new baby. They have a mortgage, small 401(k) plan, and the equivalent of about six months of spending accumulated in a money market account. They are trying to decide if they should purchase life insurance. They know that the odds of either of them dying in the near future are probably less than 100:1. Thus, they know that if they purchase life insurance, the great likelihood is that they will be transferring assets from their pockets to the pockets of the insurance company. What should they do? Pascal provides the answer. The consequences of leaving a spouse and a child with insufficient assets to provide a quality life are unthinkable. Thus, even though the odds suggest that they should not purchase insurance, the prudent decision is to do so. Again, we see that the consequences of our decisions should dominate the probability of outcomes.

A similar example relates to long-term care insurance.

Long-Term Care Insurance

It is estimated that at least 60% of people over age 65 will require some long-term care services. And, Medicare and private health insurance programs don't pay for the majority of long-term care services most people need, such as help with dressing or using the bathroom. Yet, long-term care is often overlooked as a crucial planning tool. Let's see how Pascal's wager can help us decide whether the purchase of long-term care insurance is appropriate. Consider the following example from my book, *The Only Guide You'll Ever Need for the Right Financial Plan.*

Mr. and Mrs. Smith are both 65 years old. They have financial assets of $6 million. A Monte Carlo analysis reveals that their portfolio has a high likelihood of providing sufficient assets to maintain their desired lifestyle *if* neither ever has a need for long-term care. If one or both do need long-term care for an extended period, the portfolio has a *significant* likelihood of being strained or even depleted. The Monte Carlo analysis also reveals that the costs of a long-term care insurance policy will not significantly reduce the odds of success.

The Impact of Adding Long-Term Care Insurance

Long-Term Care Scenarios	Odds the Portfolio Will Have Sufficient Assets (%)
No long-term care insurance, no need for care	94
Have long-term care insurance, no need for care	91
Have long-term care insurance coverage for 20 years, need care for 5 years (age 85–90)	83
No long-term care insurance, need care from age 85–90	74

If no insurance is needed, the costs of purchasing a long-term care policy increases the odds of running out of money by just 3% (94 to 91 percent). However, if long-term care is needed, and no insurance is purchased, the odds of running out of money increase by 20%—the odds of success fall from 94% to74%. That is almost seven times the 3% increase in likelihood of failure caused by the purchase of insurance. It seems clear that the purchase of the insurance is the prudent decision.

The same lesson applies to decisions to buy other types of insurance, be it disability, flood, earthquake, or personal liability (specifically umbrella policies, which are relatively inexpensive).

Let's turn now to the decision to purchase TIPS or nominal bonds.

TIPS Versus Nominal Bonds

If you hold long-term nominal bonds, you win if deflation shows up (or even if inflation is less than expected). You lose, however, if inflation is greater than expected because your portfolio might not provide sufficient income to maintain your desired lifestyle. However, with TIPS, you win either way. If inflation shows up, the return of your bonds keeps pace. Even with deflation, they do at least as well as in inflation because TIPS mature at par. The consequences of your decision should dominate the probability of outcomes, making TIPS the prudent choice in most cases.

Active Versus Passive Funds

If you buy an index or other passively managed fund, it should provide the market rate of return and fewer expenses (typically very low). However, if you buy an active fund, while you do have the possibility of market beating performance, you also must accept the risk of below-average performance. Given that investors are risk averse and the pain of a loss is much greater than the joy of an equivalent gain, Pascal's wager leads the way to the prudent decision being to be a passive investor.

Helping with that decision is the academic research showing both that the majority of active funds underperform and that there is no persistence of outperformance beyond the randomly expected. And studies have also found that the few funds that beat their benchmark on average do so by a relatively small amount, while those that underperform on average do so by much larger amounts (think Pascal's wager).

The Ownership of Company Stock

Every investor knows that putting too many eggs in one basket is a risky investment decision that can easily be avoided by building a diversified portfolio. Still, many executives and long-term corporate employees end up with a substantial portion of their assets in the stock of the employer. I've seen numerous cases where employees have as much as 80% to 90% of their net worth in their employer's stock. Pascal can help us decide if this is a prudent decision.

Consider two outcomes. The first is one in which the company does well. If that is the case, the employee will also likely do well regardless of whether or not he owns lots of company stock. The outlook would be bright for pay increases, bonuses, promotions, and even more stock options or stock grants. However, if the company does poorly, the employee could face a case of double jeopardy—not only will the portfolio take a devastating hit, but the employee may find themself without a job due to layoffs or even bankruptcy. The consequences of decisions should dominate the probability of outcomes.

There are many other examples of how Pascal's wager can help us make prudent financial decisions. For example, when in a low interest rate environment investors seeking incremental cash flow may decide to take more credit risk than they would normally. Pascal would say that is a bad idea because it takes a lot of interest to make up for unpaid principal. Or, those same investors might decide to extend maturities longer than they would normally to earn a term premium. But, doing so takes on increased inflation risk.

The Moral of the Tale

I have been managing or advising on the management of financial risks of various kinds (such as interest rate, credit, foreign exchange, investments, and insurance) for 50 years. Having Pascal "whispering in my ear" has prevented me from making many mistakes and helped me prevent others from making what could have turned out to be devastating mistakes, mistakes that are sometimes impossible to recover from.

The next tale demonstrates how the endowment effect causes us to make poor investment decisions.

Chapter 28

Buy, Hold, or Sell, and the Endowment Effect

The issue of holding or selling an asset is one of the more frequent risk management problems I am asked to address. I hope the following will help you address the problem from the right perspective.

Put yourself in the following situation: You are a wine connoisseur. You decide to purchase a few cases of a new release at $10 per bottle, and you store the wine in your cellar to age. Ten years later the dealer from whom you purchased the wine informs you that the wine is now selling for $200 per bottle. You have a decision to make. Do you buy more, sell your stock, or drink it?

Faced with this type of decision, few people would sell the wine—but, very few would buy more. Given the appreciation in the wine's value, some might choose to save it to drink on special occasions.

The decision not to sell, while not buying more, is not economically rational. The wine owner is being influenced by what is known as the "endowment effect." The fact that the wine is something you already own (an endowment) should not have any impact on your decision. If you would not buy more at a given price, you should be willing to sell at that price. Since you wouldn't buy any of the wine if you didn't already own any, the wine represents a poor value to you. Thus, it should be sold. The same thing is true of any investment you currently hold—in the absence of costs, the decision to hold is the same as the decision to buy.

The endowment effect often causes individuals to make poor investment decisions. For example, it causes investors to hold assets they would not purchase if they didn't already own any—either because they don't fit into the asset allocation plan or they are viewed as so highly priced that they are no longer viewed as the best alternative from a risk/reward perspective.

Perhaps the most common example of the endowment effect is that people are often reluctant to sell stocks or mutual funds that were inherited or were purchased by a deceased spouse. I have heard many people say something like, "I can't sell that stock, it was my grandfather's favorite, and he'd owned it since 1952." Or, "That stock has been in my family for generations." Or, "My husband worked for that company for 40 years, I couldn't possibly sell it." Another example of an investor subject to the endowment effect is stock that has been accumulated through stock options or some type of profit-sharing/retirement plan.

Financial assets are like the bottles of wine. If you wouldn't buy them at the market price, you should sell them. Stocks, bonds, and mutual funds are not people—they have no memory, they don't know who bought them, and they won't hate you if you sell them. An investment should be owned only if it fits into your current overall asset allocation plan. Thus, its ownership should be viewed in that context.

You can avoid the endowment effect by asking this question: If I didn't already own the asset, how much would I buy today as part of my overall investment plan? If the answer is "I wouldn't buy any" or "I would buy less than I currently hold," you should sell. That is true of a bottle of wine, a stock, bond, or a mutual fund.

The lesson is simple: in the *absence of costs*, if you would not buy the asset you are currently holding, you should sell it. For investors in mutual funds in tax-advantaged accounts, the costs of trading are either zero or so small that they can basically be ignored. However, for taxable accounts, the impact of taxes must be considered.

The Moral of the Tale

If you are faced with the decision to dispose of an "endowment asset," and there will be substantial capital gains taxes involved, you might consider donating some, or all, of the stock to your favorite charity. By donating the financial asset in place of cash you would have donated anyway, you can avoid paying capital gains taxes. Alternatively, you can place the stock in a charitable trust and then sell it, again avoiding the payment of taxes. And finally, keep this important point in mind: there is only one thing worse than having to pay taxes—not having to pay them. I have seen many large fortunes turned into small ones due to the unwillingness to pay taxes.

The next tale demonstrates how investors make errors simply because they are humans, prone to behavioral mistakes.

Chapter 29

The Drivers of Investor Behavior

During my almost 30 years as the head of financial and economic research at Buckingham Wealth Partners, I have witnessed investors make many costly mistakes. These mistakes were made for a variety of reasons, including lack of knowledge. However, some were made simply because, as human beings, investors are prone to behavioral errors. For example, as we have discussed, individuals have a strong tendency to be overconfident of their skills. And overconfidence can lead to many errors, including excessive risk taking. In order to help you avoid making such mistakes, I'll review some of the more common ones, including wanting more from investments than returns.

Ego-Driven Investments

Meir Statman is one of the leaders in the field of behavioral finance. His book, *What Investors Really Want*, exposes many of the costly errors we make as investors.[1] If you want to improve your chances of reaching your financial goals, it is a must-read. He explained that investors want more than returns from their investments: "Investments are like jobs, and their benefits extend beyond money. Investments express parts of our identity, whether that of a trader, a gold accumulator, or a fan of hedge funds. . . . We may not admit it, and we may not even know it, but our actions show that we are willing to pay money for the investment game. This is money we pay in trading commissions, mutual fund fees, and software that promises to tell us where the stock market is headed."

Statman went on to explain that some invest in hedge funds for the same reasons they buy a Rolex or carry a Gucci bag with an oversized logo—they are expressions of status, available only to the wealthy. Statman cited business and finance author John Brooks, who in 1973 wrote, "Exclusivity and secrecy were crucial to hedge funds from the first. It certifies one's affluence while attesting to one's astuteness." Statman went on to explain that hedge funds offer what he called "the expressive benefits of status and sophistication, and the emotional benefits of pride and respect." He cited the cases of investors who complain when hedge funds lower their minimums. Those expressive benefits explain both why Bernie Madoff was so successful and why high-net-worth individuals continue to invest in hedge funds despite their lousy performance—they are ego-driven investments, with demand fueled by the desire to be a "member of the club."

The Desire to Be Above Average

Jonathan Burton, in his book, *Investment Titans*, invited his readers to ask themselves the following questions:[2]

- Am I better than average in getting along with people?
- Am I a better-than-average driver?

Burton noted that, if you are like the average person, you probably answered yes to both questions. In fact, studies typically find that about 90% of respondents answer positively to those types of questions. Obviously, 90% of the population cannot be better than average in getting along with others, and 90% of the population cannot be better-than-average drivers.

While by definition only half the people can be better than average at getting along with people and only half the people can be better-than-average drivers, most people believe they are above average. Overconfidence in our abilities may in some ways be a very healthy attribute. It makes us feel good about ourselves, creating a positive framework with which to get through life's experiences. Unfortunately, being overconfident of our investment skills can lead to investment mistakes. And so does what seems to be the all-too-human desire to be above average.

In *What Investors Really Want*, Meir Statman shows how the desire to be above average leads investors to trade too much, and how costly a mistake that can be:

- The trading records of thousands of investors at an American brokerage firm showed that the returns of the heaviest traders trailed those of index investors by more than 7 percentage points a year, while the lightest traders trailed by only 0.25 percentage point per year. That means the heavy traders were taking the risks of stocks while earning Treasury bill–like returns.

However, this is not solely an American phenomenon:

- The trading records of thousands of investors at a Swedish brokerage firm revealed that on average the losses of heavy traders amounted to 4% of their net worth each year.

Statman noted that beat-the-market investors trail the market and passive (e.g., index) investors because they tend to buy high and sell low. For example:

- Investors who switched mutual funds frequently trailed buy-and-hold mutual fund investors by about 1 percentage point if they switched between large-value funds, 3 percentage points if they switched between small-growth funds, and 13 percentage points if they switched between technology funds.

- Switching hedge fund investors did no better than switching mutual fund investors, underperforming buy-and-hold hedge fund investors by about 4 percentage points a year. And those that switched among the funds with the highest returns trailed by about 9 percentage points per year.

These statistics are supporting evidence for what academic research has demonstrated: there is no persistence in outperformance beyond the randomly expected among either mutual funds or hedge funds. And while the average mutual fund underperforms its risk-adjusted benchmark by about 1.5 percentage points a year (pretax), the average hedge fund has provided risk-adjusted returns that have had a hard time keeping up with Treasury bills!

Overconfidence is such a huge problem that it even causes people to delude themselves—the truth is so painful that the delusion allows them to continue to be overconfident. Statman offered up this statistic: "Members of the American Association of Individual Investors overestimated their own investment returns by an average of 3.4 percent, and they overestimated their returns relative to the average investor by 5.1 percent."

Statman also noted that overconfidence leads to unrealistic optimism, causing investors to concentrate their portfolios in a handful of stocks rather than gain the benefits of diversification (the only free lunch in investing).[3]

Framing the Problem

Many of the errors we make as human beings and investors are a result of how we frame problems. Consider the following example from Jason Zweig's Your Money & Your Brain:[4]

- Pregnant woman are more willing to agree to amniocentesis if told they face a 20% chance of having a Down's syndrome child than if told there is an 80% chance they will have a normal baby.

Statman used the analogy of playing tennis against a practice wall to show how individuals frame the "game" of investing in the wrong way, leading to costly errors. He noted that playing tennis against a practice wall, where you can watch the ball hit the wall and place yourself at just the right spot to hit it back when it bounces, is very different from the game of investing, where you are playing against professionals who are much better players and won't tell you where they are going to hit the ball. However, Statman went on to note that "it is natural for us to adopt the frame of the beat-the-market game as tennis played against the practice wall because that frame is generally correct in our daily work. We gain competence at our work as surgeons, lawyers or teachers by study and practice just as we gain competence playing against a tennis wall. In time, with practice, we get it right." He added, "We cannot be competent surgeons with little knowledge of the human body, nor can we be competent lawyers with little knowledge of the law." However, investing is entirely different; we can be competent investors with virtually no knowledge of the companies in which we invest. While surgeons or lawyers with little knowledge in their fields cannot hope to earn average salaries, investors with no knowledge of the stocks they buy can earn market returns by simply investing in index funds. Since the average fund underperforms its benchmark index fund, and the average active investor underperforms the very funds in which they invest, by simply earning market returns, the know-nothing index investor earns above-average returns.[5]

Legendary investor Peter Lynch put it this way: "[Investors] think of the so-called professionals as having all the advantages. That is total crap. They'd be better off in an index fund."[6] Warren Buffett agrees. "By periodically investing in an index fund the know-nothing investor can actually outperform most investment professionals."[7]

There is an old saying that if you don't know who the sucker is at the poker table, it's you. The analogy for investors trying to beat the market by trading is that for every buyer there must be a seller, and only one of them can be right. And since the vast majority of trading is done by institutional investors, the other side of the trade you make is likely to be a big hedge fund, mutual fund, or other institutional investor, not another individual. Once you learn to frame the problem of trying to beat the market this way, it's easy to see who the sucker is likely to be and why individuals who trade are highly likely to underperform.

Confirmation Bias

Many of the costly errors investors (like you) make are the result of "confirmation bias"—the tendency for people to favor information confirming their preconceptions or hypothesis regardless of whether the information is true while disregarding evidence that is contrary to them. As a result, people gather evidence and recall information from memory selectively, and interpret it in a biased way. The biases appear especially in emotionally significant issues and established beliefs. They also tend to interpret ambiguous evidence as supporting their existing position. Biased search, interpretation, and/or recall have been invoked to explain "attitude polarization" (when a disagreement becomes more extreme even though the different parties are exposed to the same evidence), "belief perseverance" (when beliefs persist after the evidence for them is shown to be false), the "irrational primacy effect" (a stronger weighting for data encountered early in an arbitrary series), and "illusory correlation" (in which people falsely perceive an association between two events or situations).

Confirmation biases contribute to overconfidence in personal beliefs and can maintain or strengthen beliefs in the face of contrary evidence. Hence, they can lead to disastrous decisions, especially in companies, the military, or governments.

In his book, Meir Statman provided the following example of confirmation bias: "Investors who believe that they can pick winning stocks are regularly oblivious to their losing record, recording wins as evidence confirming their stock-picking skills but neglecting to record losses as disconfirming evidence." He quoted physicist Robert Park: "People are very good at fooling themselves. They're so sure they know the answer that they don't want to confuse people with ugly-looking data." Statman cited the case of an investor he encountered who would only realize gains on his stocks but never losses. The reason he ignored the opportunity to "harvest" losses and have Uncle Sam share the pain (via a tax deduction) was that he considered realized gains as confirming evidence of his stock-picking ability and never had to confront losses because, by his accounting, unrealized losses are no losses at all.[8]

The Moral of the Tale

As humans, we make all kinds of behavioral errors. Thus, it should not be a surprise that we make them when investing. My book, *Investment Mistakes Even Smart People Make and How to Avoid Them*, covers 77 mistakes. The unfortunate truth is that lessons are easier to teach than to learn. The moral of this tale is that smart people are humble and able to admit when they have made a mistake. In fact, they rejoice in learning that they have made a mistake because going forward they will be less wrong. They also know that what differentiates them from fools is that they don't repeat their mistakes, expecting different outcomes.

The next tale discusses one of the greatest anomalies in finance: the economically irrational investor preference for dividends.

Chapter 30

The Economically Irrational Investor Preference for Dividend-Paying Stocks

It has long been known that many investors, especially those using a cash flow approach to spending, have a preference for cash dividends. From the perspective of classical financial theory, this behavior is an anomaly. Providing you with a better understanding of the relationship between dividends and price changes will enable you to properly characterize the gains from each appropriately and avoid some of the negative consequences that can result from this anomaly.

Financial Theory

In their 1961 paper, "Dividend Policy, Growth, and the Valuation of Shares," Merton Miller and Franco Modigliani famously established that dividend policy should be irrelevant to stock returns.[1]

As they explained it, at least before trading costs and taxes, investors should be indifferent to $1 in the form of a dividend (causing the stock price to drop by $1) and $1 received by selling shares. This must be true, unless you believe that $1 isn't worth $1. This theorem has not been challenged since.

Moreover, the historical evidence supports this theory as stocks with the same exposure to common factors (such as size, value, momentum, and profitability/quality) have had the same returns whether they pay a dividend or not. Warren Buffett made this point in September 2011. After announcing a share buyback program for Berkshire, some people went after Buffett for not offering a cash dividend. In his 2012 shareholder letter he explained why he believed the share buyback was in the best interests of shareholders. He also explained that any shareholder who preferred cash can effectively create dividends by selling shares.

Despite theory, evidence, and Warren Buffett's response, many investors express a preference for dividend-paying stocks. One frequently expressed explanation for the preference is that dividends offer a safe hedge against the large fluctuations in price that stocks experience. However, this ignores that the dividend is offset by the fall in the stock price—the fallacy of the free dividend.

The Math of Cash Dividends Versus Homemade Dividends

To demonstrate the point that cash dividends and homemade dividends are equivalent consider two companies that are identical in all respects but one: Company A pays a dividend and Company B does not. To simplify the math, assume that the stocks of both companies trade at their book value (while stocks do not always do that, the findings would be the same regardless). The two companies have a beginning book value of $10. They both earn $2 a share. Company A pays a $1 dividend, while Company B pays none. An investor in A owns 10,000 shares and takes the $10,000 dividend to meet spending requirements. At the end of year one the book value of Company A will be $11 (beginning value of $10 + $2 earnings − $1 dividend). The investor will have an asset allocation of $110,000 in stock ($11 × 10,000 shares) and $10,000 in cash for a total of $120,000.

Now let's look at the investor in B. Since the book value of B is now $12 ($10 beginning book value + $2 earnings), their asset allocation is $120,000 in stock and $0 in cash. They must sell shares to generate the $10,000 they need to meet their spending needs. They sell 833 shares and generate $9,996. With the sale, they now have just 9,167 shares. With those shares now at $12, their asset allocation is $110,004 in stock and $9,996 in cash, virtually identical to that of the investor in Company A.

Another way to show that the two are equivalent is to consider the investor in Company A who instead of spending the dividend reinvests it. With the stock now at $11, their $10,000 dividend allows them to purchase 909.09 shares. Thus, they now have 10,909.09 shares. With the stock at $11 their asset allocation is the same as the asset allocation of the investor in Company B: $120,000 in stock.

It is important to understand that Company B now has a somewhat higher expected growth in earnings because it has more capital to invest. The higher expected earnings offsets the lesser number of shares owned, with the assumption being that the company will earn its cost of capital.

There is one more issue that should help to understand why dividend-based strategies are not optimal.

The Explanatory Power of Dividends

For most of the past 20 years, the workhorse model in finance was what is generally referred to as the Fama-French four model—with the four factors being beta, size, value, and momentum. The model explains the vast majority (well over 90%) of the differences in returns of diversified portfolios. If dividends played an important role in determining returns, the four-factor model would not work as well as it does since dividends are not one of the factors. If, in fact, dividends added explanatory power beyond these factors, we would have a factor model that included dividends as one of the factors. But we do not. The reason is that stocks with the same "loading," or exposure, to the four factors have the same expected return regardless of their dividend policy. This has important implications because about 60% of US stocks and about 40% of international stocks do not pay dividends. Thus, any screen that includes dividends results in portfolios that are far less diversified than they could be if dividends were not included in the portfolio design. Less diversified portfolios are less efficient because they have a higher potential dispersion of returns without any compensation in the form of higher expected returns (assuming the exposures to the factors are the same).

Taxes Matter

What is particularly puzzling about the preference for dividends is that taxable investors should favor the self-dividend (by selling shares) if cash flow is required. Unlike with dividends, where taxes are paid on the distribution amount, when shares are sold, taxes are due only on the portion of the sale representing a gain. And if there are losses on the sale, the investor gains the benefit of a tax deduction. Even in tax-advantaged accounts, investors who diversify globally (which is the prudent strategy) should prefer capital gains because in tax-advantaged accounts the foreign tax credits associated with dividends have no value. And finally, if dividends were throwing off more cash than needed to meet spending requirements, the total return approach (ignoring dividends) would benefit from not only the time value of not having to pay taxes on the "excess" amount of dividends but also dividends could push investors into a higher tax bracket.

There is another negative implication of a preference for dividends.

Diversification

Because about 60% of US stocks and about 40% of international stocks do not pay dividends, any screen that includes dividends results in portfolios that are far less diversified than they could be if dividends were not included in the portfolio design. Less-diversified portfolios are less efficient because they have a higher potential dispersion of returns without any compensation in the form of higher expected returns (assuming the exposure to investment factors are the same). These negative implications are why the preference for dividends is considered an anomaly. The field of behavioral finance has attempted to provide us with explanations for the anomalous behavior.

Attempting to Explain the Preference for Dividends

Hersh Shefrin and Meir Statman, two leaders in the field of behavioral finance, attempted to explain the behavioral anomaly of a preference for cash dividends in their 1984 paper, "Explaining Investor Preference for Cash Dividends."[2] They offered the following explanations.

The first explanation is that in terms of their ability to control spending, investors may recognize that they have problems with the inability to delay gratification. To address this problem, they adapt a cash flow approach to spending—they limit their spending to only the interest and dividends from their investment portfolio. A total return approach that would use self-created dividends would not address the conflict created by the individual who wishes to deny themself a present indulgence, yet is unable to resist the temptation. While the preference for dividends might not be optimal (for tax reasons), by addressing the behavioral issue it could be said to be rational. In other words, the investor has a desire to defer spending, but knows they don't have the will, so they create a situation that limits their opportunities and, thus, reduces the temptations.

The second explanation is based on what is called *prospect theory*. Prospect theory (otherwise referred to as loss aversion) states that people value gains and losses differently. As such, they will base decisions on perceived gains rather than perceived losses. Thus, if a person were given two equal choices, one expressed in terms of possible gains and the other in possible losses, they would choose the former. Because taking dividends doesn't involve the sale of stock, it's preferred to a total return approach, which may require self-created dividends through sales. The reason is that sales might involve the realization of losses, which are too painful for people to accept (they exhibit loss aversion). What they fail to realize is that a cash dividend is the perfect substitute for the sale of an equal amount of stock whether the market is up or down, or whether the stock is sold at a gain or a loss. It makes absolutely no difference. It's just a matter of how the problem is framed. It's form over substance. Whether you take the cash dividend or sell the equivalent dollar amount of the company's stock, at the end of the day you will have the same amount invested in the stock. It's just that with the dividend you own more shares but at a lower price (by the amount of the dividend), while with the self-dividend you own fewer shares but at a higher price (because no dividend was paid).

As the authors point out, "By purchasing shares that pay good dividends, most investors persuade themselves of their prudence, based on the expected income. They feel the gain potential is a super added benefit. Should the stock fall in value from their purchase level, they console themselves that the dividend provides a return on their cost." They also point out that if the sale involves a gain, the investor frames it as "super added benefit." However, if a loss is incurred, they frame the dividend as a silver lining with which they can "console" themself. Given that losses loom much larger in investors' minds, and they wish to avoid them, investors prefer to take the cash dividend, avoiding the realization of a loss.

Shefrin and Statman offer yet a third explanation: regret avoidance. They ask you to consider two cases:

1. You take $600 received as dividends and use it to buy a television set.
2. You sell $600 worth of stock and use it to buy a television set.

After the purchase, the price of the stock increases significantly. Would you feel more regret in the first or second case? Because cash dividends and self-dividends are substitutes for each other, you should feel no more regret in the second case than in the first. However, evidence from studies on investor behavior demonstrates that for many people the sale of stock causes more regret. Thus, investors who exhibit aversion to regret have a preference for cash dividends.

Shefrin and Statman go on to explain that people suffer more regret when behaviors are taken than when behaviors are avoided. In the case of selling stock to create the homemade dividend, a decision must be made to raise the cash. When spending comes from the dividend, no action is taken, thus less regret is felt. Again, this helps explain the preference for cash dividends. They also explained how a preference for dividends might change over the investor's life cycle. As was mentioned previously, the theory of self-control is used to justify the idea of spending only from the cash flow of a portfolio, never touching the principal. Younger investors, generating income from their labor capital, might prefer a portfolio with low dividends, as a high-dividend strategy might encourage dissavings (spending from capital). However, retired investors, with no labor income, might prefer a high-dividend strategy for the same reasons, to discourage dissavings. A study of brokerage accounts found that there was in fact a strong and positive relationship between age and the preference for dividends.

While the preference for cash dividends is an anomaly that cannot be explained by classical economic theory, which is based on investors making "rational" decisions, investors who face issues of self-control (such as being subject to impulse buying) may find that while there are some costs involved, the benefits provided by avoiding the behavioral problems may make a cash dividend strategy a rational one.

The Moral of the Tale

Both theory and historical evidence demonstrate that dividends are just another source of profit, along with capital gains, and that dividends mechanically reduce the price of stock. Yet, many investors treat the two sources of profit very differently, with negative consequences both in terms of lower returns and greater risk. Shefrin and Statman provided us with explanations demonstrating that, at least for some investors who are otherwise unable to control their spending, the negative consequences may be outweighed by the benefits in terms of controlling behavior that would have had even greater negative consequences.

The next tale explains the difference between risk and uncertainty.

Chapter 31

The Uncertainty of Investing

Even the most brilliant of mathematical geniuses will never be able to tell us what the future holds. In the end, what matters is the quality of our decisions in the face of uncertainty.
—*Peter Bernstein, "Wimps and Consequences,"*
Journal of Portfolio Management *(Fall 1999)*

One of the most important concepts to grasp is that investing is about dealing with both risk and uncertainty. University of Chicago professor Frank Knight wrote the classic book *Risk, Uncertainty, and Profit*.[1] An article from the *Library of Economics and Liberty* described Knight's definitions of risk and uncertainty as follows: Risk is present when future events occur with measurable probability. Uncertainty is present when the likelihood of future events is indefinite or incalculable.[2]

In some cases, we know the odds of an event occurring with certainty. The classic example is that we can calculate the odds of rolling any particular number with a pair of dice. Because of demographic data, we can make a good *estimate* of the odds that a 65-year-old couple will have at least one spouse live beyond

90. However, we cannot know the odds precisely because there may be future advances in medical science that could extend life expectancy. Conversely, there may arise new diseases that shorten life expectancy. Other examples of uncertainty: the odds of an oil embargo (1973) or the odds of an event such as the attacks of September 11, 2001. That concept is uncertainty.

It is critical to understand the important difference between these two concepts, risk and uncertainty. Consider the following example. An insurance company might be willing to take on a certain amount of hurricane risk in Dade and Broward Counties in Florida. They would price this *risk* based on perhaps 100 years of data, the likelihood of hurricanes occurring, and the damage they did. But only a foolish insurer would place such a large bet that if more or worse hurricanes occurred than had previously been experienced the company would go bankrupt. That would be ignoring the fact that there is actually *uncertainty* about the odds of hurricanes occurring in the future—the future might not look like the past.

Just as there are foolish insurance companies, there are foolish investors. The mistake many investors make is to view equities as closer to risk where the odds can be calculated precisely. This tendency appears with great regularity when economic conditions are good. Their "ability" to estimate the odds gives investors a false sense of confidence, leading them to decide on an equity allocation that exceeds their ability, willingness, and need to take risk.

Note that during crises the perception about equity investing shifts from one of risk to one of uncertainty. We often hear commentators use phrases like "there is a lack of clarity, or visibility." Since investors prefer risky bets (where they can calculate the odds) to uncertain bets (where the odds cannot be calculated), when the markets begin to appear to investors to become *uncertain*, the risk premium demanded rises and that is what causes severe bear markets.

The historical evidence is very clear that dramatic falls in prices lead to panicked selling as investors eventually reach their get-me-out point: the stomach screams "Don't just sit there. Do something:

get me out." Investors have demonstrated the unfortunate tendency to sell well *after* market declines have already occurred and buy well *after* rallies have long begun. The result is that they dramatically underperform the very mutual funds in which they invest.

The Moral of the Tale

One of the keys to being a successful investor is understanding that equity investing is always about uncertainty. Another is to understand the importance of choosing an equity allocation that doesn't exceed your risk tolerance. Avoiding that mistake provides investors the greatest chance of also avoiding the mistake of letting their stomachs, and not their heads, make investment decisions. Stomachs rarely make good decisions.

We now move to Part IV. It begins with a tale that takes an old story told about economists and the efficient market theory and updates it with a more accurate one.

Part Four

PLAYING THE WINNER'S GAME IN LIFE AND INVESTING

Chapter 32

The 20-Dollar Bill

The most common of all follies is to believe passionately in the palpably not true.

—*H. L. Mencken*

There is an old story about a financial economist who was a passionate defender of the efficient markets hypothesis (EMH). He was walking down the street with a friend. The friend stops and says, "Look, there is a $20 bill on the ground." The economist turns and says, "Can't be. If there were a $20 bill on the ground, somebody would have already picked it up." This joke is told by those who believe that the markets are inefficient and that investors can thus outperform the market by exploiting mispricings—finding an undervalued stock instead of a $20 bill. It is actually a misleading analogy to the EMH. The following version is a much better one.

A financial economist, and passionate defender of the EMH, was walking down the street with a friend. The friend stops and says, "Look, there is a $20 bill on the ground." The economist turns and says, "This must be our lucky day! Better pick that up quick because the market is so efficient it won't be there for long. Finding a $20 bill lying around happens so infrequently that it would be foolish to spend our time searching for more of them. Certainly, after assigning a value to the time spent in the effort, an 'investment' in trying to find money lying on the street just waiting to be picked up would be a poor one. I am certainly not aware of anyone who has achieved their wealth by 'mining' beaches with metal detectors." When he had finished, they both looked down and the $20 bill was gone!

There is also what might be called "the Hollywood version" of this story. A financial economist, and passionate defender of the EMH, was walking down the street with a friend. The friend stops and says, "Look, there is a $20 bill on the ground." The economist turns and says, "Can't be. If there were a $20 bill on the ground, somebody would have already picked it up." The friend bends down and picks up the $20 bill and dashes off. He then decides that this is an easy way to make a living. He abandons his job and begins to search the world for $20 bills lying on the ground waiting to be picked up. A year later the economist is walking down the same street and sees his long-lost friend lying on the sidewalk wearing torn and filthy clothing. Appalled to see the disheveled state into which his friend had sunk, he rushes over to find out what had happened. The friend tells that him that he never again found another $20 bill lying on the ground.

Those that tell the first version of the story fail to understand that an efficient market doesn't mean there cannot be a $20 bill lying around. Instead, it means that it is so unlikely you will find one that it does not pay to go looking for them—the costs of the effort will likely exceed the benefits. In addition, if it became known that there were lots of $20 bills to be found in a certain area, everyone would be there competing to find them. That reduces the likelihood of achieving an appropriate "return on investment."

The analogy to the EMH is that it is not impossible to uncover an anomaly (that $20 bill lying on the ground) that can be exploited (being able to buy a stock that is somehow undervalued by the market, or short one that is overvalued). Instead, one of the fundamental tenets of the EMH is that in a competitive financial environment, successful trading strategies self-destruct because they are self-limiting—when they are discovered, they are eliminated by the very act of exploiting the strategy. Andrew Lo's adaptive markets hypothesis acknowledges that while the EMH may not necessarily hold in the short run, it does predict that inefficiencies will self-correct over time as arbitrageurs exploit them post-publication.[1] Thus, financial markets trend toward efficiency in the long run.

In their 1996 paper "The Efficient Market Theory Thrives on Criticism," economics professors Dwight Lee and James Verbrugge of the University of Georgia explained the power of the efficient markets theory in the following manner:

> The efficient market theory is practically alone among theories in that it becomes more powerful when people discover serious inconsistencies between it and the real world. If a clear efficient market anomaly is discovered, the behavior (or lack of behavior) that gives rise to it will tend to be eliminated by competition among investors for higher returns. [For example:] If stock prices are found to follow predictable seasonal patterns unrelated to financially relevant considerations, this knowledge will elicit responses that have the effect of eliminating the very patterns they were designed to exploit. The implication here is rather striking. The more empirical flaws that are discovered in the efficient market theory, the more robust the theory becomes. [In effect] those who do the most to ensure that the efficient market theory remains fundamental to our understanding of financial economics are not its intellectual defenders, but those mounting the most serious empirical assault against it.[2]

The "January Effect"

The following example demonstrates how the efficiency of markets rapidly eliminates opportunities for abnormal profits. Imagine that an investor discovered that small-cap stocks historically outperformed the market in January (there is a $20 bill lying on the ground waiting to be picked up). To take advantage of this anomaly, that investor would have to buy small-cap stocks at the end of December, prior to the period of outperformance. After achieving some success with this strategy, other investors would take note— with the large dollars at stake, Wall Street is quick to copy successful strategies. An academic paper might even be published. Since the effect is now known by more than just the original discoverer of the anomaly, in order to generate abnormal profits, one would have to buy before others did. Now prices start to rise in November. But the next group of investors, recognizing this was going to happen, would have to buy even earlier.

As you can see, the very act of exploiting an anomaly has the effect of making it disappear, making the market more efficient. It is worth noting that if there ever was a January effect in small-cap stocks that could be exploited after the costs of the effort, it no longer exists.

The Moral of the Tale

While equity markets may not be perfectly efficient (it is possible to find a $20 bill waiting to be picked up), the winning investment strategy is to behave as if they were. Consider carefully these words from Richard Roll, financial economist and principal of the portfolio management firm Roll and Ross Asset Management: "I have personally tried to invest money, my client's and my own, in every single anomaly and predictive result that academics have dreamed up. And I have yet to make a nickel on any of these supposed market inefficiencies. An inefficiency ought to be an exploitable opportunity. If there's nothing investors can exploit in a systematic way, time in and time out, then it's very hard to say that information is not being properly incorporated into stock prices. Real money investment strategies don't produce the results that academic papers say they should."[3]

Investors who accept the EMH as fundamental to their investment strategy don't have to spend their time searching for the very few $20 bills lying on the ground. Instead, they earn market returns based on the amount of risk they are willing to accept (based on their exposure to common factors) and incur fewer expenses.

The next tale demonstrates that investors' worst enemy is staring at them in the mirror.

Chapter 33

An Investor's Worst Enemy

The investor's chief problem—and even his worst enemy—is likely to be himself.

—Benjamin Graham

Like many boys growing up in New York City, I spent much of my childhood and teenage years with a basketball glued to my hand. I was a fairly good athlete and even managed to make my college basketball team as a freshman. Now, that is not saying much. Baruch College was a Division III school, and I mostly sat at the end of the bench. By the end of the season, I probably had accumulated more splinters than minutes played. I also played lots of baseball, softball, and football. Unfortunately, since there were not many tennis courts in the Bronx, I did not get to play tennis often.

At the age of 25, I moved to San Francisco. Everyone there played tennis, so I became a tennis player. After a relatively short time, because of my athletic skills, I became what you might call a decent weekend player (a ranking of 3.5). However, I was often frustrated by the fact that players consistently beat me even though I was the better athlete. It was particularly frustrating when I lost to a player who was decades older. Eventually, after about 20 years, I finally figured out that while I was a better athlete, they were better tennis players—and there is a big distinction between the two.

With this "revelation," I finally decided to attend a tennis clinic. At the end of the week, each of the participants got to play for an hour with the tennis pro. During my session, I learned something that dramatically improved my tennis game. It also provided me with an insight about games in general.

Like most weekend players, my weaker shot was the backhand. During a rally, the tennis pro hit a shot deep into my backhand corner. He then came to the net, putting even more pressure on me. Amazingly, I hit a great passing shot that landed deep in the court and just inside the line. After making that shot, the pro called me to the net. I was sure he was going to compliment me. Instead, what he said was, "That shot will be your worst enemy." He explained that while it was an exceptional shot, it was not a high-percentage one for a player with my level of skill. Remembering how good that shot felt, I would try to repeat it. Unfortunately, I would be unsuccessful the vast majority of the time. He pointed out that while he could make that shot perhaps 90% of the time, I was likely to make it less than 10% of the time. The pro then asked me if I'd rather make great shots or win matches. Up until that point, I thought that one led to the other. The pro taught me otherwise.

He explained that in the game played by weekend warriors like me, most points are not won by hitting shots that can't be returned by the opponent. Instead, most points are lost when balls are hit into the net, long, or outside the lines in a failed attempt to hit those exceptional winning shots. That is why this type of strategy produces what is called a "loser's game." The pro was also polite enough to say that it's not the people who play the game who are losers—instead, it's the strategy they're following.

To improve my results, the pro told me that to find the winning strategy, I had to understand the type of game I was playing. Since, unlike professional tennis players, I'm not capable of consistently hitting winning shots, I was playing a loser's game. Instead of trying to hit winners (and likely hitting the ball long, wide, or into the net), he said I should just try to safely hit the ball back, with a bit of pace, and use the middle of the court—and let the opponent play the loser's game. Recognizing the brilliance of his advice, I immediately put it to work, with astonishingly good results. I was now regularly beating players who had previously beaten me.

What does tennis have to do with investing? Simply this: consistently successful investing requires a successful strategy. The majority of individual investors (and most professionals) try to beat the market. They do so by attempting to uncover individual securities they believe the rest of the market has somehow mispriced (the price is too high or too low). They also try to time their investment decisions so that they are buying when the market is "undervalued" and selling when it is "overvalued." Such a strategy is known as "active portfolio management." With the same infrequency of my great tennis shots, these active portfolio managers will occasionally make a killing. However, over the long run, the likelihood is they'll lose (underperform) more often than they'll win (outperform). Thus, the evidence demonstrates that while the winning strategy in tennis is different for amateurs than professionals, the winning strategy in investing is the same for all investors, whether they are individuals or institutions.

In tennis, the winning strategy is to not play the loser's game. In investing, the winning strategy is also to not play the loser's game, but to accept market returns by investing in passively managed funds.

There is an overwhelming body of evidence, such as that provided by the annual SPIVA Scorecards that demonstrates that the vast majority of professional investors succeed at beating passive benchmarks about as often as I was able to hit a shot the teaching pro was unable to return (it was the only point I won that day). The reason they fail is that they are trying to hit that great shot (finding mispriced securities) instead of just safely getting the ball back (accepting market returns). If the professionals fail with such regularity, what are the odds you will succeed?

In the face of such overwhelming evidence, the puzzling question is why people keep trying to play a game they are likely to lose. From my perspective, there are four explanations: (1) because our education system has failed investors (and Wall Street and most of the financial media want to conceal the evidence), they are unaware of the evidence; (2) while the evidence suggests that playing the game of active management is the triumph of hope over wisdom and experience, hope does spring eternal—after all, a small minority do succeed; (3) active management is exciting, while passive management is boring; and (4) investors are overconfident—a normal human condition, not limited to investing. While each investor might admit that it's hard to beat the market, each believes they will be one of the few who succeed.

University of Chicago professor Richard Thaler and Yale professor Robert Shiller noted that "individual investors and money managers persist in their beliefs that they are endowed with more and better information than others, and that they can profit by picking stocks."[1] Ninety percent think they're above average. This insight helps explain why individual investors believe they can pick stocks that will outperform the market, time the market, and identify the few active managers who will beat their respective benchmarks. Gus Sauter, who managed a wide array of index funds for Vanguard and one actively managed fund, provided this insight: "Like everybody else in this industry I have an ego large enough to believe I'm going to be one of the select few that will outperform."[2]

Perhaps the most amusing example of overconfidence is the Mensa investment club (though it could not have been amusing to them, as their results make the Beardstown Ladies investment club look like Warren Buffett). Mensa is a club that limits its membership to those individuals whose IQs are in the top 2%. If anyone has a right to be confident in their intellectual capacity to achieve superior investment results, it should be the members of Mensa.

The June 2001 issue of *Smart Money* reported that over the prior 15 years, the Mensa investment club returned just 2.5%, underperforming the S&P 500 Index by almost 13% per annum.[3] Warren Smith, an investor for 35 years, reported that his original investment of $5,300 had turned into $9,300. A similar investment in the S&P 500 Index would have produced almost $300,000. One investor described their strategy as "buy low, sell lower." The Mensa members were overconfident that their superior intellectual skills would translate into superior investment returns. Overconfidence can be very expensive.

The example of the Mensa investment club proves the wisdom of financial historian and author Peter Bernstein's insight: "The essence of investment theory is that being smart is not a *sufficient* [emphasis mine] condition for being rich."[4]

Investors would be wise to heed *Wall Street Journal* columnist Jonathan Clements, who made the following observation: "Beat the market? The idea is ludicrous. Since very few investors manage to beat the market, but in an astonishing triumph of hope over experience millions of investors keep trying."[5] Overconfidence provides the explanation for this behavior. Investors may even recognize the difficulty of the task; yet, they still believe they can succeed with a high degree of probability. As author and personal finance journalist James Smalhout put it, "Psychologists have long documented the tendency of *Homo sapiens* to overrate his own abilities and prospects for success. This is particularly true of the subspecies that invests in stocks and, accordingly, tends to overtrade."[6]

Gary Belsky and Thomas Gilovich, authors of the wonderful book, *Why Smart People Make Big Money Mistakes*, reached the following conclusion:

Any individual who is not professionally occupied in the financial services industry (and even most of those who are) and who in any way attempts to actively manage an investment portfolio is probably suffering from overconfidence. That is, anyone who has confidence enough in his or her abilities and knowledge to invest in a particular stock or bond (or actively managed mutual fund or real estate investment trust or limited partnership) is most likely fooling himself. In fact, most such people—probably you—have no business at all trying to pick investments, except perhaps as sport. Such people—again, probably you—should simply divide their money among several index mutual funds and turn off CNBC.[7]

Having been presented with several tales that provide the logic and evidence on why passive investing is the winner's game, you will allow wisdom and experience to triumph over hope and overconfidence. If, however, you are still undecided, consider the following: it is estimated that the revenues of the institutions that make their living from the capital market exceed $150 billion per year. This is the portion of the returns that the markets provide that is removed (from your pockets) by financial intermediaries. That amount might approach as much as 2% per annum of the total stock and bond markets![8] Consider these words of wisdom from author Ron Ross: "The people on Wall Street simply can't imagine how they would make a living if they weren't trying to beat the market. But that's their problem, not yours. It's not your responsibility to provide livelihoods for stock analysts. What's rational on Wall Street isn't usually aligned with the best interests of you as an investor."[9]

The Moral of the Tale

If you decide to play the loser's game of active investing, the only people you will likely enrich are your financial advisor, your broker-dealer, the manager of the actively managed mutual fund or portfolio in which you are investing, and the publisher of the newsletter, magazine, or ratings service to which you subscribe.

The next tale teaches the lesson that bear markets should be viewed as necessary evils.

Chapter 34

Bear Markets

A Necessary Evil

*The smallness of the army renders the natural strength of the community an overmatch for it; and the citizens, not habituated to look up to the military power for protection, or to submit to its oppressions, neither love nor fear the soldiery; they view them with a spirit of jealous acquiescence in a **necessary evil** [author emphasis], and stand ready to resist a power which they suppose may be exerted to the prejudice of their rights.*
                       —*Alexander Hamilton*, The Federalist Papers

A "necessary evil" can be defined as an unpleasant necessity, something that is unpleasant or undesirable but is needed to achieve a result. An example of a necessary evil is taxes. Investors should also view bear markets as a necessary evil. Let's explore why.

Perhaps the most basic principle of modern financial theory is that risk and *expected* return are related. We know that stocks are riskier than one-month Treasury bills (which is considered the benchmark riskless instrument). Since they are riskier, the only

logical explanation for investing in stocks is that they must provide a higher *expected* return. However, if stocks always provided
higher returns than one-month Treasury bills (the expected always
occurred), investing in stocks would not entail any risk—and there
would be no risk premium. In fact, in 26 of the 97 years from
1926 through 2022, or 27% of the time, the S&P 500 Index produced negative returns. In addition, there have been four periods
when the S&P 500 Index produced much greater losses than the
34% loss experienced during the COVID-19 crisis (February 19,
2020–March 23, 2020):

- January 1929–December 1932, loss of 64%
- January 1973–September 1974, loss of 43%
- April 2000–September 2002, loss of 44%
- November 2007–February 2009, loss of 51%

The very fact that investors have experienced such large losses
leads them to price stocks with a large risk premium. From 1926
through 2022, the S&P has provided an annual (compound) risk
premium over one-month Treasury bills of 8.2% and an annualized
premium of 6.9%. If the losses that investors experienced had been
smaller, the risk premium would also have been smaller. And the
smaller the losses experienced, the smaller the premium would have
been. In other words, the less risk investors perceive, the higher the
price they are willing to pay for stocks. And the higher the price-
to-earnings ratio of the market, the lower the future returns.

Demonstrating that significant declines are not rare events is
that from 1950 through 2022 there were eight calendar months
when the S&P 500 Index lost at least 10%. The worst loss, −21.5%,
was in October 1987, and the average loss was −13.6%. Over the
next 3, 6, and 12 months, the S&P 500 Index provided total returns
of 2.8%, 5.5%, and 14.7%, respectively. Investors who abandoned
their plans due to panicked selling not only missed out on those
great returns, but they were then faced with the extremely difficult decision of determining when it was safe to get back in. That's

one of the problems with market timing—you have to be right twice, not once.

The bottom line is that bear markets are necessary to the creation of the large equity risk premium we have experienced. Thus, if investors want stocks to provide high expected returns, bear markets (while painful to endure) should be considered a necessary evil. We can extend this logic to the risks of investing in small value stocks.

Small Value Stocks

We know that small value companies are riskier than the stocks in the S&P 500 Index. Therefore, the market prices them to provide higher returns. From 1927 through 2022, small value stocks (Fama-French research index) returned 14.3% per year, 4.2 percentage points greater than the return of the S&P 500 Index. However, small value stocks have not always outperformed the S&P 500 Index. If they always outperformed, there would be no risk of investing in them relative to investing in the S&P 500 Index—and there would be no risk premium. For example:

- 1969–1974: Small value stocks underperformed the S&P 500 Index by a total of 23.7 percentage points (−42.4% versus −18.7%).
- 1986–1990: Small value stocks underperformed the S&P 500 Index by a total of 46.6 percentage points (52.5% versus 5.9%).
- 1994–1998: Small value stocks underperformed the S&P 500 Index by a total of 65.4 percentage points (193.9% versus 128.5%).
- 2017–2020: Small value stocks underperformed the S&P 500 Index by a total of 68.3 percentage points (81.4% versus 13.1%).

Further evidence of the risk of investing in small value stocks is that while the small value stocks outperformed the S&P 500 by 4.2 percentage points a year, they experienced much greater volatility—their annualized standard deviation was 50% greater than that of the S&P 500 Index (28.1% versus 18.7%).

Risk Premiums and Investment Discipline

The bottom line is that the outperformance of both stocks relative to Treasury bills, and small value stocks relative to the stocks in the S&P 500 Index, is not what economists call a "free lunch"—there are risks involved. And it is a virtual certainty that the risks will show up from time to time. As much as we would like to think there is someone out there who can protect us from bear markets, there is only one being who knows when, how long, and how severe the periods of underperformance will be—and none of us gets to speak to him (or her).

It is during the periods of underperformance that investor discipline is tested. Unfortunately, the evidence suggests that most investors significantly underperform both the stock market and the very mutual funds in which they invest. The reason for the underperformance is that investors act like generals fighting the last war. Subject to recency bias (the tendency to overweight recent events/trends and ignore long-term evidence), they observe yesterday's winners and jump on the bandwagon—buying high—and they observe yesterday's losers and abandon ship—selling low. It is almost as if investors believe they can buy yesterday's returns, when they can only buy tomorrow's.

There are several explanations for this outcome. The first is that investors allow their emotions to affect their investment decisions. In bull markets, greed and envy take over, and risk is overlooked. In bear markets, fear and panic take over, and even well-thought-out plans can end up in the trash heap of emotions.

The second explanation is that investors are overconfident of their ability to deal with risk when it inevitably shows up. They believe they can stomach losses of 20%, 30%, 40%, or even 50% and stay the course, adhering to their plan. However, the evidence demonstrates that investors are as overconfident of their investment abilities as they are of their driving skills (remember: studies have found that the vast majority of people believe they are better than average drivers).

The third explanation is that investors often treat the likely (stocks will outperform Treasury bills) as certain and the unlikely (a severe bear market) as impossible. The result is that they take more risk than is appropriate. When the risks inevitably show up, they are "forced" to sell.

The Keys to Successful Investing

There is an old adage that "those who fail to plan, plan to fail." Therefore, the first key to successful investing is to have a well-thought-out plan that includes an understanding of the nature of the risks of investing. That means accepting that bear markets are inevitable, and they must be built into the plan. It also means having the discipline to stay the course when it is most difficult to do so (partly because the media will be filled with stories of economic doom and gloom). What is particularly difficult is that staying the course does not just mean buy and hold. Adhering to a plan requires that investors rebalance the portfolio, maintaining their desired asset allocation. That means that investors must buy stocks during bear markets and sell them in bull markets—which brings us to the second key to success.

While academic research has found that almost all the risk and return of a portfolio is determined by the portfolio's asset allocation, the actual returns earned by investors are determined more by the ability to adhere to whatever the allocation they chose than by the allocation itself. Thus, the second key to successful investing is to be sure you do not take more risk than you have ability (determined by your investment horizon and stability of income), willingness (risk tolerance), and need (the rate of return needed to achieve your objectives) to take. Those who avoid excessive risk taking are the ones most likely to stay the course and avoid the buy-high/sell-low pattern that bedevils most investors.

The third key to success is to understand that trying to time the market is a loser's game. Listen carefully to legendary investor Warren Buffett's statements regarding efforts to time the market:

- "Inactivity strikes us as intelligent behavior."[1]
- "The only value of stock forecasters is to make fortune-tellers look good."[2]
- "We continue to make more money when snoring than when active."[3]
- "Our stay-put behavior reflects our view that the stock market serves as a relocation center at which money is moved from the active to the patient."[4]

Buffett also observed: "Long ago, Sir Isaac Newton gave us three laws of motion, which were the work of genius. But Sir Isaac's talents didn't extend to investing: He lost a bundle in the South Sea Bubble, explaining later, 'I can calculate the movement of the stars, but not the madness of men.' If he had not been traumatized by this loss, Sir Isaac might well have gone on to discover the Fourth Law of Motion: For investors as a whole, returns decrease as motion increases."[5]

Perhaps Buffett's views on market-timing efforts are best summed up by the following:

Over the 35 years, American business has delivered terrific results. It should therefore have been easy for investors to earn juicy returns: All they had to do was piggyback Corporate America in a diversified, low-expense way. An index fund that they never touched would have done the job. Instead, many investors have had experiences ranging from mediocre to disastrous. There have been three primary causes: first, high costs, usually because investors traded excessively or spent far too much on investment management; second, portfolio decisions based on tips and fads rather than on thoughtful, quantified evaluation of businesses; and third, a start-and-stop approach to the market marked by untimely entries (after an advance has been long underway) and exits (after periods of stagnation or decline). Investors should remember that excitement and expenses are their enemies. And if they insist on trying to time their participation in equities, they should try to be fearful when others are greedy and greedy only when others are fearful.[6]

As Buffett stated, investing is simple but not easy. The simple part is that the winning strategy is to imitate the lowly postage stamp that adheres to its letter until it reaches its destination. Investors should stick to their asset allocation until they reach their financial goals. The reason it is not easy is that it is difficult for most individuals to control their emotions—greed and envy in bull markets, and fear and panic in bear markets. In fact, bear markets are the mechanisms that serve to transfer assets from those with weak stomachs and without investment plans to those with well-thought-out plans—with the anticipation of bear markets built into them—and the discipline to adhere to those plans.

The Moral of the Tale

Bear markets are a necessary evil in that their existence is the very reason the stock market has provided the large risk premium and the high returns investors had the opportunity to earn. But there is another important point investors need to understand about bear markets. Investors in the accumulation phase of their careers should view bear markets not just as a necessary evil but also as a good thing. The reason is that bear markets provide those investors (at least those who have the discipline to adhere to their plan) with the opportunity to buy stocks at lower prices, increasing expected returns. It is only those in the withdrawal phase (such as retirees) who should fear bear markets because withdrawals make it more difficult to maintain the portfolio's value over the long term. Thus, those investors have less ability to take risk, which should be built into their plan.

The bottom line for investors is this: if you don't have a plan, immediately develop one. Make sure it anticipates bear markets and outlines what actions you will take when they occur (doing so when you are not under the stress that bear markets create). Put the plan in writing in the form of an investment policy statement and an asset allocation table and sign it. That will increase the odds of your adhering to it when you are tested by the emotions caused by both bull and bear markets. And then stay the course, altering your plan only if your assumptions about your ability, willingness, or need to take risk have changed.

The next tale examines the evidence on the recommendations of CNBC investment guru Jim Cramer, teaching a lesson about the lack of worth of the investment advice from so-called market experts.

Chapter 35

Mad Money

If you're having fun investing, then there's a good chance that you're not properly diversified, you're trading too much, and you're taking too much risk.

—*Gregory Baer and Gary Gensler,*
The Great Mutual Fund Trap

Millions of people each year visit Las Vegas. With the exception of a small percentage of professional gamblers, the casinos are filled with tourists eager to test their luck. Knowing that the odds favor the house, while they hope to win, they expect to lose. The expected loss from gambling is, in effect, the price of entertainment. Of course, that entertainment not only includes what happens at the gaming tables and the roulette wheels but also the great singers, comedians, magicians, and spectacular shows from Cirque du Soleil. There are also many fantastic restaurants.

While perfectly willing to spend their hard-earned dollars on entertainment, most visitors know that it would not be prudent to invest their savings at the gambling tables—they are able to separate entertainment from investing. Once they return home, however, this is not always the case.

Jim Cramer, ex–hedge fund manager has become one of the most recognizable faces in the investment world. He dispenses rapid-fire investment advice on the show "Mad Money." Since it premiered in March 2005, it has been one of CNBC's most watched shows. In September 2005, *Variety* reported that "the free-wheeling investor show hosted by Jim Cramer, increased the net's 6 p.m. [performance] by 141% in the third quarter and became the financial net's highest-rated show in primetime."[1] But, has his advice been as successful for the investors who follow it?

Unlike many other personalities in financial entertainment Cramer actually manages a portfolio that invests in many of the stock recommendations he makes on TV. Established in August 2001 with approximately $3 million, the Action Alerts PLUS (AAP) portfolio has been the centerpiece of Cramer's media company, TheStreet, which sells his financial advice, giving subscribers who number in the millions access to each trade the portfolio makes ahead of time.

In March 2005, upon the launch of Cramer's "Mad Money" show, the AAP portfolio was converted into a charitable trust, adopting the policy that any dividend or other cash distributions would be donated to charity. Cramer lists himself as a co-manager of the AAP portfolio. Jonathan Hartley and Matthew Olson, authors of the 2018 study "Jim Cramer's *Mad Money* Charitable Trust Performance and Factor Attribution," examined the AAP portfolio's historical performance.[2] Their study covered the period from August 1, 2001, the AAP portfolio's inception, through December 31, 2017. They found that the AAP portfolio underperformed the S&P 500 Index's total return both since inception and since the debut of "Mad Money." From inception, the AAP portfolio provided a total return of 97% (4.1% on annualized basis), underperforming the S&P 500 Index's return of 204% (6.8% on annualized basis). Over the full period, the AAP portfolio produced a Sharpe ratio (a measure of risk-adjusted returns) of 0.16, half the size of the S&P 500 Index's Sharpe ratio of 0.32.

The preceding findings on Cramer's performance are consistent with those from prior studies.

Other Evidence

In their study "How Mad Is *Mad Money*?," which appeared in the Summer 2012 issue of *The Journal of Investing*, Paul Bolster, Emery Trahan, and Anand Venkateswaran examined Cramer's buy and sell recommendations for the period from July 28, 2005, through December 31, 2008.[3] They also constructed a portfolio of his recommendations and compared it to a market index.

Their study covered 1,592 clear buy and 700 clear sell recommendations. They then assembled an equal-weighted portfolio. To try to capture prices available to the typical retail investor, they based their trades on closing prices on the following day. Stocks remained in the portfolio until there was a sell recommendation. They then adjusted the absolute returns for the portfolio's exposure to the market beta, size, value, and momentum factors. Following is a summary of the authors' findings:

- Investors are paying attention, as the stocks returned an abnormal and statistically significant 1.88% on the day following Cramer's buy recommendation.
- The returns for recommended stocks were positive and significant for both the day of the show (0.38%) and the 30 days prior to the show (3.9%).
- However, the returns were negative and significant, at −0.33% and −2.1%, for days 2 through 5 and days 2 through 30 following the recommendation. After 30 days, the results are insignificant.

The bottom line is that, over this period, Cramer recommended stocks with momentum, both positive and negative. His recommendations affect price, with the impact reversing quickly, consistent with pricing pressure caused by viewers jumping on his buy recommendations.

Cramer's sell recommendations also affect prices, though the impact doesn't quickly reverse.

- The abnormal returns were negative (−0.73%) and statistically significant on the day when his sell recommendations hit the market. They were also negative (−3.24%) and statistically significant in the 30 days prior. Again, this suggests Cramer picked stocks based on momentum.
- Unlike with his buy recommendations, returns remain negative and statistically significant for days 1 through 5 (−1.22%) and days 1 through 30 (−3.11%) following the sell recommendation.

Over the full period, a portfolio of Cramer's picks lost 7.3%, slightly better than the S&P 500 Index's loss of 8.7%. In other words, there is no evidence of any stock-picking skill—his picks are neither good nor bad. In the end, it's just entertainment.

The results of this study basically replicated the findings of a May 2005 study, "Is the Market Mad? Evidence from *Mad Money*," by Joseph Engelberg, Caroline Sasseville, and Jared Williams.[4] They found that after Cramer recommended a stock, its volume typically soared. For example, they found that on the smallest quartile of stocks, volume was almost nine times more than on the day after his recommendation (and stayed above normal for about three days, with the effect decreasing with time). The increased demand led to an overnight rise in prices of about 5% for the smallest stocks (where they can have the greatest impact) and about 2% for the entire sample of the 246 unconditional recommendations examined between July 28, 2005, and October 14, 2005.

Unfortunately, those gains turned out to be temporary. For example, price gains for stocks in the smallest quartile completely reversed within 12 trading days. The original gains turned into nothing more than market impact costs. In other words, after costs, Cramer's picks typically had negative value to naive investors who reacted to the buy recommendations.

However, because the market is so efficient, a different category of investors may have benefited from Cramer's picks. For example, while the demand for Cramer's stock picks increased, there was also an increase in the volume of short selling (bets that the stocks will fall). In the opening minutes of the day following one of his recommendations, short sales increased to almost seven times their normal levels, and they remained elevated for three days. Who are these short sellers? Likely candidates are hedge funds, who are exploiting the naivete of individual investors. Through their actions, short sellers are helping to keep the market efficient.

The authors also found that the stocks that Cramer recommended had excess returns for the three days prior to his actual recommendation. They provided two explanations for this behavior. Their first explanation was that Cramer was recommending stocks with short-term momentum (of which there is some evidence, although after trading costs the positive momentum would be difficult, if not impossible, to exploit). Their second explanation was that information pertaining to some of the stocks he recommended was released before the television show aired each day (during market hours), which the authors attributed to either Cramer's daily radio show or web columns.

There is one other study, "Shorting Cramer," to review. In a 2007 column, *Barron's* reported that they studied 1,300 recommendations and found, over the prior two years, viewers holding Cramer's stock picks would have been up 12% while the Dow Jones Industrial Average rose 2% and the S&P 500 Index 16%.[5]

The research makes it clear that being highly intelligent (and entertaining, in Cramer's case) is not a sufficient condition to outperform the market. The reason is simple. There are many other highly intelligent money managers whose price discovery actions work to keep the market highly efficient (meaning market prices are the best estimate we have of the right price). That makes it unlikely any active money manager will outperform on a risk-adjusted basis.

Cramer himself provides a fitting conclusion. In a 2007 issue of *New York* magazine, Cramer stated: "God knows why, but there seems to be a market for this kind of idiocy."[6]

Before concluding, there is one more study we need to review. Thanks to research by CXO Advisory Group, we also have insight into Cramer's market-timing skills.[7] CXO set out to determine if stock market experts, whether self-proclaimed or endorsed by others (such as in the financial media), reliably provide stock market–timing guidance.

To find the answer, from 2005 through 2012, they collected and investigated 6,584 forecasts for the US stock market offered publicly by 68 experts (including Cramer), employing technical, fundamental, and sentiment indicators. Their collection included forecasts, all of which were publicly available on the internet, that went back as far as the end of 1998. They selected experts, both bulls and bears, based on web searches for public archives with enough forecasts spanning enough market conditions to gauge accuracy.

The researchers' methodology was to compare forecasts for the US stock market to the return of the S&P 500 Index over the future interval(s) most relevant to the forecast horizon. They excluded forecasts that were too vague and forecasts that included conditions requiring consideration of data other than stock market returns. They matched the frequency of a guru's commentaries (such as weekly or monthly) to the forecast horizon, unless the forecast specifies some other timing. Importantly, they took into account the long-run empirical behavior of the S&P 500 Index. For example, if a guru said investors should be bullish on US stocks over the current year, and the S&P 500 Index went up by just a few percentage points, they judged the call incorrect because the long-term average annual return has been much higher. Finally, they graded complex forecasts with elements proving both correct and incorrect as both right and wrong (not half right and half wrong).

The following is a summary of CXO's findings:

• Across all forecasts, accuracy was worse than the proverbial flip of a coin—just under 47%.

- The average guru, and Cramer specifically, also had a forecasting accuracy rate of about 47%. Cramer finished 39th out of the 68 experts.
- The distribution of forecasting accuracy by the gurus looks very much like a bell curve—what you would expect from random outcomes. That makes it difficult to tell if there is any skill present.

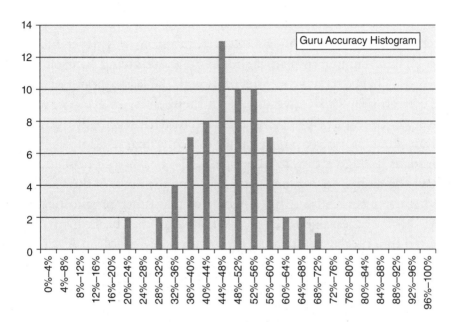

Of course, there were a few with fairly good records, which is what you would randomly expect. But only 5 of the 68 gurus posted scores above 60% (the highest score was 68%) while 12 had scores below 40% (the lowest score was 22%). Remember as well that strategies based on forecasts have no costs, but implementing them does.

The research shows that whether it involves predicting economic growth, interest rates, currencies, or the stock market, or even picking individual stocks, gurus' only value is to make weathermen look good. Keep this in mind the next time you find yourself paying attention to some guru's latest forecast. You're best served by ignoring it.

The Moral of the Tale

The moral of this tale is that while it is fine to render unto Caesar's Palace your entertainment dollar, you should not be rendering unto Wall Street your investment dollars. While Cramer might be providing entertainment, those following his recommendations are like lambs being led to be sheared by more sophisticated institutional investors.

Both CNBC and Cramer attempt to make investing entertaining so you will pay attention. And, they hope you forget that your actions make them money. However, investing was never meant to be entertaining. Instead, it should be about giving yourself the greatest chance to achieve your goals with the least amount of risk. Research shows that investors harm themselves, on average, with every trade inspired by paying attention to what is actually nothing more than "noise" (which Cramer certainly makes a lot of). The prudent strategy is thus to develop a well-thought-out plan and to have the discipline to adhere to it, ignoring the noise of the market, whether it comes from Jim Cramer or any other prognosticator. As Steve Forbes, publisher of the magazine that bears his name, stated in a presentation at UCLA's Anderson School on April 15, 2003: "You make more money selling the advice than following it. It's one of the things we count on in the magazine business—along with the short memory of our readers."

The next story is about individual investors allowing themselves to be influenced by the herd mentality, or the "madness of crowds."

Chapter 36

Fashions and Investment Folly

Fashion is the great governor of this world; it presides not only in matters of dress and amusement, but in law, physics, politics, religion, and all other things of the gravest kind; indeed, the wisest of men would be puzzled to give any better reason why particular forms in all these have been at certain times universally received, and at other times universally rejected, than that they were in or out of fashion.

—*Henry Fielding,* The True Patriot

Psychologists have long known that individuals allow themselves to be influenced by the herd mentality, or the "madness of crowds," as Charles MacKay, author of *Extraordinary Popular Delusions and the Madness of Crowds*, described it back in 1841. The "herd mentality" may be defined as a desire to be like others, to be part of the action or scene. This mentality manifests itself in the fashion world where, like the length of a skirt or the width of a tie, fashions seem to come into and go out of favor for no apparent reason. But fads are not limited to the world of fashion. Fads come and go in most endeavors. For example, in the

1950s westerns dominated television screens. Today there are no westerns to be found. Later, situation comedies became the staple of network television. Today we have reality shows. Even with diets fashions come and go, from the grapefruit diet to the South Beach diet to the low carbohydrate diet.

Since fashions affect social behavior, is it not logical to believe they affect investment behavior as well? Charles MacKay put it this way: "Every age has its peculiar folly: some scheme, project, or fantasy into which it plunges, spurred on by the love of gain, the necessity of excitement, or the force of imitation."[1] And as mentioned previously, Sir Isaac Newton was reported to have said this about the investment mania of his day, the South Sea Company: "I can calculate the motions of heavenly bodies, but not the madness of people."[2]

When it comes to investing, otherwise perfectly rational people can be influenced by a herd mentality. The potential for large financial rewards plays on the human emotions of greed and envy. In investing, as in fashion, fluctuations in attitudes often spread widely without any apparent logic. But whereas changing the length of a skirt or width of a tie won't affect your net worth in any appreciable manner, allowing your investment decisions to be influenced by the madness of crowds can have a devastating impact on your financial statement.

Perhaps one of the most amazing statistics about the world of investing is that there are many more mutual funds than there are stocks, and there are also more hedge fund managers than there are stocks. There are also thousands of separate account managers. The question is, Why are there so many managers and so many funds? There are several explanations for this phenomenon. The first is the all-too-human tendency to fall subject to "recency."

As we age, our long-term memory skills tend to remain strong, while our short-term memory skills erode. Unfortunately, individuals don't benefit from that tendency when it comes to investing. It seems to be a common human failing to fall prey to recency, the tendency to give too much weight to recent experience while ignoring the lessons of long-term historical evidence. Investors subject to recency make the mistake of extrapolating the most recent past into the future, almost as if it is preordained the recent trend will continue. The result is that whenever there is a hot sector, investors rush to jump on the bandwagon and money flows into that sector. Inevitably, the fad (fashion) passes and comes to a bad ending. The bubble inevitably bursts. The result is that investors follow a strategy of buying high and selling low—not exactly a recipe for investment success. But that is a matter of perspective. While investors almost invariably do poorly, mutual funds collect huge fees, advertising revenues of financial publications soar as Wall Street's marketing machines gear up to exploit the latest frenzy, and subscription revenues skyrocket as investors yearn to learn how they can become rich quickly.

The advertising machines of Wall Street's investment firms are great at developing product to meet demand. The record indicates they are even great at creating demand where none should exist. For example, when the biotechnology craze occurred, investment firms rushed to create biotech mutual funds. When the technology craze hit, technology funds were created by the hundreds. Then telecom became the hot industry, and scores of telecom funds were created. The internet became the greatest craze of all, and internet funds were created to exploit the demand. How many investors made their fortunes investing in these sectors? Surely it is safe to say that more fortunes were lost than were made. The latest fashions include cloud computing, electric vehicles, and artificial intelligence.

At various times in history, the financial craze has been for Japanese funds, emerging market funds, small-cap funds, value funds, and so on. When the craze eventually petered out, while some of the funds disappeared, the vast majority stayed alive (at least for some period of time). Hence the number of funds tends to grow over time. However, this trend, at least for mutual funds, has changed, and there are now fewer funds than there were at the height of the internet frenzy. This is a result of many poor performers being either merged out of existence (to make their track record disappear) or simply closed due to lack of sufficient funds to keep them alive.

It is rare for a new fund to be brought to market when an asset class has performed poorly. A perfect example is the asset class of emerging markets. When the asset class was providing great returns in the period 1987 through 1993 (about 35% per year), there was a tremendous proliferation of emerging market funds. The asset class performed poorly after that, producing negative returns from 1994 through 2002. By the end of 2003, Morningstar was able to list only 16 emerging market funds with a 10-year track record.

There is a second reason for the proliferation of funds. The Wall Street machines know that the track record of active managers is one of inconsistent (and poor) performance. Thus, a family of funds may create several funds in the same category in the hope that at least one will be randomly hot at any given time.

One explanation might be that investors often feel trapped by taxes (the shares they own have a relatively low cost). Thus, they won't sell shares in an underperforming fund—but they won't invest any new money, either. To attract new assets, there has to be a fund with a record of recent hot performance, allowing it to attract the performance-chasing dollars. Thus, there is not only the need for a number of funds (hoping at least one will be randomly hot) but also the need to regularly create new ones.

One of the great things about our capitalist society is that we have freedom of choice. Unfortunately, that can be a bad thing if investors are not educated about how the world of investing works. A lack of education allows investment firms to exploit investors who are constantly seeking the "holy grail" of outperforming the market. The end result in most cases is poor investment results for the investor and large profits for investment management and brokerage firms.

The Moral of the Tale

Investors are best served by first developing an investment plan that addresses their ability, willingness, and need to take risk. The next step is building a globally diversified portfolio and adhering to that plan, ignoring the noise of the market and the emotions that are aroused—emotions like greed and envy whenever and wherever bull markets occur, and fear and panic when bear markets happen.

Investors are also best served by using passively managed funds to implement the plan; this is the only way to ensure they do not underperform the market. By minimizing this risk, they give themselves the best chance to achieve their goals. If investors adopt the winner's game of passive investing, they will no longer have to spend time searching for that hot fund. They can spend time on far more important issues.

The next tale explains why another bit of conventional wisdom is based on a false premise.

Chapter 37

Sell in May and Go Away

Financial Astrology

O ne of the more persistent investment myths is that the winning strategy is to sell stocks in May and wait until November to buy back into the market. It is likely that the source of the myth is that it is true that stocks have provided greater returns from November through April than they have from May through October. The average annual premium of the S&P 500 Index over one-month Treasury bills averaged 8.3 percentage points per year from January 1926 through June 2023. From November through April the average annual premium was 5.7% compared to just 2.6% for the May through October period. In other words, the equity risk premium from November through April has been more than twice the premium from May through October. Furthermore, the premium was negative more frequently for the May through October portfolio, with 33% of the six-month periods having a negative result compared to 28% of the six-month periods for the November through April portfolio.

However, what is most important is that the May through October portfolio had a positive equity risk premium of 2.6% per year, which means the stocks still outperformed Treasury bills on average. In fact, a strategy that invested in the S&P 500 Index from November through April and then invested in riskless one-month Treasury bills from May through October would have returned 8.3% per year over this period, underperforming the S&P 500 Index by 1.9 percentage points per annum. And that's even before considering any transactions costs, let alone the impact of taxes (the conversion of what would otherwise be long-term capital gains into short-term capital gains, which are taxed at the same rate as ordinary income).

Prior to 2022, the last year the sell in May strategy was profitable was 2011. Given the results it is amazing that the myth persists. However, you can be sure that since the sell in May strategy outperformed in 2022, with the S&P 500 losing 12.6% while the one-month Treasury bill returned 0.6%, in following years the financial media will be raising the myth once again.

The Moral of the Tale

For an investor to believe in an investment strategy there must be a logical explanation for believing the strategy will outperform. A basic tenet of finance is that there's a positive relationship between risk and expected return. To believe that stocks should produce lower returns than Treasury bills from May through October, you would also have to believe that stocks are less risky during those months—a nonsensical argument. That makes "sell in May" the financial equivalent of astrology.

The next tale demonstrates that chasing spectacular performance is not a prudent strategy.

Chapter 38

Chasing Spectacular
Fund Performance

T he year 2020 was a typical one in that the vast majority
of actively managed funds underperformed their index
benchmarks. For example, Fidelity's Total Market Index
Fund (FSKAX), with an expense ratio of just 0.01%, currently the
leader for lowest expense ratio among total stock market index
funds, returned 20.8% and outperformed 80% of actively managed
funds in its Morningstar category. However, there were 18 funds
that gained more than 100% that year, the most since 2008. Even
more impressive is that 17 of those 18 funds had earned positive
returns over the prior three years, with the average of those funds
gaining more than 23% per year from 2017 through 2019.

Such spectacular success attracts investor attention and cash
flows. Those 18 funds attracted $19 billion in new cash flows in
2020. Which raises the question, How did funds with such outsized
returns perform in the future? To answer that question, Morningstar's Jeffrey Ptak conducted a study into equity funds that gained
more than 100% in a calendar year.[1] He found that of the 123
stock funds that gained at least 100% between 1990 and 2016, just
24 made money in the three years following their big gain. Much

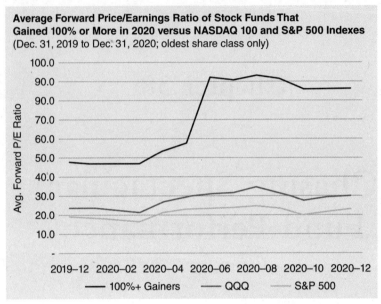

Average Forward Price/Earnings Ratio of Stock Funds That Gained 100% or More in 2020 versus NASDAQ 100 and S&P 500 Indexes (Dec. 31, 2019 to Dec. 31, 2020; oldest share class only)

Source: Morningstar Analysts.

worse was that the average fund proceeded to lose about 17% per year. Ptak also found that funds that lost money in the years before their big gain were far likelier to earn a positive return in the years after that big year than funds that made money in the run-up to their big gain! One explanation for the poor performance in the years following spectacular success is that Ptak found that the 18 funds that earned more than 100% in 2020 tended to invest in stocks that were extremely expensive. In fact, he found that on average they were recently trading at around three times the valuation of the Nasdaq-100 Index.

The Moral of the Tale

The moral of the tale is that while it is possible to outperform the market on a risk-adjusted basis, in the long term the odds of doing so are very much against it. Smart investors know that since investing is all about uncertainty, the best you can do is to put the odds in your favor by investing in low-cost, passive (or systematic) strategies. And the evidence is very clear that you should avoid chasing the performance of "hot funds."

The next tale is about the definition of being rich is knowing that you have "enough."

Chapter 39

Enough

To know you have enough is to be rich.

— *The Tao Te Ching*

Author Kurt Vonnegut related this story about fellow author Joseph Heller: "Heller and I were at a party given by a billionaire on Shelter Island. I said, 'Joe, how does it make you feel to know that our host only yesterday may have made more money than your novel *Catch-22* has earned in its entire history?' Joe said, 'I've got something he can never have.' And I said, 'What on earth could that be, Joe?' And Joe said, 'The knowledge that I've got *enough*.'"[1]

In 2009, I was asked to do an investment seminar for the TIGER 21 Group. According to their current website, "TIGER 21 Members are part of a trusted, confidential community that enables ultra-high-net-worth individuals to learn from each other to navigate the issues and opportunities that stem from success."[2]

One of the issues the group asked me to address was, How do the rich think about risk and how should they think about it? What follows is my answer.

Unless one inherits their wealth, the most common way large fortunes are created is by taking lots of risk, often concentrating that risk in a personally owned business. Thus, high-net-worth individuals are typically successful entrepreneurs. By definition, they are risk takers who have known success. That provides them with confidence in their ability to take risk. That confidence often creates the willingness to take risks. In addition, given that they have large fortunes, they also have the ability to take risk. And that combination can lead people to continue to take risks.

However, the ability and willingness to take risk are only two of the three criteria one should consider when deciding on an investment policy. There is a third, often overlooked, criterion— the *need* to take risk. A great irony is that the very people who have the most ability and willingness to take risk have the least need to take it.

Those with sufficient wealth to meet all their needs should consider that the strategy to get rich is entirely different than the strategy to stay rich. The strategy to get rich is to take risks, typically in one's own business. But the strategy to stay rich is to minimize risk, diversify the risks you take, and avoid spending too much.

I explained that given that the objective of the TIGER 21 members was now to stay rich, it was important to create a new investment plan incorporating that goal. The new plan should be based on the fact that the inconvenience of going from rich to poor is unthinkable.

When deciding on the appropriate asset allocation, investors should consider their *marginal utility of wealth*—how much any potential incremental wealth is worth relative to the risk that must be accepted in order to achieve a greater *expected* return. While more money is always better than less, at some point most people achieve a lifestyle with which they are very comfortable. At that point, taking on incremental risk to achieve a higher net worth no longer makes sense: the potential damage of an unexpected negative outcome far exceeds the potential benefit gained from incremental wealth.

Each investor needs to decide at what level of wealth their unique utility of wealth curve starts flattening out and begins bending sharply to the right. Beyond this point there is little reason to take incremental risk to achieve a higher *expected* return. Many wealthy investors have experienced devastating losses (Does the name Madoff ring a bell?) that could easily have been avoided if they had the wisdom to know what author Joseph Heller knew.

The lesson about knowing when enough is enough can be learned from the following incident. In early 2003, I met with a 71-year-old couple with financial assets of $3 million. Three years earlier their portfolio was worth $13 million. The only way they could have experienced that kind of loss was if they had held a portfolio that was almost all equities and heavily concentrated in US large-cap growth stocks, especially technology stocks. They confirmed this. They then told me they had been working with a financial advisor during this period—demonstrating that while good advice does not have to be expensive, bad advice almost always costs you dearly.

I asked the couple if, instead of their portfolio falling almost 80%, doubling it to $26 million would have led to any meaningful change in the quality of their lives? The response was a definitive no. I stated that the experience of watching $13 million shrink to $3 million must have been very painful and they probably had spent many sleepless nights. They agreed. I then asked why they had taken the risks they did, knowing the potential benefit was not going to change their lives very much but a negative outcome like the one they experienced would be so painful. The wife turned to the husband and punched him, exclaiming, "I told you so!"

Some risks are not worth taking. Prudent investors don't take more risk than they have the ability, willingness, or *need* to take. The important question to ask yourself is, If you've already won the game, why are you still playing?

Needs Versus Desires

One reason people continue to play a game they have already won is that they convert what were once desires (nice things to have, but not necessary to enjoy life) into needs. That increases the need to take risk. That causes an increase in the required equity allocation. And, that can lead to problems when the risks show up, as they did in 1973–1974, 2000–2002, 2007–2008, during the COVID-19 crisis, and in 2022.

The Moral of the Tale

Failing to consider the need to take risk is a mistake common to many wealthy people, especially those who became wealthy by taking large risks. However, the mistake of taking more risk than needed is not limited to the very wealthy. The question you need to ask yourself is how much money buys happiness? Most people would be surprised to find that the figure is a lot less than they think. For example, psychologists have found that once you have enough money to meet basic needs like food, shelter, and safety, incremental increases have little effect on your happiness. Once you have met those requirements the good things in life (the really important things) are either free or cheap. For example, taking a walk in a park with your significant other, riding a bike, reading a book, playing bridge with friends, or playing with your children/grandchildren doesn't cost very much if anything. And whether you drink a $10 or a $100 bottle of wine, or eat in a restaurant that costs $50 or $500 for dinner for two won't really make you any happier.

The next tale explains why passive (systematic) investing is the winning strategy in life as well as investing.

Chapter 40

The Big Rocks

As I traipse around the country speaking to investing groups, or just stay in my cage writing my articles, I'm often accused of "disempowering" people because I refuse to give any credence to anyone's hope of beating the market. The knowledge that I don't need to know anything is an incredibly profound form of knowledge. Personally, I think it's the ultimate form of empowerment. You can't tune out the massive industry of investment prediction unless you want to: otherwise, you'll never have the fortitude to stop listening. But if you can plug your ears to every attempt (by anyone) to predict what the markets will do, you will outperform nearly every other investor alive over the long run. Only the mantra of "don't know, and I don't care" will get you there.

—Jason Zweig

An expert in time management was speaking to a group of graduate business students. After a brief introduction, she produced a large mason jar and set it on the table. Then she brought out a box filled with big rocks. She removed the rocks from the box and began to carefully place them, one at a time, into the jar. When no more rocks would fit inside the jar, she asked the class, "Is this jar full?" Everyone yelled, "Yes." She replied, "Oh, really?"

243

She pulled out a bucket of gravel from under the table and dumped some into the jar. Pieces of gravel moved into the spaces between the big rocks. She continued this process until no more gravel could be placed into the jar. She asked again, "Is the jar full?" One student answered, "Probably not."

She then reached under the table, brought out a bucket of sand, and dumped the sand into the jar. The sand began to fill the spaces between the rocks and the gravel. She continued until no more sand could fit into the jar. Once again she asked, "Is this jar full?" Everyone shouted, "No!"

Finally, she filled the jar with water and asked, "What is the point of this demonstration?" An eager student said, "The point is that no matter how full your schedule, you can always fit in one more meeting!"

Once the laughter had died down, the speaker replied, "That's not the point. This demonstration teaches us that if you don't put in the big rocks first, you'll never get them into the jar at all. What are the big rocks in your life? Time with your loved ones, your faith, your education, your dreams, your career, a worthy cause, teaching or mentoring others?" She concluded by repeating the important message: "Remember to put these big rocks in first, or you'll never get them in at all."

Individual investors following an active management strategy spend much of their precious leisure time watching the latest business news, studying the latest charts, scanning and posting on internet investment discussion boards, reading financial trade publications and newsletters, and so on. What they are really doing is focusing on the gravel, the sand, and the water, leaving insufficient time for the big rocks. However, investors who adopt a passive investment strategy ignore the "noise" (the sand, the gravel, and the water). They are playing the winner's game and focusing on the big rocks, the really important things in their lives.

Consider these words of wisdom from Paul Samuelson, probably the most famous economist of our time: "You shouldn't spend much time on your investments. That will just tempt you to pull up your plants and see how the roots are doing, and that's bad for the roots. It's also very bad for your sleep."[1] The following true story demonstrates these points better than a fictional story would.

Shortly after my first book on the winning strategy was published in 1998, a doctor called and related this story. He had been in practice a few years and had a wife, a young child, and one more on the way. Many of his friends had generated large profits from trading stocks, and he became caught up in the euphoria of the bull market.

After putting in a long day at the office, he would come home to his computer and the internet. He spent hours studying charts and investment reports and following the chat boards. He was caught up in the excitement of the bull market, a technology revolution that was changing the world, access to information the internet provided, the hype surrounding the success of day traders, and so on. The expansion of the coverage of financial markets by the financial media helped fuel the interest in active management and the "take control of your portfolio" mentality. Within just a few months, he had turned his small initial investment into about $100,000.

Unfortunately, his wife no longer saw her husband, and his child no longer had a father; the doctor was now "married" to his computer and his investments. His wife began to seriously question their marriage. Luckily, he lost all his profits within a few months.

Fortunately, the doctor recognized that he was not paying attention to the most important part of his life—his family. He also realized that his original gains were a result of luck, similar to a hot hand at the craps table. Someone suggested that he read my book, *The Only Guide to a Winning Investment Strategy You'll Ever Need*. After doing so, he called to thank me. He told me that he recognized his error and had designed a portfolio of index funds and sworn off active investing.

The following is another true story. It too made me realize how adopting passive investing as the basis for one's investment strategy can improve the quality of one's life as well.

About one year after my first book was published, I met a colleague and sophisticated investor with an MBA from Wharton, University of Pennsylvania, and a BBA from Wake Forest. He had about 30 years of experience in financial management, including his last position as assistant treasurer at a major corporation. After meeting with my firm, and having read my book, he was so convinced this was the winning strategy that he wanted to help others benefit from adopting its principles. Eventually, he became a financial advisor. In short order, he completed the extensive educational requirements for his Certified Financial Planner certification. He later related the following story.

He told me that he used to spend many hours every day reading various financial publications, researching individual stocks, and watching the financial news. And this was after spending a long and full day at the office. After learning of and adopting the principles of modern portfolio theory, the efficient market hypothesis, and passive investing, he found that he no longer needed to do those things. He recognized that he was paying attention to what was really nothing more than noise that would, at best, distract him from the winner's game.

He sat down with his wife and calculated that by adopting a passive investment approach, he had recaptured six weeks of his life per year. It is one thing to decide to spend six weeks a year on productive activities. However, as he had now learned, not only were the activities in which he had been engaged nonproductive, they were actually counterproductive because of the expenses and taxes incurred as a result of his active strategy. And that didn't even include placing a value on his most precious resource: time. He only had a limited amount of it and did not want to spend it on less than optimal activities.

Don't Sweat the Small Stuff

I became the head of economic and financial research at Buckingham Wealth Partners because I wanted to provide investors with the knowledge needed to make prudent investment decisions. I wanted to help prevent the wolves of Wall Street from shearing (and in some cases slaughtering) investors, as if they were sheep. Through my writings and interactions with investors, I believe I have accomplished that objective—though there is still a lot more work to be done.

Helping clients ignore the noise of the market and the investment pandering of Wall Street by arming them with knowledge of how markets really work and a custom, tailored investment plan for their unique situation has resulted in one of the greatest pleasures I have received from my efforts: helping clients improve their quality of life.

In my particular case, I was able to spend my time coaching my children's sports teams. Over the years I have coached my daughters in soccer, basketball, and softball. I also have been able to attend their sporting events and dance recitals. I am also an avid reader. While I read about 10 to 20 investment books a year as part of my research, I also read another 50 to 60 books annually, ranging from popular spy novels to great literature.

Indexing and passive investing have the "disadvantage" of being boring. I admit it. However, if anyone really needs to get their excitement in life from investing, I'd suggest they might want to consider getting another life.

Personally, my life is enriched by participating in and attending sporting events. And I get excitement from my passion, whitewater rafting. There is no question in my mind that I get all the excitement I need from life staring a Class V+ rapid in the face. I have been on over 40 whitewater adventures, on more than 30 different rivers, in 10 different states, many of them containing Class V and Class V+ rapids. I have even experienced the thrill of going overboard on a Class V rapid on the Youghiogheny River in Maryland, and a similar thrill going down a Class V section of the Arkansas River in Colorado, which, by the way, is one thrill I can do without.

And, more importantly, I have been able to share many of those experiences with my family, especially my oldest daughter, Jodi.

She loves the sport so much, she took canoeing classes while attending Emory University and trained to be a guide.

While it is a tragedy that the majority of investors unnecessarily miss out on market returns that are available to anyone by adopting a passive investment strategy, the really great tragedy in life is that they also miss out on the important things in pursuit of the "holy grail of outperformance." If you find that you need excitement from your investments, you should set up a special "entertainment" account. The assets inside that account should not exceed more than a few percent of your total portfolio. Invest the rest of your assets in what I believe to be the winner's game.

The Moral of the Tale

The moral of this tale is that indexing, and passive investing in general, not only allows you to earn market returns in a low-cost and tax efficient manner but also frees you from spending any time at all watching CNBC and reading financial publications that are basically not much more than what Jane Bryant Quinn called "investment porn."

Instead, you can spend your time with your family, perform community service, read a good book, or pursue your favorite hobby. Remember, investing was never meant to be exciting despite what Wall Street and the financial media want you to believe. Investing is supposed to be about achieving your financial goals with the least amount of risk.

The next tale explains why investors who have implemented the types of passive strategies recommended in this book have experienced "the best of times." However, for those who continue to play the game of active investing, in general, it has been the "worst of times."

Chapter 41

A Tale of Two Strategies

Wall Street doesn't have to keep confessing its sins. It just has to stop committing them.
—James Surowiecki, "The Talking Cure," New Yorker
(December 9, 2002)

"It was the best of times, it was the worst of times." These are among the most famous words in all of literature. They are the opening lines of *A Tale of Two Cities*, Charles Dickens's tale of the French Revolution. However, those words apply just as well today to the world of investing.

For those investors who believe in active management as the winning strategy, it is the worst of times. As we previously discussed, the percentage of active managers who are able to persistently outperform has collapsed. For example, in 1998, when Charles Ellis wrote his famous book *Winning the Loser's Game*, he estimated that only about 20% of actively managed funds were generating statistically significant outperformance (alpha) on a risk-adjusted basis.[1] However, the 2010 study "Luck Versus Skill in the Cross-Section of Mutual Fund Returns" found that fewer active managers (about 2%) were able to outperform their risk-adjusted benchmark than would be expected by chance.[2] And that was even before considering the negative impact of taxes, which are typically the greatest expense for actively managed funds held in taxable accounts—even greater than the expense ratios and trading costs. And the 2014 study "Conviction in Equity Investing" found that the percentage of fund managers showing net alphas had fallen from about 20% in 1993 to just 1.6%.[3]

However, for investors who believe that markets are efficient and that passive investing is the winning strategy, it has been the best of times. There has been a dramatic increase in the availability of passively managed funds—index funds, exchange-traded funds (ETFs), and passive asset class funds. More fund choices are available in more asset classes and providing exposure to more factors (such as value, size, momentum, profitability, quality, and low volatility) enabling investors to more effectively diversify their portfolios. In addition, while passively managed funds are almost by definition relatively more tax efficient than actively managed funds (because of their relatively low turnover), several fund families have introduced passively managed funds that are tax managed as well, further improving after-tax returns. And ETF versions make the funds even more tax efficient.

While actively managed funds have been delivering on average poor performance, passively managed funds have been delivering market returns at already low costs and yet lowering fees. The intense competition for market share among such fund families as Black Rock, Fidelity, and Vanguard has led to a dramatic fall in their expense ratios. For example, as its name suggests, Fidelity's ZERO Large Cap Index (FNILX) has a 0.00% expense ratio. These fund families are actually delivering on the promise of economies of scale.

The Moral of the Tale

When Dickens wrote those famous opening words perhaps he knew that they would be applicable to all times. They certainly are applicable to investors today. For the majority of those who continue to place their faith in the practice of active management, it has been the "age of foolishness, the season of Darkness, and the winter of despair." However, for those that have adopted a passive investment strategy it has been "the age of wisdom, the season of Light, and the spring of hope." And that is the moral of this tale.

The final tale provides guidance to those investors who believe they are best served by working with a financial advisor. It provides the road map to help you identify one you can trust.

Chapter 42

How to Identify an Advisor You Can Trust

When it comes to home repairs individuals can be categorized into two broad groups. The first group is what we might call the "Home Depot Crowd," the do-it-yourselfers (DIYers). This group has many subgroups. One subgroup belongs because they believe they can do it cheaper than the cost of hiring a professional. Another belongs because they like the work, have the skills to do the work well, and enjoy seeing the fruits of their labor.

Some of the individuals who belong to the DIY group should not be there. These individuals belong because they are trying to save money (though they might even enjoy doing the work), but, unfortunately, they don't have the skills required to be sure that the job will be well done. And if something is not done right the first time, the cost of correcting errors can far exceed what it would have cost to pay a professional to do it right in the first place. Those people who belong to the second group should follow what I call the Swedroe principle: if something is worth doing, it is worth paying someone to do it for you. It might be that you follow that principle because you place a high value on your free time and can afford to pay to have the work done. It might also be that you don't enjoy doing the work. And, if you are like me, you belong because if there is a way to screw it up, you will find it.

When it comes to investing there are also those same two groups. Within the DIY group you have the same types of sub-groups. You have those who belong because they don't want to pay a professional for something they believe they can do just as well. Unfortunately, the evidence from academic studies demonstrates that there are few individuals with the investment knowledge and discipline to be successful investors. Had those studies compared the two skills, it is likely that they would have found that DIYers who attempt to perform home repairs fare better than their DIY investor counterparts. And the costs of making bad investment decisions almost certainly exceeds the costs of repairing that leaky faucet.

There are also individuals who recognize that they have neither the knowledge nor the discipline required to be successful on their own. They also recognize that a good financial advisor can add value in many ways. There are also individuals who would rather have someone else focus on financial matters so that they can focus more of their attention on the more important things in their lives, their big rocks. They know that even if they had the skills to do it themselves, the time spent on financial matters is time not spent with family, friends, doing community service, and so on. And they place a greater value on that time than on the cost of an advisor.

For those who wish to go it alone, this book has provided you not only with the winning strategy of global diversification and passive investing. The Appendix provides a list of recommended investment vehicles to use. For those who recognize the value of a good financial advisor the following advice is offered.

One of the most important decisions an investor can make is the choice of a financial advisor. When making this selection, surveys show that along with the financial expertise of the advisor, investors look for someone they can trust. However, trust is an intangible quality that cannot be as easily quantified as, for example, a baseball player's batting average. Thus, when interviewing a potential financial advisor, require them to make the following 11 commitments to you. Doing so will give you the greatest chance of avoiding conflicts of interest and the greatest chance of achieving your financial goals.

1. The firm should be able to demonstrate that its guiding principle is to provide investment advisor services that are in the client's best interests.
2. The firm follows a fiduciary standard of care—a fiduciary standard is often considered the highest legal duty that one party can have to another. This differs from the suitability standard present in many brokerage firms. That standard requires only that a product or service be suitable—it does not have to be in the investor's best interest.
3. The firm serves as a fee-only advisor—avoiding the conflicts that commission-based compensation can create. With commission-based compensation, it can be difficult to know if the investment or product recommended by the advisor is the one that is best for you, or the one that generates greater compensation for the advisor.
4. All potential conflicts are fully disclosed.
5. Advice is based on the latest academic research, not on opinions.
6. The firm is client centric—advisors focus on delivering sound advice and targeted solutions. The only requirement they have in offering particular solutions is whether the client's best interests will be served.
7. Advisors deliver a high level of personal attention and develop strong personal relationships—and clients benefit from a team of professionals to help them make sound financial decisions.
8. Advisors invest their personal assets (including the firm's profit-sharing plan) based on the same set of investment principles and in the same or comparable securities that they recommend to their clients.
9. They develop investment plans that are integrated with estate, tax, and risk management (insurance) plans. The overall plans are tailored to each client's unique personal situation.

10. Their advice is goal oriented—evaluating each decision not in isolation, but in terms of its impact on the likelihood of success of the overall plan.
11. Comprehensive wealth management services are provided by individuals that have the CFP, PFS, or other comparable designations.

The Moral of the Tale

There are certainly some individuals who have the knowledge, time, interest, and discipline to develop a well-thought-out investment plan. But that is only the necessary condition for success. The sufficient condition is to also be able to integrate the investment plan with a carefully planned estate, tax, and risk management plan. They also have to be able to manage the plan (rebalance and tax loss harvest) on an ongoing basis in a cost and tax efficient manner. And that is not all. They must also be able to adapt the plan to meet changing circumstances and the passage of time. Unfortunately, the evidence is that fewer people have those skills than believe they have them. As we have discussed, overconfidence is a common human trait.

Fortunately, for those who recognize that they would be best served by hiring a professional advisor, good advice doesn't have to be expensive. However, bad, or untrustworthy, advice almost always will cost you dearly, no matter how little you pay for it. Therefore, you should perform a thorough due diligence before choosing a financial advisor. That due diligence should not only include requesting the advisor make the aforementioned 11 commitments to you but also should include a careful review of form ADV—a disclosure document setting forth information about the advisor, including the investment strategy, fee schedules, conflicts of interest, regulatory incidents, and so on. Careful due diligence will minimize the risk of having to make expensive repairs.

Conclusion

One of my favorite films is *The Man Who Shot Liberty Valance*. The film is a western about a greenhorn, pacifist lawyer (Jimmy Stewart) who stands up to and then shoots and kills the villain, Liberty Valance (Lee Marvin). The story is told using the device of a flashback. Stewart, a US senator, returns to his hometown to attend the funeral of his best friend (John Wayne). In an interview with a young newspaper reporter, Stewart finally tells the true story of the legendary gunfight. The reporter learns that it was not Stewart who actually killed Liberty Valance. Instead, it was John Wayne. Excited about his great discovery, the reporter races off to his editor. When the editor finishes reading this incredible tale, he rips the reporter's notes to shreds and tells him, "When the legend becomes fact, print the legend."

Wall Street and the financial media need and want to keep alive the myth that active investing is the winning strategy. Thus, they fight extremely hard to keep the legends and myths about active investing alive. The goal of this book was to kill the legends by exposing them as myths. The introduction set forth three objectives to achieve that goal:

- Demonstrate through the use of stories and analogies how markets really work, exposing many investment legends as nothing more than investment propaganda.
- Change the way you think about investing and how markets work.
- Provide you with sufficient knowledge to begin to make informed and prudent investment decisions—in other words, to stop throwing your hard-earned money away.

Hopefully, the book has been successful in meeting those objectives. If it has, your next step should be to develop a well-thought-out financial plan that identifies your unique ability, willingness, and need to take risk. The financial plan should also be integrated with an estate, tax, and risk management (insurance) plan. And the plan should include an asset allocation table, such as this one:

	Conservative	Moderate	Moderately Aggressive	Highly Aggressive
Equity (%)	40	60	80	100
US stocks (%)	28	42	56	70
Large (%)	6	9	12	15
Large Value (%)	6	9	12	15
Small (%)	6	9	12	15
Small Value (%)	6	9	12	15
Real Estate (%)	4	6	8	10
International Stocks (%)	12	18	24	30
Large (%)	2	3	4	5
Large Value (%)	4	6	8	10
Small (%)	2	3	4	5
Small Value (%)	2	3	4	5

	Conservative	Moderate	Moderately Aggressive	Highly Aggressive
Emerging Markets (%)	2	3	4	5
Fixed Income (%)	**60**	**40**	**20**	**0**
Bonds (%)	60	40	20	0

The table might also include alternative assets (such as reinsurance, private credit, and long-short factor funds) that serve as diversifiers of the risks of stocks and bonds.

When designing your portfolio, it is critical that you remember that we live in a world of uncertainty. Despite what Wall Street and the media would like you to believe, there are no clear crystal balls, only cloudy ones. And in a world of uncertainty, the best defense is broad global diversification across many different asset classes. For the equity allocation of your portfolio that means including some exposure to domestic and international stocks (including emerging markets), small-cap and large-cap stocks, value and growth stocks, and perhaps real estate.

After writing your plan, it is also important that you sign it, demonstrating your commitment to the plan. Having done so you should implement the plan by purchasing passively managed funds—index funds (including ETFs) or other non–actively managed factor-based (or asset class) funds. Then, unless an underlying assumption of your plan has changed, the only actions you should be taking are to regularly rebalance the portfolio to the allocation targets you established and to tax loss harvest whenever the opportunity arises. Fortunately, these should be easy things to do. The hard part for most investors is ignoring the noise of the market, the Wall Street establishment, the media, and the emotions caused by all the noise. Unfortunately, emotions, like greed and envy in bull markets and fear and panic in bear markets, have often caused even the best laid out plans to end up in the trash heap.

Thus, one last bit of advice is offered: cancel all subscriptions to mass media investment publications and newsletters, turn off CNBC, and, finally, focus on the BIG ROCKS in your life. By doing so, you are likely to have not only a richer portfolio but a richer life as well. That is why passive investing is the winner's game in life as well as investing.

In closing, one of the great pleasures for me has been hearing from so many readers of my 18 other books. If you have any questions, or if you would like to discuss any of the concepts covered in this book, feel free to e-mail me at lswedroe@bucking hamgroup.com.

Appendix A

Implementation: Recommended Investment Vehicles

The following list of funds has been approved by the investment policy committee at Buckingham Strategic Wealth.[1] Thus, these are the products we believe you should consider first when constructing your portfolio. Where more than one share class for a mutual fund is available, the lowest-cost version is shown. That fund version may not be available to all investors because minimums may be required. AQR, Bridgeway, and Dimensional funds are available through approved financial advisors and in retirement and 529 plans. (Note that for some AQR funds, lower-cost R Share versions may be available to some investors.)

Considerations for selecting a fund should include how much exposure it provides to each desired/targeted factor, its expense ratio, and the amount of diversification it offers (that is, the number of securities held and their weightings). For ETFs, the liquidity of the fund is an added consideration. Our recommendation is that the ETFs you consider have more than $100 million in assets and an average daily trading volume in excess of $5 million.

Single-Style Funds

Market Beta

Domestic
- Dimensional US Equity (DFUS)
- Fidelity Total Market Index (FSKAX)
- Schwab Total Stock Market Index (SWTSX)
- Schwab U.S. Broad Market (SCHB)
- SPDR Portfolio Total Stock Market (SPTM)
- Vanguard Russell 3000 (VTHR)
- Vanguard Total Stock Market Index (VTI/VTSAX)
- iShares Core S&P Total U.S. Stock Market (ITOT)
- iShares Russell 3000 (IWV)

International Developed Markets
- Fidelity Global ex-U.S. Index (FSGGX)
- Fidelity Total International Index (FTIHX)
- SPDR MSCI ACWI ex-U.S. (CWI)
- SPDR Portfolio Developed World ex-U.S. (SPDW)
- Vanguard Developed Markets Index (VEA/VTMGX)
- Vanguard FTSE All-World ex-US (VEU/VFWAX)
- Vanguard Total International Stock (VXUS/VTIAX)
- Schwab International Equity (SCHF)
- iShares Core MSCI International Developed Markets (IDEV)
- iShares Core MSCI Total International Stock Market (IXUS)
- iShares MSCI ACWI ex-U.S. (ACWX)

Emerging Markets
- DFA Emerging Markets (DFEMX)
- Fidelity Emerging Markets Index (FPADX)
- Schwab Emerging Markets (SCHE)
- SPDR Portfolio Emerging Markets (SPEM)
- Vanguard Emerging Markets Stock Index (VWO/VEMAX)
- iShares Core MSCI Emerging Markets (IEMG)

Small

Domestic
- Bridgeway Ultra-Small Company Market (BRSIX)
- DFA US Micro Cap (DFSCX)
- DFA US Small Cap (DFSTX)
- Dimensional US Small-Cap (DFAS)
- Fidelity Small-Cap Index (FSSNX)
- Schwab Small-Cap Index (SWSSX)
- Schwab U.S. Small Cap (SCHA)
- SPDR Portfolio S&P 600 Small-Cap (SPSM)
- SPDR S&P 600 Small-Cap ETF (SLY)
- TIAA-CREF Small-Cap Blend Index (TISBX)
- Vanguard Russell 2000 Index (VTWO/VRTIX)
- Vanguard S&P Small-Cap 600 Index (VIOO/VSMSX)
- Vanguard Small Cap Index Fund (VB/VSMAX)
- Vanguard Tax-Managed Small-Cap Index (VTSIX/VTMSX)
- iShares Core S&P Small-Cap (IJR)
- iShares Micro-Cap (IWC)
- iShares Russell 2000 (IWM)

International Developed Markets
- DFA International Small Company (DFISX)
- Dimensional International Small-Cap (DFIS)
- Schwab International Small-Cap Equity (SCHC)
- SPDR S&P International Small Cap (GWX)
- Vanguard FTSE All-World ex-U.S. Small-Cap (VSS/VFSAX)
- iShares MSCI EAFE Small-Cap (SCZ)

Emerging Markets
- DFA Emerging Markets Small-Cap (DEMSX)
- SPDR S&P Emerging Markets Small-Cap (EWX)

Large and Value

Domestic

- DFA US Large Cap Value III (DFUVX)
- Dimensional US Marketwide Value (DFUV)
- Dimensional US Large-Cap Value (DFLV)
- Fidelity Large-Cap Value Enhanced Index (FLVEX)
- Fidelity Large-Cap Value Index (FLCOX)
- Schwab Fundamental U.S. Large Company Index (FNDX/ SFLNX)
- Schwab U.S. Large-Cap Value Index (SCHV/SWLVX)
- SPDR S&P 500 Value (SPYV)
- TIAA-CREF Large-Cap Value Index (TILVX)
- Vanguard Mega-Cap Value Index (MGV/VMVLX)
- Vanguard Russell 1000 Value Index (VONV/VRVIX)
- Vanguard S&P 500 Value (VOOV)
- Vanguard Value Index (VTV/VVIAX)
- iShares Core S&P U.S. Value (IUSV)
- iShares Edge MSCI USA Value Factor (VLUE)
- iShares Russell 1000 Value (IWD)
- iShares Russell Top 200 Value (IWX)
- iShares S&P 500 Value (IVE)

International Developed Markets

- DFA International Value III (DFVIX)
- Dimensional International Value (DFIV)
- DFA World ex-US Value (DFWVX)
- FlexShares Morningstar Developed Markets ex-U.S. Factor Tilt Index (TLTD)
- Schwab Fundamental International Large Company Index (FNDF/SFNNX)
- iShares MSCI EAFE Value (EFV)
- iShares MSCI International Value Factor (IVLU)

Emerging Markets
- DFA Emerging Markets Value (DFEVX)
- Schwab Fundamental Emerging Markets Large Company Index (FNDE/SFENX)

Small and Value

Domestic
- Bridgeway Omni Small-Cap Value (BOSVX)
- EA Bridgeway Omni Small-Cap Value (BSVO)
- DFA US Small-Cap Value (DFSVX)
- Dimensional US Small-Cap Value (DFSV)
- Dimensional US Targeted Value (DFAT)
- DFA US Targeted Value (DFFVX)
- Fidelity Small-Cap Value Index (FISVX)
- Schwab Fundamental U.S. Small Company Index (FNDA/SFSNX)
- SPDR S&P 600 Small-Cap Value ETF (SLYV)
- Vanguard Russell 2000 Value (VTWV)
- Vanguard S&P Small-Cap 600 Value (VIOV)
- Vanguard Small Cap Value (VBR/VSIAX)
- iShares Russell 2000 Value ETF (IWN)
- iShares S&P Small-Cap 600 Value (IJS)

International Developed Markets
- DFA International Small Cap Value (DISVX)
- DFA World ex-US Targeted Value (DWUSX)
- DFA International Vector Equity (DFVQX)
- Dimensional International Small-Cap Value (DISV)
- Schwab Fundamental International Small Company Index (FNDC/SFILX)

Emerging Markets
- DFA Emerging Markets Targeted Value (DEMGX)

Large and Momentum

Domestic
- AQR Large-Cap Momentum (QMORX)
- iShares Edge MSCI USA Momentum Factor (MTUM)

International Developed Markets
- AQR International Momentum (QIORX)
- iShares MSCI International Momentum Factor (IMTM)

Small and Momentum

Domestic
- AQR Small-Cap Momentum (QSMRX)

Profitability / Quality

Domestic
- DFA US High Relative Profitability (DURPX)
- Dimensional US High Profitability (DUHP)
- iShares Edge MSCI USA Quality Factor (QUAL)

International Developed Markets
- DFA International High Relative Profitability (DIHRX)
- Dimensional International High Profitability (DIHP)
- iShares Edge MSCI International Quality Factor (IQLT)

Term
- DFA Five-Year Global Fixed Income (DFGBX)
- DFA Intermediate Government Fixed Income (DFIGX)
- Fidelity Intermediate Treasury Bond Index (FUAMX)
- iShares 3–7 Year Treasury Bond (IEI)
- iShares 7–10 Year Treasury Bond (IEF)
- iShares U.S. Treasury Bond (GOVT)
- Schwab Intermediate-Term Treasury (SCHR)
- SPDR Portfolio Intermediate-Term Treasury (SPTI)
- Vanguard Intermediate-Term Treasury Index (VGIT/VSIGX)

Multi-Style Funds

Large and Value and Profitability/Quality

Domestic
- Avantis US Equity (AVUS/AVUSX)
- Avantis US Large-Cap Value (AVLV)
- DFA US Core Equity 1 (DFEOX)
- Dimensional US Core Equity Market (DFAU)

International
- Avantis International Equity (AVDE/AVDEX)
- Dimensional International Core Equity Market (DFAI)

Emerging Markets
- Avantis Emerging Markets Equity (AVEM/AVEEX)
- DFA Emerging Markets Core Equity (DFCEX)
- Dimensional Emerging Markets Core Equity Market (DFAE)

Small and Value and Profitability/Quality

Domestic
- Avantis US Small-Cap Value (AVUV/AVUVX)
- DFA US Core Equity 2 (DFQTX)
- Dimensional US Core Equity 2 (DFAC)

International
- Avantis International Small-Cap Value (AVDV/AVDVX)
- DFA International Core Equity (DFIEX)
- DFA World ex-US Core Equity (DFWIX)
- Dimensional World ex-US Core Equity 2 (DFAX)
- Dimensional International Core Equity 2 (DFIC)

Emerging Markets
- Dimensional Emerging Markets Core Equity 2 (DFEM)

Value and Momentum and Profitability/Quality

Domestic
- AQR Large Cap Multi-Style (QCERX)
- iShares Edge MSCI Multifactor USA (LRGF)
- Goldman Sachs ActiveBeta U.S. Large-Cap Equity (GSLC)
- Vanguard U.S. Multifactor (VFMFX)

International
- AQR International Multi-Style (QICRX)
- Goldman Sachs ActiveBeta International Equity (GSIE)
- Hartford Multifactor Developed Markets ex-U.S. (RODM)
- iShares Edge MSCI Multifactor International (INTF)

Emerging Markets
- AQR Emerging Multi-Style II (QTERX)
- Goldman Sachs ActiveBeta Emerging Markets Equity (GEM)
- iShares MSCI Emerging Markets Multifactor (EMGF)

Small + Value + Momentum + Profitability/Quality

Domestic
- AQR Small-Cap Multi-Style (QSERX)
- iShares Edge MSCI Multifactor USA Small-Cap (SMLF)

Trend-Following (Stocks, Bonds, Currencies and Commodities)
- AQR Managed Futures (AQMRX)
- AQR Managed Futures HV (QMHRX)

Alternative Funds

Value + Momentum + Quality + Defensive (Stocks, Bonds, Currencies and Commodities)
- AQR Style Premia Alternative (QSPRX)

Value + Momentum + Quality + Defensive + Trend + Variance Risk Premium (Stocks, Bonds, and Currencies)

- AQR Alternative Risk Premia (QRPRX)

Reinsurance

- Pioneer ILS Interval (XILSX)
- Stone Ridge HighYield Reinsurance Risk Premium (SHRIX)
- Stone Ridge Reinsurance Risk Premium Interval (SRRIX)

Alternative Lending

- Cliffwater Corporate Lending (CCLFX)
- Cliffwater Enhanced Lending (CELFX)
- Stone Ridge Alternative Lending Risk Premium (LENDX)

Diversified Alternatives

- AQR Diversified Arbitrage (QDARX)
- Stone Ridge Diversified Alternatives (SRDAX)

Notes

Introduction

1. Moshe Levy, "The Deadweight Loss of Active Management," *The Journal of Investing* (July 2023).

Chapter 1: The Determinants of the Risk and Return of Stocks and Bonds

1. Michael Lewis, *Moneyball* (Norton, 2003), p. 67.
2. Eugene Fama and Kenneth French, "The Cross-Section of Expected Stock Returns," *The Journal of Finance* (June 1992).
3. Andrea Frazzini, David Kabiller, and Lasse Pedersen, "Buffett's Alpha," *Financial Analysts Journal* (September 2018).
4. Eugene Fama and Kenneth French, "Luck Versus Skill in the Cross-Section of Mutual Fund Returns, *The Journal of Finance* (September 2010).

Chapter 2: How Markets Set Prices

1. William J. Bernstein, *The Four Pillars of Investing* (McGraw-Hill, 2002), p. 297.
2. Raymond D. Sauer, "The Economics of Wagering Markets," *Journal of Economic Literature* 36, pp. 2021–64.
3. Daniel C. Hickman, ""Efficiency in the Madness? Examining the Betting Market for the NCAA Men's Basketball Tournament," *Journal of Economics and Finance* (July 2020).
4. Guy Elaad, James Reade, and Carl Singleton, "Information, Prices and Efficiency in an Online Betting Market," *Finance Research Letters* (July 2020).
5. James Suroweicki, *The Wisdom of Crowds* (Doubleday, 2004), pp. 13–14.
6. Brad Barber and Terrance Odean, "Trading Is Hazardous to Your Wealth: The Common Stock Investment Performance of Individual Investors," *Journal of Finance* (April 2000).
7. Brad Barber and Terrance Odean, "Boys Will Be Boys: Gender, Overconfidence and Common Stock Investment," *Quarterly Journal of Economics* (February 2001).
8. Brad Barber and Terrance Odean, "Trading Is Hazardous to Your Wealth."
9. Brad Barber and Terrance Odean, "Too Many Cooks Spoil the Profits: Investment Club Performance," *Financial Analysts Journal* (January/February 2000).
10. Andrew Tobias, *The Only Investment Book You Will Ever Need* (Harcourt, 1978).
11. Eugene F. Fama and Kenneth R. French. "Luck Versus Skill in the Cross-Section of Mutual Fund Returns." *Journal of Finance* 65, no. 5 (October 2010), p. 1915.
12. Philipp Meyer-Brauns, "Mutual Fund Performance Through a Five-Factor Lens," Dimensional Fund Advisors White Paper (2016).

13. Andrew Berkin and Larry E. Swedroe, *The Incredible Shrinking Alpha* (Harriman House, 2020).
14. James Surowiecki, *The Wisdom of Crowds* (Doubleday, 2004), p. 51.
15. William Berlind, "Bookies in Exile," *New York Times* (August 17, 2003).

Chapter 3: Persistence of Performance

1. Dr. Mark Rubinstein, "Rational Markets: Yes or No? The Affirmative Case," *Financial Analysts Journal* (May–June 2001).
2. Ron Ross, *The Unbeatable Market* (Optimum Press, 2002), p. 57.
3. Dr. Mark Rubinstein, "Rational Markets."
4. Raymond Fazzi, "Going Their Own Way," *Financial Advisor* (March 2001).
5. Charles Ellis, "The Rise and Fall of Performance Management," *Financial Analysts Journal* (2014).
6. Ibid.
7. Tim Riley, "Timothy Riley, author of Can Mutual Fund Stars Still Pick Stocks? A Replication and Extension of Kosowski, Timmermann, Wermers, and White (2006)." *Critical Finance Review* 10, no. 2 (2021), pp. 251–61.
8. Robert Kosowski, Allan Timmermann, Russ Wermers, and Hal White, "Can Mutual Fund 'Stars' Really Pick Stocks? New Evidence from a Bootstrap Analysis," *Journal of Finance* (December 2006)
9. Ibid.
10. Tim Riley, "Timothy Riley."
11. Ibid.
12. Ralph Wanger, *A Zebra in Lion Country* (Simon & Schuster, 1997).
13. Peter Bernstein, *Against the Gods* (Wiley, 1996).

Chapter 4: Why Is Persistent Outperformance So Hard to Find?

1. Amit Goyal and Sunil Wahal, "The Selection and Termination of Investment Management Firms by Plan Sponsors," *Journal of Finance* (July 2008).
2. Jonathan B. Berk, "Five Myths of Active Portfolio Management," *The Journal of Portfolio Management* 31, no. 3 (Spring 2005), 27–31.
3. Ibid.
4. Roger Edelen, Richard Evans, and Gregory B. Kadlec, "Scale Effects in Mutual Fund Performance: The Role of Trading Costs" (March 17, 2007). http://dx.doi.org/10.2139/ssrn.951367.
5. Ibid.

Chapter 6: Market Efficiency and the Case of Pete Rose

1. Charles D. Ellis, *Winning the Loser's Game: Timeless Strategies for Successful Investing* (McGraw-Hill, 1998).
2. John Dowd et al., "In the Matter of Peter Edward Rose, Manager of Cincinnati Reds Baseball Club," (1989).
3. Douglas Coate, "Market Efficiency in the Baseball Betting Market: The Case of Pete Rose," Rutgers University Newark Working Paper 2008–003 (January 2008).
4. Raymond D. Sauer, "The Economics of Wagering Markets," *Journal of Economic Literature* 36, pp. 2021–64.
5. James Surowiecki, *The Wisdom of Crowds* (Doubleday, 2004), pp. 13–14.

Chapter 7: The Value of Security Analysis

1. Joseph Engelberg, David McLean, and Jeffrey Pontiff, "Analysts and Anomalies," *Journal of Accounting and Finance* (February 2020).

Chapter 8: Be Careful What You Ask For

1. *Encyclopedia Mythica.*
2. Jim Davis, "Economic Growth and Emerging Market Returns" (August 2006).

Chapter 9: The Fed Model and the Money Illusion

1. Andrew Lo, "Can You Really Time the Market?" *Kiplinger's Personal Finance* (February 1997).
2. David Leinweber, "Butter Production in Bangladesh Is No Predictor of S&P 500," *Wall Street Journal* (April 5, 1996).
3. The Federal Reserve, "Humphrey-Hawkins Report, Section 2: Economic and Financial Developments in 1997 Alan Greenspan" (July 22, 1997).
4. William Bernstein, "The Efficient Frontier" (Summer 2002).
5. Clifford S. Asness, "Fight the Fed Model: The Relationship Between Stock Market Yields, Bond Market Yields, and Future Returns" (December 2002). http://dx.doi.org/10.2139/ssrn.381480.

Chapter 10: When Even the Best Aren't Likely to Win the Game

1. Richard Ennis, "Institutional Investment Strategy and Manager Choice: A Critique," *Journal of Portfolio Management* 46, no. 5 (2020).

Chapter 11: The Demon of Chance

1. Karen Damato and Allison Bisbey Colter, "Hedge Funds, Once Utterly Exclusive, Lure Less-Elite Investors," *Wall Street Journal* (January 3, 2002).
2. Jonathan Clements, *25 Myths You've Got to Avoid* (Simon & Schuster, 1998), p. 86.
3. Nassim Nicholas Taleb, *Fooled by Randomness* (Random House, 2005)

Chapter 12: Outfoxing the Box

1. Robert D. Arnott, Andrew L. Berkin, and Jia Ye, "How Well Have Taxable Investors Been Served in the 1980s and 1990s?" *Journal of Portfolio Management* (Summer 2000).
2. Charles Ellis, *Investment Policy: How to Win the Loser's Game* (Irwin, 1993), p. 24.

Chapter 13: Between a Rock and a Hard Place

1. Herman Brodie and Klaus Harnack, *The Trust Mandate* (Harriman House, 2018).
2. Howard Jones and Jose Vicente Martinez, "Institutional Investor Expectations, Manager Performance, and Fund Flows," *Journal of Financial and Quantitative Analysis* (December 2017).
3. Amit Goyal and Sunil Wahal, "The Selection and Termination of Investment Management Firms by Plan Sponsors," *Journal of Finance* (August 2008).
4. Tim Jenkinson, Howard Jones, and Jose Vicente Martinez, "Picking Winners? Investment Consultants' Recommendations of Fund Managers," *Journal of Finance* (October 2016).
5. George Santayana, *The Life of Reason: Vol. 1: Reason in Common Sense* (London, Constable, 1905).

Chapter 14: Stocks Are Risky No Matter How Long the Horizon

1. Terry Burnham, *Mean Markets and Lizard Brains* (Wiley, 2005), p. 169.
2. Jeremy Siegel, *Stocks for the Long Run: The Definitive Guide to Financial Market Returns & Long-Term Investment Strategies*, 6th ed. (McGraw-Hill, 2022).
3. Nassim Nicholas Taleb, *Fooled by Randomness* (Random House, 2005), p. 108.

Chapter 15: Individual Stocks Are Riskier Than Investors Believe

1. Longboard Asset Management, "The Capitalism Distribution Observations of Individual Common Stock Returns, 1983–2006."
2. Hendrik Bessembinder, "Do Stocks Outperform Treasury Bills?" *Journal of Financial Economics* (September 2018).
3. Ibid.

Chapter 16: All Crystal Balls Are Cloudy

1. Didier Sornette, *Why Stock Markets Crash* (Princeton University Press, 2002), p. 322.
2. Ibid, p. 321.

Chapter 17: There Is Only One Way to See Things Rightly

1. John Ruskin, "The Two Paths" (1859).

Chapter 18: Black Swans and Fat Tails

1. Nassim Nicholas Taleb, *Fooled by Randomness* (Texere, 2001).
2. Javier Estrada, "Black Swans and Market Timing: How Not to Generate Alpha" (November 2007).
3. Ibid.
4. Eugene Fama, "The Distribution of the Daily Differences of the Logarithms of Stock Prices," PhD Dissertation, University of Chicago (1964).
5. Nassim Nicholas Taleb, *Black Swans* (Random House, 2007).

Chapter 19: Is Gold a Safe Haven Asset?

1. Claude Erb and Campbell Harvey, "The Golden Dilemma," *Financial Analysts Journal* (July/August 2013).

2. Claude Erb and Campbell Harvey, "The Golden Constant" Duke I&E Research Paper No. 2016–35 (May 2019).
3. Goldman Sachs, "Over the Horizon," *2013 Investment Outlook* (January 2013),
4. Pim van Vliet and Harald Lohre, "The Golden Rule of Investing" (June 2023).

Chapter 20: A Higher Intelligence

1. W. Scott Simon, *The Prudent Investor Act* (Namborn Publishing, 2002), p. 125.

Chapter 21: You Can't Handle the Truth

1. Jason Zweig, *Your Money & Your Brain* (Simon & Schuster, 2007), pp. 85–86.
2. Jonathan Fuerbringer, "Why Both Bulls and Bears Can Act So Bird-Brained," *New York Times* (March 30, 1997).
3. Jonathan Burton, *Investment Titans* (McGraw-Hill, 2000).
4. *Money*, "Did You Beat the Market?" (January 1, 2000).
5. Don A. Moore, Terri R. Kurtzberg, Craig R. Fox, and Max H. Bazerman, "Positive Illusions and Forecasting Errors in Mutual Fund Investment Decisions," Harvard Business School Working Paper 99–123.
6. Markus Glaser and Martin Weber, "Why Inexperienced Investors Do Not Learn: They Don't Know Their Past Portfolio Performance" (July 21, 2007).
7. Zweig, *Your Money & Your Brain*, p. 102

Chapter 22: Some Risks Are Not Worth Taking

1. Laurence Gonzalez, *Deep Survival* (W. W. Norton & Company, 2003), p. 134.

Chapter 23: Framing the Problem

1. Jason Zweig, *Your Money & Your Brain* (Simon & Schuster 2007), pp. 134–35.

Chapter 24: Why Do Smart People Do Dumb Things?

1. Itzhak Ben-David, Jiacui Li, Andrea Rossi, and Yang Son, "Ratings Driven Demand and Systematic Price Fluctuations" (September 2021).
2. Bradford Cornell, Jason Hsu and David Nanigian, "Does Past Performance Matter in Investment Manager Selection?" *Journal of Portfolio Management* (Summer 2017).
3. Ibid.
4. Ibid.
5. Rob Bauer, Rik Frehen, Hurber Lum, and Roger Otten, "The Performance of U.S. Pension Plans" (2008).
6. Amit Goyal and Sunil Wahal, "The Selection and Termination of Investment Management Firms by Plan Sponsors," *Journal of Portfolio Management* (August 2008).
7. Molly Mercer, Alan R. Palmer, and Ahmed E. Taha, "Worthless Warnings? Testing the Effectiveness of Disclaimers in Mutual Fund Advertisements," *Journal of Empirical Legal Studies* (September 2010).

Chapter 25: Battles Are Won Before They Are Fought

1. *Wall Street Journal*, "One 'Quant' Sees Shakeout for the Ages—'10,000 Years'" (August 11–12, 2007).
2. Roger Lowenstein, *When Genius Failed* (Random House, 2000), p. 71.
3. Peter L. Bernstein, *The Portable MBA in Investment* (Wiley, 1995).

4. Peter Lynch, "Fear of Crashing," *Worth* (September 1995).
5. Stephen Gould, *Full House: The Spread of Excellence from Plato to Darwin* (Harmony Books, 1996).

Chapter 26: Dollar Cost Averaging

1. George Constantinides, "A Note on the Suboptimality of Dollar Cost Averaging as an Investment Policy," *The Journal of Financial and Quantitative Analysis* (June 1979).
2. John Ross Knight and Lewis Mandell, "Nobody Gains from Dollar Cost Averaging: Analytical, Numerical and Empirical Results," *Financial Services Review* 2, no. 1 (1992–1993), pp. 1–71.
3. Gerstein Fisher, "Does Dollar Cost Averaging Make Sense for Investors?" (2011).

Chapter 27: Pascal's Wager and the Making of Prudent Financial Decisions

1. Jonathan Clements, *The Little Book of Main Street Money* (Wiley, 2009), p. xvii.
2. Nassim Nicholas Taleb, *Fooled by Randomness* (W. W. Norton & Company, 2001).

Chapter 29: The Drivers of Investor Behavior

1. Meir Statman, *What Investors Really Want* (McGraw-Hill, 2010).
2. Jonathan Burton, *Investment Titans* (McGraw-Hill, 2000).
3. Meir Statman, *What Investors Really Want*.
4. Jason Zweig, *Your Money and Your Brain* (Simon and Schuster, 2008).
5. Meir Statman, *What Investors Really Want*.
6. Peter Lynch, "Is There Life After Babe Ruth," *Barron's* (April 2, 1990).
7. 1993 Annual Report of Berkshire Hathaway.
8. Meir Statman, *What Investors Really Want*.

Chapter 30: The Economically Irrational Investor Preference for Dividend-Paying Stocks

1. Merton Miller and Franco Modigliani, "Dividend Policy, Growth, and the Valuation of Shares," *Journal of Business* (October 1961).
2. Hersh Shefrin and Meir Statman, "Explaining Investor Preference for Cash Dividends," *Journal of Financial Economics* (June 1984).

Chapter 31: The Uncertainty of Investing

1. Frank Knight, *Risk, Uncertainty, and Profit* (Houghton Mifflin, 1921).
2. Ross Emmett, "Frank H. Knight and Risk, Uncertainty and Profit," *Library of Economics and Liberty* (2014).

Chapter 32: The 20-Dollar Bill

1. Andrew Lo, "The Adoptive Markets Hypothesis," *The Journal of Portfolio Management* (2004).
2. Dwight Lee and James Verbrugge, "The Efficient Market Theory Thrives on Criticism," *Journal of Applied Corporate Finance* (Spring 1996).
3. Burton G. Malkiel, "Are Markets Efficient? Yes, Even If They Make Errors," *Wall Street Journal* (December 28, 2000).

Chapter 33: An Investor's Worst Enemy

1. Jonathan Fuerbringer, "Why Both Bulls and Bears Can Act So Bird-Brained," *New York Times* (March 30, 1997).
2. Robert McGough, "The Secret (Active) Dreams of an Indexer," *Wall Street Journal* (February 25, 1997).
3. Eleanor Laise, "The Mensa Investment Club: A Cautionary Tale," *Smart Money* (June 2021).
4. Peter Bernstein, *The Portable MBA in Investment* (Wiley, 1995).
5. Jonathan Clements, *25 Myths You've Got to Avoid* (Simon & Schuster, 1998), p. 55.

6. James H. Smalhout, "Too Close to Your Money?" *Bloomberg Personal* (November 1997).
7. Gary Belsky and Thomas Gilovich, *Why Smart People Make Big Money Mistakes* (Simon & Schuster, 1999).
8. Peter L. Bernstein and Aswath Damodaran (eds.), *Investment Management* (Wiley, 1998), p. 252.
9. Ron Ross, *The Unbeatable Market* (Optimum Press, 2002), p. 16.

Chapter 34: Bear Markets

1. 1996 Annual Report of Berkshire Hathaway.
2. 1992 Annual Report of Berkshire Hathaway.
3. 1996 Annual Report of Berkshire Hathaway.
4. 1991 Annual Report of Berkshire Hathaway.
5. 2006 Annual Report of Berkshire Hathaway.
6. 2004 Annual Report of Berkshire Hathaway.

Chapter 35: Mad Money

1. Michael Learmonth, "Ratings Flood for Fox, CNN," *Variety* (September 27, 2005).
2. Jonathan Hartley and Matthew Olson, "Jim Cramer's *Mad Money* Charitable Trust Performance and Factor Attribution," *The Journal of Retirement* (Summer 2018).
3. Paul Bolster, Emery Trahan, and Anand Venkateswaran, "How Mad Is *Mad Money?*" *The Journal of Investing* (Summer 2012).
4. Joseph Engelberg, Caroline Sasseville, and Jared Williams, "Is the Market Mad? Evidence from *Mad Money*" (March 22, 2006).
5. Bill Alpert, "Shorting Cramer," *Barron's* (August 20, 2007).
6. Ben McGrath, "The Rise and Rise of Jim Cramer," *New York Magazine* (October 22, 2007).
7. CXO Advisory Group, "Guru Grades." www.cxoadvisory.com/gurus.

Chapter 36: Fashions and Investment Folly

1. Charles MacKay, *Extraordinary Popular Delusions and the Madness of Crowds* (Barnes and Noble, 1994).
2. Quoted in Edward Chancellor, *Devil Take the Hindmost* (Farrar, Straus and Giroux, 1999), p. 69.

Chapter 38: Chasing Spectacular Performance

1. Jeffrey Ptak, "What Happens After Fund Managers Crush It?" *The Evidence Based Investor* (January 18, 2001). www.evidence investor.com/what-happens-after-fund-managers-crush-it.

Chapter 39: Enough

1. Kurt Vonnegut's obituary for Joseph Heller, *The New Yorker* (May 16, 2005).
2. Tiger 21 website. https://tiger21.com/.

Chapter 40: The Big Rocks

1. Paul Samuelson, quoted in Jonathan Burton, *Investment Titans* (McGraw-Hill, 2001).

Chapter 41: A Tale of Two Strategies

1. Charles D. Ellis, *Winning the Loser's Game: Timeless Strategies for Successful Investing* (McGraw-Hill, 1998).
2. Eugene Fama and Kenneth French, "Luck Versus Skill in the Cross-Section of Mutual Fund Returns," *The Journal of Finance* (October 2010).
3. Mike Sebastian and Sudhakar Attaluri, "Conviction in Equity Investing," *The Journal of Portfolio Management* (Summer 2014).

Appendix A: Implementation: Recommended Investment Vehicles

1. Provided for informational purposes only and is not intended to serve as specific investment or financial advice. This list of funds does not constitute a recommendation to purchase a single specific security and it should not be assumed that the securities referenced herein were or will prove to be profitable. Prior to making any investment, an investor should carefully consider the fund's risks and investment objectives and evaluate all offering materials and other documents associated with the investment.

Acknowledgments

This book reflects the wisdom gained over my almost 30 years as head of economic and financial research at Buckingham Strategic Wealth. I have learned so much from so many people that it would be impossible to list them all. Thus, my apologies if I have left you off the following short list. With that said, I am especially thankful to have had the opportunity to work with and learn from Cliff Asness and Toby Moskowitz (and the rest of the research team at AQR), Andrew Berkin, Vladimir Masek, and Wes Wellington (and the rest of the research team at Dimensional). I am deeply grateful for the time you have shared. I also want to thank Josh Ernst for helping with the data.

I also thank my wife, Mona, the love of my life, for her tremendous encouragement and understanding during the lost weekends and many nights I have sat at the computer well into the early morning hours. She has always provided whatever support was needed—and then some. Walking through life with her has truly been a gracious experience. And, finally, I thank Sandy Hickman for her editing work. She has been a great partner.

Index

A

AAP (Action Alerts PLUS) portfolio, 220
Aces Gold Casino, 25
Action Alerts PLUS (AAP) portfolio, 220
Active investing, 67–71
    avoiding, in prudent strategy, 6
    as conventional wisdom, xxii
    and diversification, 95
    as loser's game, 70–71
    as myth, 257–258
    and overconfidence, 128
    passive investing vs., 171
    and persistent outperformance, 36–37
    risks of, 79–81
    time commitment of, 244–246
    and winning strategy, 205–210
ALI (American Law Institute), 122, 150
Allen, Woody, 11
Alphas, 47–48, 80
Alternative funds, 268–269
Alternative lending funds, 269
American Law Institute (ALI), 122, 150
"Analysts and Anomalies" (Engelberg
    et al.), 53
Annuities, indexed, 138–141
Argentina, 90

Arkhipov, Vasily, 87
Army basketball, 9–13
The Art of War (Sūn Wǔ. Tzu), 153
Asness, Clifford S., 63
Asset allocation, 168, 215, 258–259
Attitude polarization, 182
Average, being above, 178–180

B

Baer, Gregory, 219
Baker, David, 77
Barber, Brad, 23
Barron's, 223
Baseball, 3–4, 7, 27–29, 32, 48–49
Basketball, 9–25
Bauer, Rob, 147, 148
Beane, Billy, 4
Bear markets, 153–159, 211–218
Behavior, drivers of, 177–183
Behavioral finance, xxiv, 125–195
    and cash dividends, 185–192
    dollar cost averaging, 161–165
    drivers of investor behavior, 177–183
    emotions in markets, 153–159
    endowment effect, 173–175
    framing, 137–142

Behavioral finance (*continued*)
  ignoring warnings, 143–151
  overconfidence, 127–131
  risk assessment, 133–135
  risk management, 167–172
  and uncertainty, 193–195
Belief perseverance, 182
Belsky, Gary, 209–210
Bensman, Miriam, 73
Berk, Jonathan, 36–37
Berkin, Andrew, 30, 48, 80
Bernstein, Peter, 33, 97, 128, 157, 193, 209
Bernstein, William, 11, 167
Bessembinder, Hendrik, 93–95
Billings, Josh, xxi
The Bill James Handbook (James), 3
The Black Swan (Taleb), 112
Black swans, 109–113
"Black Swans and Market Timing"
  (Estrada), 110
Blyleven, Bert, 29
Bolster, Paul, 221
Bonds, Barry, 27–29, 32
Book-to-market (BtM) ratio, 19–22
Boston Red Sox, 7
Brodie, Herman, 84
Brooks, John, 178
BtM (book-to-market) ratio, 19–22
Buckingham Strategic Wealth, 85, 261
Buckingham Wealth Partners, 177, 246–247
Buffett, Warren, 3, 5, 39, 158, 181,
  186, 216–217
"Buffett's Alpha" (Frazzini et al.), 5
Burnham, Terry, 87
Burton, Jonathan, 178

C
Calendar cycles, 233–234
"Can Mutual Fund 'Stars' Really Pick Stocks?
  New Evidence from a Bootstrap
  Analysis." (Kosowski et al.), 30–31
"Can Mutual Fund Stars Still Pick Stocks?
  A Replication and Extension of
  Kosowski, Timmermann, Wemers,
  and White" (Riley), 30–31
Capital gains taxes, 175
"The Capitalism Distribution" (Longboard
  Asset Management), 91–92
Cardano, Girolamo, 79
Cash dividends, 185–192

Chamfort, Nicholas, 59
Chance, 73–78
Chomsky, Noam, 87–88
Clemens, Roger, 29
Clements, Jonathan, 67, 143, 167, 209
CNBC, 220
The Coffeehouse Investor (Schultheis), 79
Collective wisdom, of markets, 28–29
College basketball, 9–25
Companies:
  active vs. passive investment in, 39–41
  small vs. large, 41–42
Competition, true nature of, 32
Confirmation bias, 182–183
Constantinides, George, 162
Contentment, 239–242
Conventional wisdom, xxii–xxiii, 61, 233–234
"Conviction in Equity Investing," 250
Cornell, Bradford, 52
Correlation, during financial crises, 156
COVID-19 pandemic, 112, 153, 168
Cramer, Jim, 220–226
"The Cross-Section of Expected Stock
  Returns" (Fama and French), 4
Cruise, Tom, 127
Cuban Missile Crisis, 87–88
CXO Advisory Group, 224–225

D
Data mining, 59–60, 74
Davis, Jim, 56
DCA (dollar cost averaging), 161–165
"The Deadweight Loss of Active
  Management" (Levy), xxii
Deep Survival (Gonzalez), 133
Delayed gratification, 189–190
Desires, needs vs., 241–242
De Vlamingh, Willem, 110
Dickens, Charles, 249
Diversification:
  and active investing, 95
  and dividends, 189
  during financial crises, 156
  and risk, 134
"Dividend Policy, Growth, and the
  Valuation of Shares" (Miller and
  Modigliani), 185
Dividends, 185–192
"Does Dollar Cost Averaging Make Sense for
  Investors" (Gerstein Fisher), 162

"Does Past Performance Matter in Investment
Manager Selection?," 144–147
Dollar cost averaging (DCA), 161–165
"Do Stocks Outperform Treasury Bill?"
(Bessembinder), 93
Dowd Report, 48–49
Dow Jones Industrial Index, 110–111
Drivers, of investor behavior, 177–183
Duke University, 9–13

E

Earnings, 42–45
Economic growth rates, 55–57
Edelen, Roger, 37–38
Efficient market hypothesis (EMH), 36,
37, 199–203
"The Efficient Market Theory Thrives
on Criticism" (Lee and Verbrugge),
201
Ego-driven investments, 177–178
Egyptian equities, 89–90
Elaad, Guy, 15
Ellis, Charles, 29–30, 47, 70, 81, 249
Emerging markets, 230
EMH, *see* Efficient market hypothesis
Emotions, markets driven by, 153–159, 214
Endowment effect, 173–175
Engelberg, Joseph, 53–54, 222
Ennis, Richard, 69–70
Enough, having, 239–242
Equity risk premium (ERP), 52–53
Erb, Claude, 115, 116
Estrada, Javier, 110, 111
Evans, Richard, 37–38
Evidence:
for correlation of economic growth rates
and stock returns, 56–57
examining, 14–16
in security analysis, 53–54
Expected returns:
and Fed Model, 61
and marginal utility of wealth, 240–241
and risk, 4, 44–45, 211–212
risk-adjusted, 20
Experts, 219–226
"Explaining Investor Preference for Cash
Dividends" (Shefrin and
Statman), 189
*Extraordinary Popular Delusions and the Madness
of Crowds* (McKay), 227

F

Fama, Eugene, 4, 23, 154–155
Fama-French four model, 187–188
Fat tails, 109–113
Federal Reserve, 60
Fed Model, 59–64
A Few Good Men (film), 127
Fidelity Total Market Index Fund
(FSKAX), 235
Fidelity ZERO Large Cap Index (FNILX), 250
Fielding, Henry, 227
Financial advisor selection, 253–256
Financial crazes, 229–230
Financial crises, 155–156
Financial ratios, 21–22
"Five Myths of Active Management"
(Berk), 36–37
Fixed-income portfolios, 4
FNILX (Fidelity ZERO Large Cap
Index), 250
Fooled by Randomness (Taleb), 78, 110, 112
Football, 25
Forbes, 150
Forbes, Steve, 226
Forecasting, 55–57, 97–104
Fortune, 150
44 Wall Street Equity Fund, 77
44 Wall Street Fund, 77
Fox, Loren, 39
Framing, 137–142, 180–182, 190
Franklin, Benjamin, 83, 133
Frank Russell, 69, 84
Frazzini, Andrea, 5
Frehen, Rik, 147, 148
French, Kenneth, 4, 23
FSKAX (Fidelity Total Market Index
Fund), 235
Fuerbringer, Jonathan, 128
Full House (Gould), 159

G

Gensler, Gary, 219
Gerstein Fisher, 162–163
Gilovich, Thomas, 209–210
Glaser, Markus, 129
Gold, 115–119
"The Golden Constant" (Erb and
Harvey), 116
"The Golden Dilemma" (Erb and
Harvey), 115

"The Golden Rule of Investment" (van Vliet and Lohre), 117
Goldman Sachs, 69, 116
Gonzalez, Laurence, 133
Gould, Stephen, 159
Goyal, Amit, 84, 148
Graham, Benjamin, 205
Grand Forks, North Dakota, 97–98
Great Financial Crisis (2008), 153, 168
Greenspan, Alan, 60, 103

H
Hamilton, Alexander, 211
Hammer-heading, 133
Harnack, Klaus, 84
Harvey, Campbell, 115, 116
Hedge funds, 156–157, 178
Hedging, with gold, 118–119
Heller, Joseph, 239
Hennessy Funds, 77
Hennessy Total Return Fund, 77
Herd mentality, 227–231
Hickman, Daniel C., 14–15
High-return investments, 39–45
Holy Grail, 35–36
Horse racing, 15–16
"How Mad is Mad Money?" (Bolster et al.), 221
Hubbell, Carl, 29
Hugo, Victor, 121

I
IAs (indexed annuities), 138–141
Illmanen, Antti, 56
Illusions, 59–64
Illusory correlation, 182
The Incredible Shrinking Alpha (Swedroe and Berkin), 47, 80
Indexed annuities (IAs), 138–141
Individual investors:
   choosing to be, 253–254
   and competition, 28
   overconfidence of, 128–129
   and price setting, 17, 23
   time spent by, 244
Individual stocks, 91–96
Inflation, 62
"Information, Prices and Efficiency in an Online Betting Market" (Elaad et al.), 15

Initial public offerings (IPOs), 19
Inside information, 17–18
Insider trading, 17–18
"Institutional Investment Strategy and Manager Choice" (Ennis), 69
"Institutional Investor Expectations, Manager Performance, and Fund Flows" (Jones and Martinez), 84
Institutional investors:
   and competition, 28
   lack of outperformance by, 80–81
   and price setting, 17, 23–24
Intel, 134
International markets, 111–112
"In the matter of Peter Edward Rose, Manager of Cincinnati Reds Baseball Club," 48–49
Investment discipline, 159, 214–215, 259
Investment managers:
   criteria for selection of, 151
   hiring and firing of, 148–149
Investment Policy (Ellis), 81
Investment returns, 42–45
Investment Titans (Burton), 178
Investment vehicles, 261–269
Investor behavior, drivers of, 177–183
IPOs (initial public offerings), 19
Irrational primacy effect, 182
"Is the Market Mad? Evidence from Mad Money" (Engelberg et al.), 222

J
James, Bill, 3–4, 7
"January effect," 201–202
Japan, 90
Jenkinson, Tim, 84
Johnson, Randy, 29
Jones, Howard, 84
The Journal of Financial and Quantitative Analysis, 162

K
Kabiller, David, 5
Kadlec, Gregory, 37–38
Knight, Frank, 193
Knight, John, 162
Kohl's, 19–21, 43–45
Kosowski, Robert, 30–31
Krzyzewski, Mike (Coach K), 9–10

L

Large companies, 41–42
Large multi-style funds, 267
Large single-style funds, 264–266
Lee, Dwight, 201
Legg Mason Value Trust, 76, 78
Lehman Holdings Inc., 154
Leinweber, David, 60
Levy, Moshe, xxii–xxiii
Lewis, Michael, 4
Life insurance, 169
Limra, 139
Lindner Large-Cap Fund, 76–77
The Little Book of Main Street Money
        (Clements), 167
Lo, Andrew, 60
Lohre, Harald, 117–118
Longboard Asset Management, 91
Long-Term Capital Management
        (LTCM), 154, 157
Long-term care insurance, 169–170
Loss aversion, 190
LSI (lump sum investing), 163
LTCM (Long-Term Capital Management),
        154, 157
Luck, 73–78
"Luck Versus Skill in the Cross-Section of
        Mutual Fund Returns," 6, 249
Lum, Hurber, 147, 148
Lump sum investing (LSI), 163
Lynch, Peter, 77, 158, 181

M

McKay, Charles, 227, 228
McLean, David, 53–54
Maddux, Greg, 29
"Mad Money" (television program), 220
Madoff, Bernie, 178
Magellan Fund, 77
Mandell, Lewis, 162
The Man Who Shot Liberty Valance (film), 257
Marginal utility of wealth, 240
Markets, xxiii–xxiv, 1–64
        and economic growth rates, 55–57
        emotions in, 153–159
        Fed Model, 59–64
        high-return investments, 39–45
        lack of understanding of, xxi–xxii
        market efficiency, 47–50
        outperformance of, 35–38

persistence of performance, 27–33
        price setting, 9–25
        research on, 3–7
        security analysis, 51–54
        timing the market, 157–158, 216–217
Market beta funds, 262
Market efficiency, 47–50
        and basketball betting, 14–15
        betting against, 24
        and price setting, 16–18, 24–25
Market experts, 219–226
Markowitz, Harry, 105, 106
Martinez, Jose Vicente, 84
Matterhorn Growth Fund, 77
May, selling in, 233–234
MC (Monte Carlo) simulations,
        100–103, 141–142
Mencken, H. L., 199
Mensa investment club, 208–209
Meriwether, John, 154
Merton, Robert, 154
Meyer-Brauns, Philipp, 23
Miller, Bill, 76
Miller, Merton, 185–186
Modern portfolio theory (MPT), 105–107
Modigliani, Franco, 185–186
Momentum multi-style funds, 268
Momentum single-style funds, 266
Moneyball (Lewis), 4
Money magazine, 128
Monte Carlo (MC) simulations, 100–103,
        141–142
Morningstar, 230, 235, 236
MPT (modern portfolio theory), 105–107
MSCI World Index, 112
Murphy, Eddie, 12
"Mutual Fund Performance Through a
        Five-Factor Lens" (Meyer-Brauns), 23
Mutual funds:
        active investing vs. chance for, 75–76
        performance of, 148
        SEC warnings about, 143–144
        warnings about, 149

N

Napoleon, 158
Nash, Steve, 105–106
Needs, desires vs., 241–242
New England Patriots, 25
Newton, Sir Isaac, 216, 228

NFL Super Bowl, 25
Nicholson, Jack, 127
1977 Baseball Abstract (James), 3
"Nobody Gains from Dollar Cost Averaging"
  (Knight and Mandell), 162
Nominal bonds, 170–171
Nominal growth rate of economy, 62
"A Note on the Suboptimality of Dollar Cost
  Averaging as an Investment Policy"
  (Constantinides), 162

O
Oakland Athletics, 4
Odean, Terrance, 23
O'Reilly, Gerard, 30
Otten, Roger, 147, 148
"Outfoxing the box" game, 79–81
Outperformance, 6, 35–38
Overconfidence, 127–131, 178–180,
  208–209, 214–215

P
Park, Robert, 183
Pascal, Blaise, 167
Pascal's wager, 167–172
Passive investing:
  active investing vs., 171
  as safe bet, 24
  as winning strategy, 243–248
Past performance, 73–78, 83–85, 144–147
Pedersen, Lasse, 5
Pension plans, 68–70, 147–148
P/E (price-to-earnings) ratio, 19–22
Performance:
  chasing, 235–237
  outperformance, 6, 35–38
  past, 73–78, 83–85
  persistence of, 27–33
"The Performance of U.S. Pension Plans"
  (Bauer et al.), 147
Perry, Gaylord, 29
Phoenix Suns, 105
"Picking Winners? Investment Consultants'
  Recommendations of Fund
  Managers" (Jenkinson et al.), 84
Planning, 215, 259
Point spreads, 11–16
Pontiff, Jeffrey, 53–54
The Portable MBA in Investment
  (Bernstein), 157

Portfolio management, xxiv, 65–124
  active investing, 67–71
  black swans and fat tails, 109–113
  designing your portfolio, 258–260
  forecasting, 97–104
  gold, 115–119
  modern portfolio theory, 105–107
  and past performance, 73–78, 83–85
  prudent strategies for, 121–124
  riskiness of stocks, 87–96
  risks of active investing, 79–81
"Positive Illusions and Forecasting Errors in
  Mutual Fund Investment
  Decisions," 129
Price setting, 9–25
  financial ratios, 21–22
  and individual investor performance, 23
  and institutional investor performance,
    23–24
  and market efficiency, 16–18, 24–25
  point spreads, 13–16
  and sports betting, 9–13
  stocks, 19
Price-to-earnings (P/E) ratio, 19–22
Profitability/quality multi-style
  funds, 267, 268
Profitability/quality single-style funds, 266
Prospect theory, 190–191
Prudent Investor Rule (American Law
  Institute), 122, 150
Prudent strategies:
  based on academic research, 6
  and having enough, 241
  for portfolio management, 121–124
Ptak, Jeffrey, 235–236

Q
Quality, of stocks, 5
Quality of life, improving, 245–248
Quinn, Jane Bryant, 248

R
"Ratings-Driven Demand and Systematic
  Price Fluctuations," 144
Reade, James, 15
Real growth rate of economy, 62
Real interest rates, 62–64
Recency bias, 214, 228–229
Regret avoidance, 191
Reinsurance funds, 269

Repetto, Eduardo, 30
Riley, Timothy, 30
"The Rise and Fall of Performance
    Management" (Ellis), 29–30
Risk(s):
    of active investing, 79–81
    adjusting for, 45
    avoiding unnecessary, 215
    and expected returns, 4, 44–45, 211–212
    sequence risk, 98–103
    of stocks, 87–96, 155
    and uncertainty, 193–195
Risk, Uncertainty, and Profit (Knight), 193
Risk-adjusted expected returns, 20
Risk assessment, 133–135
Risk management, 167–172
Risk premiums, 212, 214–215
Ritter, Jay, 56
Roll, Richard, 202
Rose, Pete, 17–18, 48–49
Ross, Ron, 29, 210
Rothman, Matthew, 154
Rubinstein, Mark, 28, 47
Ruskin, John, 107
Russell, Bertrand, 161
Russell 3000 Index, 92

S

Sabermetricians, 4
Safe haven, gold as, 115–119
Samuelson, Paul, 9, 244–245
Santayana, George, 85
Sasseville, Caroline, 222
Sauer, Raymond, 14, 49
Sauter, Gus, 208
"Scale Effects in Mutual Fund Performance"
    (Edelen et al.), 37
Scholes, Myron, 154
Schultheis, Bill, 79
Security analysis, 51–54
SEI, 69, 84
"The Selection and Termination of Invest-
    ment Management Firms by Plan
    Sponsors" (Goyal and Wahal), 84, 148
Selling in May, 233–234
Selling stock, 186–187
Sentimentality, 174
Sequence risk, 98–103
Shefrin, Hersh, 189–192
Sher, Michael, 123–124

Shiller, Robert, 128, 208
"Shorting Cramer" (Barron's), 223
Siegel, Jeremy, 56, 88
Singleton, Carl, 15
Sinquefield, Rex, 29
Sisyphus, 83, 85
Skewness, of stocks, 94
Small companies, 41–42
Small multi-style funds, 267, 268
Small single-style funds, 263, 265, 266
Small value stocks, 213
Smart Money, 209
Smith, Adam, 28
Smith, Warren, 209
Sports betting, 9–25, 48–49
St. Louis Rams, 25
Standard and Poor's Active Versus Passive
    Scorecards (SPIVA), 207
Statman, Meir, 177–183, 189–192
Stengel, Casey, 103
Stewart, Martha, 17
Stocks:
    cash dividends paid by, 185–192
    in Fed Model, 60–61
    and gold, 117
    historical returns on, 154–155
    individual stocks, 91–96
    and Pascal's wager, 171–172
    price setting, 19
    riskiness of, 87–96, 155
    selection of, 5
    small value stocks, 213
Stockbrokers, 11
Stocks for the Long Run (Siegel), 88
Sūn Wŭ. Tzu, 153
Surowiecki, James, 49, 249
Systematic strategy, xxiv

T

Taleb, Nassim Nicholas, 78, 90, 109, 110, 168
A Tale of Two Cities (Dickens), 249
The Tao Te Ching, 239
Taxes:
    capital gains taxes, 175
    and dividends, 188
    and proliferation of funds, 230
Thaler, Richard, 128, 208
Third Restatement of Trusts, 122–123
Thirteen Days in October (film), 87–88
Three-factor model, 4

TIGER 21 Group, 239
Time management, 243–244
Timing the market, 157–158, 216–217
Timmermann, Allan, 30–31
TIPS (Treasury inflation-protected securities), 62, 170–171
Trading Places, 12
Trahan, Emery, 221
Treasury bills, 93–94
Treasury inflation-protected securities (TIPS), 62, 170–171
The Trust Mandate (Brodie and Harnack), 84
2013 Investment Outlook (Goldman Sachs), 116
Two-factor model, 4

U

The Unbeatable Market (Ross), 29
Unbiased estimators, 13–14
Uncertainty, 193–195, 259
Uniform Prudent Investor Act, 123

V

Value multi-style funds, 267–269
Value single-style funds, 264–265
Vanguard 500 Index Fund (VFNIX), 106–107, 134
Vanguard Emerging Markets Index Fund (VEIEX), 106–107
Van Vliet, Pim, 117–118
Venkateswaran, Anand, 221
Verbrugge, James, 201
Vigorish, 11, 13
Vonnegut, Kurt, 239

W

Wahal, Sunil, 84, 148
Walmart, 19–21, 43–45

Wanger, Ralph, 32
Warnings:
  about indexed annuities, 140
  ignoring, 143–151
Weber, Martin, 129
Wermers, Russ, 30–31
What Investors Really Want (Statman), 177, 179
White, Hal, 30–31
"Why Inexperienced Investors Do Not Learn" (Glaser and Weber), 129
Why Smart Pepe Make Big Money Mistakes (Belsky and Gilovich), 209
Williams, Jared, 222
Winning strategy, xxiv, 158, 159, 197–256
  and active investing, 205–210
  bear markets, 211–218
  chasing fund performance, 235–237
  and efficient market hypothesis, 199–203
  financial advisor selection, 253–256
  having enough, 239–242
  and herd mentality, 227–231
  and market experts, 219–226
  with passive investing, 243–248
  selling in May, 233–234
Winning the Loser's Game (Ellis), 47, 70, 249
The Wisdom of Crowds (Surowiecki), 49
"Worthless Warnings? Testing the Effectiveness of Disclaimers in Mutual Fund Advertisements," 149

Y

Yardeni, Edward, 60, 61, 63
Your Money & Your Brain (Zweig), 138, 180

Z

Zweig, Jason, 138, 180–181, 243